IN

CCTV and Policing

CLARENDON STUDIES IN CRIMINOLOGY

Published under the auspices of the Institute of Criminology,
University of Cambridge; the Mannheim Centre, London School of
Economics; and the Centre for Criminological Research,
University of Oxford.

GENERAL EDITOR: PER-OLOF WIKSTRÖM (*University of Cambridge*)

EDITORS: ALISON LIEBLING AND MANUEL EISNER
(*University of Cambridge*)

DAVID DOWNES, PAUL ROCK, AND JILL PEAY
(*London School of Economics*)

ROGER HOOD, LUCIA ZEDNER, AND RICHARD YOUNG
(*University of Oxford*)

CCTV and Policing

Public Area Surveillance and Police Practices in Britain

Benjamin J. Goold

OXFORD
UNIVERSITY PRESS

OXFORD
UNIVERSITY PRESS

Great Clarendon Street, Oxford OX2 6DP

Oxford University Press is a department of the University of Oxford.
It furthers the University's objective of excellence in research, scholarship,
and education by publishing worldwide in

Oxford New York

Auckland Bangkok Buenos Aires Cape Town Chennai
Dar es Salaam Delhi Hong Kong Istanbul Karachi Kolkata
Kuala Lumpur Madrid Melbourne Mexico City Mumbai Nairobi
São Paulo Shanghai Singapore Taipei Tokyo Toronto

Oxford is a registered trade mark of Oxford University Press
in the UK and in certain other countries

Published in the United States
by Oxford University Press Inc., New York

© B. J. Goold, 2004

First published 2004

British Library Cataloguing in Publication Data
Data available

Library of Congress Cataloging in Publication Data
Data available
ISBN 0–19–926514–3

1 3 5 7 9 10 8 6 4 2

Typeset by Kolam Information Services Pvt. Ltd, Pondicherry, India
Printed in Great Britain
on acid-free paper by
Biddles Ltd, King's Lynn

For Lisa

General Editor's Introduction

The *Clarendon Studies in Criminology* was inaugurated in 1994 under the auspices of the centres of criminology at the Universities of Cambridge and Oxford and the London School of Economics. It was the successor to *Cambridge Studies in Criminology*, founded by Sir Leon Radzinowicz and J.W.C. Turner almost sixty years ago.

Criminology is a field of study that covers everything from research into the causes of crime to the politics of the operations of the criminal justice system. Researchers in different social and behavioural sciences, criminal justice and law, all make important contributions to our understanding of the phenomena of crime. The *Clarendon Series in Criminology* aim to reflect this diversity by publishing high-quality theory and research monographs by established scholars, as well as by young scholars of great promise from all kinds of academic backgrounds.

In *CCTV and Policing* Goold makes two central claims. The first is that the introduction of CCTV may not have significantly changed the way the police operate on a day-to-day basis. Goold presents some interesting empirical evidence for this thesis from his own study of the police in the Southern region of England. The second, following on from this observation, is that this fact should lead us to rethink the 'conventional wisdom' in criminology and social science, and among civil libertarians, about the relationship between policing and surveillance technology. Goold states that, 'there is a pressing need for us to re-examine the ways in which we think about surveillance and to resist the pull of dystopic visions when looking at the impact of technologies like CCTV. Cameras are not in and of themselves intrusive—they only become so when used in particular settings and in particular ways' (p. 210).

In Goold's book, *CCTV and Policing*, we have an important, and partly controversial contribution to the ongoing discussion of the role of the police and policing in the emerging surveillance society. It will most surely attract the attention of both practitioners and academics interested in the difficult issues relating to policing and surveillance technologies.

Per-Olof H Wikström,
University of Cambridge
January 2004

Acknowledgements

This book began its life as a doctoral thesis, which would never have been finished without the guidance, patience, and faith of my supervisor Professor Roger Hood. It is my enormous privilege to have been his student, and I am indebted to him for sharing his experience and insights with me. I also owe a great deal to Lucia Zedner, who first introduced me to criminology and has been an invaluable source of advice and encouragement ever since.

Thanks must also go to the police officers, camera operators, scheme managers, and local officials involved with CCTV in the Southern Region. Their cooperation and good humour made the fieldwork not only possible, but enjoyable. I also wish to express my appreciation for the support provided by the following institutions: the Rhodes Trust, the Oxford Centre for Criminological Research, the Centre de Recherches Sociologiques sur le Droit et les Institutions Pénales, the Max Planck Institute for Foreign and International Criminal Law, John Jay College of Criminal Justice at the City University of New York, and the Niigata University Faculty of Law.

I am grateful to the editors and publishers concerned for their permission to use material from earlier articles of mine. 'Public Area Surveillance and Policing: the Impact of CCTV on police behaviour and autonomy' (2003) *Surveillance and Society* 2(1), pp. 191–203 (http://www.surveillance-and-society.org) is reproduced here by kind permission of *Surveillance and Society*. 'Privacy Rights and Public Spaces: CCTV and the Problem of the "Unobservable Observer"' (2002) 21(1) *Criminal Justice Ethics* 21(1), [Summer/Fall 2002], pp. 21–7, is reprinted here by kind permission of the Institute for Criminal Justice Ethics, 555 West 57th Street, Suite 601, New York, NY 1019–1029. I would also like to thank Ashgate Publishing Group for permission to reproduce the information in Table 1.1 in Chapter 1, which is taken from B.C.M. Koch (1998) *The Politics of Crime Prevention* (Aldershot: Ashgate) 50. I would also like to acknowledge John Louth, Gwen Booth, and the

x Acknowledgements

the preparation and publication of this book.

Finally, I would like to say thank you to the many people who
read drafts of the manuscript, offered advice, and provided much-
needed support and encouragement along the way: Andrew Ash-
worth, Simon Cole, David Goold, Imogen Goold, David Gourd,
Karen Gourd, Lisa Gourd, Heath Grant, Carolyn Hoyle, Susan
James, Dennis Kenney, John Kleinig, Liora Lazarus, Mark Matz,
Bob Panzarella, Fusako Sekura, Tadashi Sekura, Andrew Sanders,
Matthew Silverstein, Phyllis Silverstein, Maja Strbac, Teiko
Tamaki, Hannah Young, and Richard Young. I count myself lucky
to have had such good friends, family, and colleagues.

Contents

Table of Cases

Table of Statutes and Legislation

List of Tables

1

Under Surveillance

⌐ The advantages of CCTV, properly managed, speak for themselves: crime prevention, the deterrent effect of knowing that
there is observation, the alerting of police at an early stage to
stop dangerous situations escalating, the operational assistance to the police in sizing up a situation, the safer convictions
that can be obtained—the savings in court time can be enormous—and, above all, the fact that people's confidence is
renewed, which has led to many town centres being revital-
ised. Vulnerable groups in particular feel the advantage.

Alun Michael, Minister of State[1] ⌐

We have to think carefully about the implications of this new
weapon against crime. It is time for national discussion. We
have a right to ask the tough questions: Who controls the
technology? Who owns the images? And, most important of
all, who will protect our rights? This is not a question of sacri-
ficing privacy for safety. It is our right to enjoy both. And it is a
duty to demand both.

Caught in the Act, Kulter Films Inc.[2]

1.1 Introduction

Over the past ten years, the United Kingdom has become the most
watched citizenry in Europe.[3] Since the late 1980s, over 1 million

---

[1] A. Michael (Minister of State) (30 July 1997) *Hansard House of Commons
Debates* (London: HMSO), col. 41.

[2] Kulter Films Inc. (1995) *Caught in the Act*. Quoted in S. Davies (1998) 'CCTV: a
new battleground for privacy' in C. Norris, J. Moran, and G. Armstrong (eds.)
Surveillance, Closed Circuit Television and Social Control (Aldershot: Ashgate),
243, 246.

[3] Looking beyond Europe, it has also been suggested by some commentators that
the United Kingdom is now the most watched citizenry in the world. According to
Barbara Morgan, the former Director of the National CCTV Users Group, there are

closed circuit television (CCTV) cameras have been installed in towns and cities across Britain, with an estimated 500 or more being added to this figure every week.[4] As a consequence, CCTV cameras can now be found in most urban high streets, town squares, and shopping centres, as well as in many offices, car parks and stores.[5] Although Britain may not have reached the stage where there is a camera on every street corner, that day is perhaps not so far away.

This rapid expansion in the use of video surveillance has meant that for many citizens, whether they like it or not, going about their daily business under the watchful eye of CCTV has become a fact of life. Every time we go shopping, walk into a bank, or casually stop to talk with friends in the street, there is the possibility that our actions are being observed and recorded. In many cases, these cameras are owned and operated by private organizations. Retailers and banks were among the first to use video surveillance as a means of protecting property and premises, and today the private sector remains the principal user of CCTV.[6] Increasingly, however, police

'more cameras here in proportion to the population than anywhere else, including the United States. The UK is the largest user of CCTV in the world.' Quoted in D. Gadher (1999) 'Smile, you're on 300 candid cameras...' (14 Feb.) *The Sunday Times*.

[4] Gadher (1999). According to one recent estimate, an average of £361 m. per year was spent on CCTV in Britain between 1996 and 2000: M. McCahill and C. Norris (2002b) 'Working paper No. 3: CCTV in Britain', Urban eye project: On the threshold to urban Panopticon? Analysing the employment of CCTV in European cities and assessing its social and political impacts (Berlin: Centre for technology and society, Technical University Berlin), 14. See also B. Appleyard (2001) 'Nowhere to hide' (15 Apr. 2001) *The Sunday Times Magazine*; and I. Drury (2001b) 'More peaks to scale as UK market reaches plateau' *CCTV Today* (Nov./Dec.).

[5] As Norris *et al.* have noted, all cities in Britain with a population in excess of 500,000 (with the exception of Leeds) had installed public area CCTV schemes by the end of 1996, and, according to research cited by Fay, by January 1998 a total of 450 British towns had introduced some form of CCTV surveillance system. See C. Norris, J. Moran, and G. Armstrong (1998) 'Algorithmic surveillance: the future of automated visual surveillance' in Norris *et al.* (1998b), 255; and C. Norris and G. Armstrong (1998) 'Introduction: power and vision' in Norris *et al.* (1998b), 3. See also S. J. Fay (1998) 'Tough on crime, tough on civil liberties: some negative aspects of Britain's wholesale adoption of CCTV surveillance during the 1990s' *Law, Computers & Technology* 12(2): 315.

[6] See S. Narayan (1996) 'What's happening?' *CCTV Today* (Nov.), 26. According to the British Security Industry Association (quoted in Narayan), in the years between 1989 and 1994 the market for video surveillance systems and equipment almost quadrupled, with annual spending on CCTV and related technology reaching £170 m. on conservative estimates.

forces and local councils have also turned to video surveillance in their efforts to control crime and maintain public order. Cameras are now routinely used in the hope that they will help to detect and deter crimes such as car theft, shoplifting, and assault, as well as to combat public drunkenness, vagrancy, and other forms of 'anti-social behaviour'. In the minds of many senior police officers and local councillors, CCTV represents a new and valuable weapon in the fight against crime and public disorder.

Gathering information and generating intelligence for the purpose of controlling crime and maintaining order has always been a key aspect of police work. Prior to the advent of CCTV, the extent of police surveillance was limited by the number of officers on the street and the willingness of the public and police informers to report and cooperate in the investigation of crime. Public-area CCTV, however, has the potential to free the police from this state of 'information dependency', at least as far as crime committed in public view is concerned.[7] Cameras can be used to monitor a city or town centre 24 hours a day, 365 days a year, providing the police with a wealth of information about suspect populations, criminal activity, and the community at large.[8] Known offenders, as well as those suspected of criminal behaviour, can be followed and their activities recorded, in many cases without their knowledge. Buildings and car parks can be kept under constant watch, in the hope of either catching a burglar or car thief or simply deterring them. In short, CCTV gives the police greater control over information and their environment. Examining the extent to which this shift in control has altered the organization and practice of policing in Britain, and the relationship of the police to other government agencies, is the central concern of this work.

---

[7] P. Manning (1992) 'Information technologies and the police' in M. Tonry and N. Morris (eds.) *Modern Policing* (Chicago: University of Chicago Press), 349. According to Manning (p. 355), technologies like CCTV are attractive to the police because they offer the prospect of freedom from 'the burdens of directly managing the human condition'.

[8] For an illustration of the amount of information generated by a typical CCTV system, see J. Ansell (1998) 'Closed circuit television: the human element', unpublished M.Sc. diss. (Scarman Centre for the Study of Public Order, Leicester University), 2. See also C. Norris and G. Armstrong (1999*b*) *The Maximum Surveillance Society: The Rise of CCTV* (Oxford: Berg), 210–11.

This book examines the ways in which CCTV cameras are currently being used by the police and their partners. It describes the impact that the introduction of CCTV has had on police practices, considers the various factors that affect police CCTV use, and explores the relationship between public surveillance, policing, and social control.[9] In addition, it also considers how the emergence of surveillance technologies such as CCTV is likely to shape policing over the coming century.

Increasingly, many criminologists have come to regard the growing use of public surveillance by the police as part of a more general trend towards what has been called 'risk-based policing'. According to this view, collecting and disseminating information that can be used in the assessment and management of risk has become one of the core functions of the modern police force, progressively replacing more traditional concerns about law enforcement and crime control:

> In risk society, policing is not just a matter of repressive, punitive, deterrent measures to control those who are morally wrong. It is also a matter of surveillance, of producing knowledge of populations that is useful for administering them. The focus is on knowledge that allows selection of thresholds that define acceptable risks and on forms of inclusion and exclusion based on this knowledge.[10]

It has been argued that the police, along with local authorities and the private security industry, have been instrumental in the gradual commodification of insecurity that has characterized late twentieth-century life.[11] According to social theorists such as David Garland, the growing popularity of surveillance technologies like CCTV owes much to policies aimed at shifting responsibility for crime and the management of risk away from the state to local governments, community partnerships, and non-government agencies.[12] The

---

[9] Note that this book is concerned primarily with the use of *public area* CCTV by the police. For an examination of the use of CCTV cameras in police custody suites, see T. Newburn and S. Hayman (2002) *Policing, Surveillance, and Social Control: CCTV and the Police Monitoring of Suspects* (Cullompton, Devon: Willan Publishing).

[10] R. Ericson, and K. Haggerty (1997) *Policing the Risk Society* (Oxford: Clarendon Press), 41.

[11] See M. McCahill (1998) 'Beyond Foucault: towards a contemporary theory of surveillance' in Norris *et al.* (1998*b*), 41.

[12] D. Garland (2001) *The Culture of Control: Crime and Social Order in Late Modernity* (Oxford: Oxford University Press).

extent to which the introduction of public area CCTV may be seen as part of a movement towards risk-based policing and greater local governance of crime is a key question for this book. In particular, it examines the claim that far from reassuring the public that crime is under control, CCTV and other surveillance technologies simply confirm the conviction that more security is needed.[13]

An even more evocative and persistent claim is that greater levels of surveillance necessarily lead to more authoritarian and disciplinary methods of policing. In part, this claim derives from the assumption that there is an inherent relationship between surveillance and totalitarianism. According to Anthony Giddens, for example, totalitarianism is 'first of all, an extreme focusing of surveillance'.[14] Almost inevitably, any discussion of video surveillance conjures up a variety of disturbing images. 'Orwellian nightmares' of a society in which 'total surveillance' is the norm have passed not only into popular consciousness, but also into the mainstream discourses of sociology and criminology. Indeed, it is rare to find a critical discussion of policing and electronic surveillance that does not at some point either invoke the image of 'Big Brother' or rely on metaphors drawn directly from the world of *Nineteen Eighty-Four*:

Surveillance continues to have sinister and secretive overtones for many of us. We need look no further than our well-thumbed copies of Orwellian fiction and the all encompassing eyes and ears of Big Brother to satisfy our paranoid anxieties about the intrusive state. We feel threatened, even more so now that much fictional imagery appears to have become practical reality, routinised and part of the everyday.[15]

[13] For claims of this nature, see: K. Stenson and R. Sullivan (eds.) (2001) *Crime, Risk and Justice* (Cullompton, Devon: Willan Publishing); M. Feeley and J. Simon (1994) 'Actuarial justice: the emerging new criminal law' in D. Nelken (ed.) *The Futures of Criminology* (London: Sage), 173; M. Davies (1998) *City of Quartz: Excavating the Future in Los Angeles* (London: Pillico); McCahill (1998).

[14] A. Giddens (1985) *The Nation-State and Violence* (Cambridge: Polity), 303. On the relationship between surveillance and democracy, see also C. Dandeker (1990) *Surveillance Power and Modernity* (Cambridge: Polity); D. Lyon (1994) *The Electronic Eye: The Rise of Surveillance Society* (London: Polity), 11–14; and J. Rule (1973) *Private Lives, Public Surveillance* (London: Allen-Lane).

[15] P. Francis and J. Braggins (1995) 'Editorial' *Criminal Justice Matters* (summer) (20): 2. For further examples of the use of Orwellian imagery, see I. Lloyd (1996) 'Review of *Big Brother: Britain's Web of Surveillance and the New Technological Order* by Simon Davies' *Journal of Information, Law and Technology* 3. For an analysis of the influence that Orwell's *Nineteen Eighty-Four* has had on discussions

That this is the case is hardly surprising. Given the speed at which technological change has taken place within police forces across Britain over the past thirty years, academics and other commentators have at times struggled to make sense of the effect successive technological innovations have had on the nature of modern policing. For many, the comfortable image of *Dixon of Dock Green* has been gradually replaced by that of a new generation of police who rely less and less on the goodwill of the community for their authority or information, and increasingly on an expanding array of 'high-tech' law-enforcement and surveillance devices.[16] In addition, the apparent failure of successive governments to consider the possible effects of many of these changes on individual liberties has helped to heighten concerns that the trend towards greater use of CCTV surveillance may represent a further shift towards a more intrusive and authoritarian form of 'techno-policing':

There is a grave risk that the CCTV industry is out of control. Fuelled by fear of crime, the systems take on a life of their own, defying quantification and quashing public debate. In a very short time, the systems have challenged some fundamental tenets of justice, and created the threat of a surveillance society. Once more traditional approaches to law enforcement and social justice are being undermined without due process.[17]

This statement from the advocacy group Privacy International is particularly interesting because it highlights many of the key concerns that have accompanied the spread of CCTV in recent years. The notion that the technology of surveillance possesses a life of its

of the relationship between the power of technology and social control, see Lyon (1994), 11–14, 57–63. As Lyon notes at p. 11, 'the influence of Orwell's *Nineteen Eighty-Four* has been felt far beyond the merely literary. The metaphor of "Big Brother", in particular, now expresses a profound cultural fear in areas quite remote from what Orwell originally had in mind.'

[16] See in particular S. Manwaring-White (1983) *The Policing Revolution: Police Technology, Democracy and Liberty in Britain* (Brighton: Harvester).

[17] Statement from Privacy International, September 1995, quoted in S. Davies (1996a) *Big Brother: Britain's Web of Surveillance and the New Technological Order* (London: Pan Books), 190. A more detailed account of this argument can be found in Manwaring-White (1983), as well as in C. Walker (1983) 'Review of *The Policing Revolution: Police Technology, Democracy and Liberty in Britain*' *Public Law* 694. As Walker notes, one of the primary objections to this view is that it is based on the assumption that technology is 'inherently malevolent'.

own, and as such is in constant danger of escaping from our control, is a theme that runs through much of the literature of policing and social control.[18] More authoritarian policing is seen as an unavoidable consequence of greater levels of surveillance, no matter how well-intentioned the initial decision to embrace such technology might be. In addition, invoking the spectre of a 'surveillance society'—in which due process and justice have been subordinated to an overriding concern with crime control—invites us not only to imagine the sort of society envisaged by Orwell, but also to see its emergence as inevitable and insidious.

At the heart of this book is an ethnographic study of the way in which the technology of CCTV has been integrated into policing practices and organization. Based on extensive observation of CCTV systems and interviews with police officers, camera operators, and local authority employees in the south of England, this study seeks to understand both how CCTV surveillance is carried out by the police and how the information generated by CCTV is ultimately used. Ironically perhaps, just as the emergence of public area CCTV has greatly increased the extent to which the police can 'keep tabs' on the public and suspect communities, it has given the public the means to scrutinize the police as well. This book therefore also explores the extent to which placing the police under direct surveillance has affected their working practices and the exercise of police powers and discretion.

In order to understand the impact that the introduction of CCTV has had on policing in Britain, it is first necessary to look at the development of this technology and examine the reasons behind its rapid expansion in this country and abroad. This opening chapter traces the history of public area surveillance, considers the social and political forces that were behind its spread during the 1990s, and explains how within the space of less than ten years Britain became the most extensive user of CCTV in the world. Before turning to a historical account of the rise of CCTV, this chapter begins with an account of what CCTV is, what it is not, and what is meant by public area surveillance.

[18] One of the most disturbing portrayals of computer technology as both self-augmenting and out of control can be found in D. Burnham (1983) *The Rise of the Computer State* (New York: Vintage).

1.2   What is CCTV?

Although a great deal has been written about CCTV in recent years, it is surprisingly difficult to find a definition of closed circuit television in the literature of surveillance or crime prevention. Many writers appear to assume that because 'we all know what we're talking about', there is no reason to define exactly what a CCTV system is. Yet ensuring that everyone is in fact talking about the same thing is crucial. One of the most striking features of the current debate over the legality and effectiveness of CCTV is the extent to which different sides of the discussion make very different assumptions about what constitutes a typical CCTV system. For example, according to Privacy International, CCTV systems involve sophisticated technology.

Features include night vision, computer assisted operation, and motion detection facilities which allow the operator to instruct the system to go on red alert when anything moves in view of the cameras. Camera systems increasingly employ bullet-proof casing, and automated self defence mechanisms. The clarity of the pictures is usually excellent, with many systems being able to read a cigarette packet at a hundred metres. The systems can often work in pitch blackness, bringing images up to daylight levels.[19]

While it is true that there are systems in England that possess some of these features, and a very small number that have them all, the vast majority of CCTV schemes currently in operation are nowhere near as sophisticated as this description suggests. Indeed, the above account reads more like the average scheme manager's wish-list than an accurate description of a typical CCTV system. Similarly, describing the modern surveillance camera as 'truly awesome', as Simon Davies does in his book *Big Brother: Britain's Web of Surveillance and the New Technological Order*, is an exaggeration.[20] While it may be true that once connected to a 'moderately

---

[19] Privacy International (1997*b*) 'Statement on closed circuit television (CCTV) surveillance devices' (London: Privacy International). See also statements made by Simon Davies in his capacity as the Director General of Privacy International to the House of Lords Select Committee on Science and Technology (1997), recorded in House of Lords Paper 64, 'Enquiry into digital images as evidence: oral evidence' (London: HMSO), 31.

[20] Davies (1996*a*), 195. In the same chapter, under the heading 'The next generation of cameras', Davies also discusses the future of Computerized Facial Recognition (CRF), claiming that by 1997 technological advances will have made it possible for CCTV systems to 'scan a database of 50 million faces in less than a minute'.

priced computer [CCTV cameras] can achieve what the Stasi could only dream about', this says more about the technology of the former Democratic Republic of Germany than it does about the capabilities of most camera systems in Britain.[21]

More recently, a number of civil liberties organizations have also taken to speculating on the possible future of public area surveillance. As various anti-CCTV groups noted ominously in a leaflet entitled '10 reasons to stop the cameras':

Your local camera network involves sophisticated military technology. It may have infra-red night vision, automatic tracking, remote control, audio channels, and a zoom so powerful that it can scrutinise your facial blemishes in full colour at two hundred yards. Central control rooms are being equipped with sophisticated computer and telecommunications technology which link directly to police computer systems. And the technology being planned is even more frightening. In the near future, many camera systems will incorporate parabolic microphones to detect conversations on the street, in parks, in shops and in restaurants. And sophisticated software already on the market will allow the cameras to analyse the movement and activities of individuals or groups in public places.[22]

While it is true that technology such as that described above does exist, as yet there is little evidence to indicate that the introduction of this kind of advanced surveillance is likely to occur in the near future. Closer to the mark is the National Council for Civil Liberties' description of the modern camera as being closely equivalent to 'a person equipped with night-vision binoculars'.[23] However, even

Writing in 1995, Davies appears to be suggesting that the widespread introduction of CRF technology can be expected to take place within the very near future, despite the fact that there is little evidence to suggest that a fully functional CRF system is likely to be commercially available within the next few years or possibly much later. As Norris et al. observed in 1998, 'the prospect of being able to match a face from a city centre surveillance scene with one held on a computerised data base is advancing but still a long way off'. See Norris et al. (1998b), 266.

[21] Davies (1996a), 195.

[22] Privacy International (1997a) '10 reasons to stop the cameras', Pamphlet (London: Privacy International). The same statement also appears in an article posted in April 1997 by Simon Davies on KDIS Online (http://merlin.legend.org.uk/-brs/cctv/tenreasons.html) entitled '10 Reasons why public CCTV schemes are bad'.

[23] Liberty (1989) 'Who's watching you? Video surveillance in public places', Liberty Briefing Paper No. 16 (London: Liberty), 4. While this briefing is now somewhat out of date, the account of CCTV employed remains a fairly accurate description of the average system.

this description presupposes that there is someone actually looking at the image being recorded by the camera—a situation which is often unlikely where a system consists of more than a few cameras. It does nonetheless give some sense of the type of picture generated by the average system and the depth of surveillance that is possible using current technology. This exception aside, however, many civil liberties organizations and anti-CCTV groups continue to present a particularly frightening picture of the technology of CCTV surveillance, based on a very selective description of the kinds of systems actually in operation and an overstated account of what they can in fact do.[24]

Unfortunately, the descriptions of CCTV to be found in the reports and promotional literature available from local councils and other operators of public area systems are often no more accurate than those used by their detractors. Typically, the literature distributed by local authorities and the police avoids reference to the actual technology of surveillance, and instead focuses on the benefits that CCTV has to offer. The following extract from a pamphlet produced by the Borough of Windsor and Maidenhead to promote their CCTV system is a good example of the 'genre': 'The system for Windsor and Eton town centres covers an extensive area of the town. The cameras are carefully positioned to ensure that whilst public areas are covered, the cameras do not overlook private dwellings or any other areas where privacy is expected.'[25]

While making no mention of the type of technology used or the capabilities of the system—and at the time the Windsor and Maidenhead scheme was one of the most advanced in the country— the pamphlet instead focuses on the 'human element' of CCTV and

[24] Further illustrations of this kind of description can be found, for example, at the website of the UK Public CCTV Surveillance Regulation Campaign (at http// www.spy.org.uk/). Included among the new technologies discussed at this site are: advanced motion sensors; automated tracking software; 'biosensors' (what these are exactly is not made clear); 'millimetre wave radar'; and CCTV-operated sniper rifles (which the site notes were 'presented as a possibility in the Wim Wenders' film *The End of Violence*', and then alleges are 'actually already designed and tested "for use by security authorities" @£30,000 each by a company that designs and builds undersea robot submersibles').

[25] Royal Borough of Windsor and Maidenhead (1996) 'CCTV: Closed circuit television making Windsor and Eton safer places', Pamphlet (Windsor: Royal Borough of Windsor and Maidenhead).

Under Surveillance 11

the safeguards put in place to protect the community from abuse of the system: 'Specially trained staff monitor the CCTV pictures in a secure control room 24 hours a day, every day of the year... All staff operating the CCTV system have been specially vetted and trained and the system operates under a stringent Code of Practice designed to safeguard an individual's rights and privacy.'[26]

Significantly, nowhere in the pamphlet is there a description of how the system works, how many cameras it consists of, or exactly what it is that the operators are able to see and how it is that privacy is in fact protected.[27] In this sense, the Windsor and Maidenhead approach is common: benefits are emphasized and technical features played down or left out altogether. Given the type of information distributed by local councils and their partners, interested members of the public could be forgiven for thinking that a CCTV system consists of little more than a few cameras perched on top of buildings and poles, a video recorder, and a security guard locked away in a small, dark room. In its own way, the image is as misleading as the high-tech picture painted by opponents of CCTV.

Of course, the fact that these different groups all make use of very different descriptions and definitions of CCTV is hardly surprising. Those strongly against the use of public area surveillance are unlikely to draw attention to the fact that most CCTV schemes are in reality quite limited in terms of their surveillance capacity, just as those in favour of cameras are more likely to emphasize the benefits of surveillance rather than focus on the limits of the technology or its potential threat to civil liberties. For the purposes of this study, however, it is important to frame the discussion of video surveillance and policing in terms of the existing technology available and how that technology is *actually* being used in the majority of local authority and police-run schemes throughout Britain. To date, the debate over the use of public area surveillance has been marred by an excess of dogmatism and speculation on both sides, with the result that most discussions about the future of CCTV fail to take

[26] Royal Borough of Windsor and Maidenhead (1996).

[27] It is, however, important to note that the pamphlet does give some information about videotape management within the system: 'All video tapes are strictly managed and erased/destroyed as appropriate at regular intervals, providing they are not required by the police for use as evidence in court actions or by the Council for managing its services'. What exactly 'Council services' are in this context is not explained. See Royal Borough of Windsor and Maidenhead (1996).

into account the current reality. Understanding the present situation is, however, essential to analysing trends and accurately predicting the future. This book is not a speculative examination of public area surveillance; instead it focuses on how CCTV is being used now, and the impact that it has had on police organization and policing practices.

It is also important to be clear about the level of police involvement in the design, control, and development of public area CCTV. As will be discussed in more detail later in this book, contrary to what a number of academic commentators and civil liberties groups would have the public believe, we are in fact a long way from living in an 'Orwellian State'. While the technology of CCTV may be advancing rapidly, many factors have worked to constrain the police in making use of these new surveillance technologies. Organizational and cultural factors all play a role in the way in which an institution approaches innovation and new technology. The larger the organization and the more entrenched its organizational and cultural goals, the slower it is to change. Indeed, one of the great criticisms of the British police over the past twenty years has been their apparent resistance to change and outside pressures to reform. Yet as far as video surveillance is concerned, the picture painted by anti-CCTV groups is often starkly different, with the police frequently being portrayed as highly responsive to technological change and almost hawkish in their pursuit of new techniques of social control. Thus, in order to avoid mischaracterizing any discussion of CCTV and policing, it is first important to ensure that we know what CCTV is, and to be clear about what it can and cannot do.

As the name suggests, closed circuit television is a system in which a number of video cameras are connected in a closed circuit or loop, with the images produced being sent to a central television monitor or recorder. While the term CCTV was originally used to distinguish this type of 'private' system from broadcast television—where any correctly tuned receiver can pick up the picture signal sent from the cameras—it has since come to refer to virtually any form of monitoring system that uses video cameras as a means of surveillance. At present, CCTV cameras can be found in a wide variety of settings. Current applications range from the use of cameras to assist with traffic management and road monitoring, to the installation of CCTV by large supermarket chains to collect information on customers and shopping patterns.[28] Cameras are used in hospital operating theatres to observe surgeons at work, in maternity wards to check on the progress of premature infants, and on factory assembly lines to monitor production control.[29] Yet despite the fact that CCTV is found in some of the most unlikely of places, most commercially available systems are still used for security purposes. As the security industry is quick to point out, watching people and places is what CCTV does best.

Although in theory a CCTV system can be as simple as a single stationary camera, a monitor, and a recorder, in practice most public CCTV schemes consist of a number of cameras placed in and around a town or city centre. The location of these cameras are normally decided after consultation between local authorities, the police, and retailers, and depending on the aims of the scheme, they are positioned to provide the maximum possible amount of surveillance 'coverage'. Increasingly, however, public area CCTV is seen as forming part of more general strategies aimed at improving security through the use of urban design.[30] Ensuring that CCTV systems are integrated with measures such as street lighting and the creation of pedestrian areas has gradually become a key priority in many town and city management schemes across the country.[31]

[28] For the former, see M. Constant and P. Turnbull (1994) *The Principles and Practice of Closed Circuit Television* (Hertfordshire: Paramount Publishing Ltd.), 1. The practice of 'store tracking' and the use of CCTV cameras for video-based consumer research is discussed in The *Scotsman* (3 Dec. 1998). At the time of writing, 'store tracking' remains a relatively new practice, and one which has attracted little attention from civil libertarians or researchers.

[29] According to *The Sunday Times*, 'spy-in-the-theatre' cameras have been proposed by the Chairman of the Federation of NHS Trusts in order to monitor the performance of surgeons and record any 'mistakes'. See *The Sunday Times*, (19 Mar. 1995; 8 Oct. 1995). See also J. Moran (1998) 'A brief chronology of photographic and video surveillance' in Norris *et al.* (1998*b*), 277, 284. For CCTV use in factories, see Constant and Turnbull (1994), 1.

[30] See R. Tunstall (1994) 'Video surveillance in town centres: the implications for urban design', unpublished MA thesis (Oxford: Oxford Brookes University). See also A. Reeve (1998*a*) 'The panopticisation of shopping: CCTV and leisure consumption' in Norris *et al.* (1998*b*), 69, 79–84.

[31] See Reeve (1998*a*); Tunstall (1994); and S. Graham (1998*c*) 'Towards a fifth utility? On the extension and normalisation of public CCTV' in Norris *et al.* (1998*b*), 89.

While the majority of public area CCTV systems use overt cameras, the degree of camera visibility can vary considerably. Pole- or wall-mounted cameras, such as those typically found in car parks and many early public CCTV schemes, are perhaps the most obvious and obtrusive. As the movement and direction of this type of camera can be clearly seen, for the most part it is easy for members of the public to know whether or not they are being watched or followed by these cameras. In contrast, CCTV cameras mounted in domes and other forms of protective housing are not only less immediately visible from the street, but also far more difficult to 'read'. Even standing directly under one of these cameras, it is almost impossible to tell whether one is being observed. In addition, many such cameras make use of 'dummy lenses', which are deliberately designed to mislead as to the direction of the camera.[32] Contrary to the claims made by some civil liberties groups, however, at present the use of truly covert cameras in public areas is extremely rare. Although stories of cameras hidden in mail boxes, under park benches, and in trees abound, in reality few public authorities or police forces appear to have seriously considered using covert systems for public area surveillance. Similarly, claims that many systems will soon incorporate some form of sound-recording facility are premature.[33]

In most CCTV systems, the video pictures generated by closed circuit cameras are sent back to a central control room by way of an underground cable or microwave signal. In the control room, an operator faces a bank of television screens, each one displaying images from anywhere between one and sixteen different cameras. If the cameras are capable of being moved by remote control, the operator is free to position the cameras as he or she sees fit and to determine exactly which areas are under surveillance at any given time. Additionally, the operator can take control of an individual camera and use it to 'patrol' an area of interest, or to follow an

[32] For a discussion of the privacy implications of covert cameras, see B. J. Goold (2002b) 'Privacy rights and public spaces: CCTV and the problem of the "unobservable observer"' *Criminal Justice Ethics* 21(1): 21.

[33] In a leaflet entitled '10 reasons to stop the cameras' (1997) various anti-CCTV campaigning groups including Privacy International claimed, without reference to any evidence, that: 'In the near future, many camera systems will incorporate parabolic microphones to detect conversations on the street, in parks, in shops and in restaurants'. Quoted in Davies (1998), 248.

individual or group who may have attracted his or her attention. Almost all public area CCTV systems have the capacity to take a 'real-time' recording from at least one camera at a time, with more advanced systems now making use of digital technology to enable multiple cameras to record in 'real time'.[34]

As has been noted above, much has been made of the speed with which the technology of CCTV has advanced in recent years and the implications this may have for the type and level of surveillance undertaken. It is, however, often forgotten that even the simplest public area CCTV system is capable of generating an enormous amount of information. One camera recording constantly over a 24-hour period will produce 1,440 minutes of surveillance data, and if that camera is located on a central shopping street, on a busy day it could conceivably record the movements of literally thousands of people.[35] Given that the Local Government Association (LGA) has estimated that the average public area CCTV scheme consists of at least 29 cameras, then the total amount of information collected within a 24-hour period by such a system is enormous.[36] In light of this, it is hardly necessary to conjure up images of fully or semi-automated, high-tech systems in order to raise the prospect of CCTV being used for 'mass surveillance'. Indeed, by focusing on the technical capabilities of some of the more advanced systems available, there is perhaps a danger that the 'human aspect' of public area CCTV is obscured. Irrespective of how advanced a CCTV system may be, two factors remain constant. First, a large amount of information will be generated. Secondly, and perhaps more importantly, even in those systems that employ some form of automated tracking technology, the decision as to what the cameras look at or look out for is ultimately decided by those responsible for managing the system and their employees. This relationship— between the technology and the human element of public area

---

[34] Real-time recording is to be contrasted with multiplex recording, where images from more than one camera are stored on the same video film by a process of switching between images in a set sequence. Using a multiplex system to manage six cameras would, for example, result in a recording of every sixth frame of footage from each of the six cameras being recorded, with a resulting loss in video quality and the amount of information recorded.

[35] This example is taken from Ansell (1998), 2.

[36] Local Government Association (1998) *Local Government Association (LGA) CCTV Directory 1997/1998* (London: Local Government Association), p. vii.

surveillance—provides the key to understanding both how the police and their partners currently use CCTV and what we can expect from this technology in the future.

1.3   The rise of public area CCTV

Although in recent years the video surveillance debate has been marred by a number of exaggerated claims from both supporters and opponents of public area CCTV, one point frequently made by both the pro- and anti-CCTV lobbies is undeniably true: the expansion in CCTV surveillance over the past decade has been unprecedented. Words like 'explosive' and 'epidemic' are commonly used to describe the speed with which public area surveillance has spread throughout Britain, without any hint of overstatement. Before attempting to understand why this expansion has taken place, however, it is important to develop an accurate picture of how public area CCTV has gone from being something of a technical novelty to a ubiquitous feature of the urban landscape.

Although private CCTV systems have been in operation throughout Britain since the late 1960s, public area surveillance is a relatively recent phenomenon.[37] In August 1985, Bournemouth City Council launched what is generally regarded as Britain's first public CCTV system, ostensibly in an effort to counter rising levels of vandalism on the city's waterfront.[38] Prior to this, while cameras had been used by the police for specific surveillance operations—as in the case of the 1984–5 miners' strike—few forces or local authorities had considered the possibility of installing their own dedicated,

---

[37] According to *Photoscanner: The Journal of Photoscan*, Issue No. 23, Photoscan was the first company to market CCTV systems to retailers in Britain, having been established in 1967. See also Narayan (1996), 20; and McCahill and Norris (2002b), 14.

[38] Moran (1998), 280. 'Public area' CCTV cameras had already been in use on the London Underground since 1975, when cameras were installed on the Northern and Victoria lines in an effort to combat theft and assaults on staff. It is questionable as to whether these cameras can rightly be regarded as part of a 'public area' surveillance system, given that access to these areas was under the control of the London Underground Corporation. For the purpose of this book, a public space is defined as one to which the public normally have unrestricted access and right of way, following the definition used in M. Bulos and C. Sarno (1994) *Closed Circuit Television and Local Authority Initiatives: The First National Survey* (London: School of Land Management and Urban Policy, South Bank University London), 7.

public area CCTV systems.[39] Less than a decade later, the landscape had changed considerably. According to a survey undertaken by Bulos and Sarno, by 1993 some 39 towns and cities had CCTV cameras.[40] This number had swelled to 79 by August 1994.[41] In March 1995, the *Guardian* reported that over 90 schemes were in operation across Britain.[42] By August of the following year this number was estimated to be in excess of 200.[43] In a little over ten years, Britain had raced from a standing start to become the most extensive user of public area CCTV in Europe, if not the world.[44]

This rapid spread in the use of CCTV has been accompanied by a parallel trend, namely an increase in the depth of video surveillance. In the early 1980s, most commercially available camera systems were only capable of producing low-resolution black and white pictures, with images being stored on conventional videotape using a combination of real-time and time-lapse recorders.[45] The

[39] In 1980, a feasibility report commissioned by the Liverpool City Crime Prevention Panel recommended the installation of a police-operated, public CCTV scheme in Liverpool's city centre. See Liberty (1989), 1.

[40] Bulos and Sarno (1994). It is important to note that while the survey undertaken included London boroughs and metropolitan authorities, only a sample of district councils were considered. As such, it is possible that the actual number of schemes active in England at the time the survey was completed may have been higher.

[41] Home Office (1994) 'CCTV: Looking out for you', Pamphlet (London: HMSO).

[42] The *Guardian* (22 Mar. 1995).

[43] C. Norris, J. Moran, and G. Armstrong (1996) 'Algorithmic surveillance: The future of automated visual surveillance' Paper presented at the conference CCTV Surveillance and Social Control (University of Hull, 9 July 1996). See also S. Graham, J. Brooks, and D. Heery (1996b) 'Towns on the television: closed circuit TV in British towns and cities' *Local Government Studies* 22(3): 3. As Graham *et al.* have noted, by 1996 every major city in Britain with the exception of Leeds had installed some form of public area CCTV system.

[44] Graham *et al.* (1996b). By way of contrast, France, Europe's second-biggest user of public area CCTV, is said to have installed approximately 150,000 cameras, less than half the equivalent number in Britain. See A. Vitalis (1998) 'Big Brother is watching you: they see you but you don't see them' *Le Monde Diplomatique* (Sept.), 15.

[45] In most public area CCTV systems, a time-lapse recorder is used to extend the life of a scheme's videotapes. A type of industrial video recorder, time-lapse VCR operates by moving the tape mechanism in steps and recording one frame at a time, thereby allowing for up to 480 hours of images to be stored on a conventional three-hour video cassette. For example, a time-lapse recorder set on 72-hour mode will record only three frames per second, instead of the normal 25 frames per second associated with 'real-time' recording. The consequence of this method of recording is

now infamous but grainy pictures of the abduction of James Bulger from a shopping centre in Liverpool are fairly representative of the image quality produced by these early systems.[46] Recent advances in video technology have, however, led to the development of considerably more advanced systems of surveillance. Many cameras are now fitted with full pan, tilt, and zoom capabilities, and record in high-resolution colour, while a small but gradually increasing number also utilize sophisticated night vision, motion detection, and automatic tracking technologies.[47] While this does not mean that the average CCTV system can be accurately described as a 'military system', an increasing number of CCTV schemes are making use of advanced technologies in an effort to improve the quality of pictures produced by their cameras.

As the demand for more advanced CCTV systems has grown, technological innovations have also been drawn from an increasingly diverse range of industries. In the City of London, an automated licence plate recognition system, initially developed to solve problems of traffic management, was deployed in 1996 in conjunction with existing CCTV cameras to create what has since been called the 'Ring of Steel'.[48] Consisting of some ninety cameras, the system is capable of tracking all vehicles coming in and out of the square mile of London, automatically recording their licence plate numbers and raising an alarm if any vehicle behaves 'suspiciously'.[49] Similarly, advances in information technology and digital imaging

---

a trade-off between image quality and recording time, with an increasing amount of information being lost as the number of frames recorded per second decreases. See Constant and Turnbull (1994), 245.

[46] See *R v Secretary of State for the Home Department, ex parte Venables* and *R v Secretary of State for the Home Department, ex parte Thompson* (The Bulger Case) [1996] COD 365; (1996) 93(18) LSG 37; (1996) 146 NLJ 786; (1996) 140 SJLB 127; *The Times* (7 May 1996); The *Independent* (10 June 1996).

[47] Davies (1998), 244.

[48] The system was first established after the Bishopsgate bombing in 1993, in an effort to provide some protection for the financial centre of London from further terrorist attacks. For a more detailed description of the system see The *Guardian* (4 Aug. 1993), as well as Norris *et al.* (1998*b*), 262.

[49] Examples of 'suspicious' behaviour that will trigger a response from the system include travelling the wrong way through a one-way system and failing to leave the city area after a designated period of time. The lenses used by the system are capable of screening out glare and reflection from windscreens, and can clearly identify the occupants of any given vehicle within view of the cameras.

have also had an impact on CCTV use. Both the Police Foundation and the Forensic Science Service have been looking into the viability of facial recognition systems since 1996,[50] with the first such system being installed in the London Borough of Newham in October 1998.[51] Although there have been suggestions that this technology could soon be linked to some form of national database of faces, as yet such a system remains in the planning stage.[52]

Throughout this period, the level of police involvement in public area surveillance has varied considerably. Whereas in the United States police forces have been quick to make use of advances in video surveillance technology, in Britain the police initially approached public area CCTV with a degree of caution.[53] As will be discussed in more detail in later chapters, during the early days of

[50] The *Daily Telegraph* (22 May 1996). Facial recognition software produces pictures of surveillance subjects based on the areas of light and shade created by each person's unique facial structure (thus eliminating identification problems created by vagaries of hairstyle and the wearing of glasses), which are then digitized and can be matched against a central database. Systems based on this technology have been in operation in Britain since the mid-1990s. One of the earliest efforts to link CCTV with offender identification was the 'Football Intelligence System', in use at Manchester City's Maine Road ground. See G. Armstrong and R. Giulianotti (1998) 'From another angle: police surveillance and football supporters' in Norris *et al.* (1998b), 113, 130; and Norris *et al.* (1998a), 267.

[51] BBC News (13 Oct. 1998). According to the report, the system (which consists of 140 street cameras plus an additional 11 mobile cameras) is capable of scanning a street scene or crowd and then identifying individual targets by comparing the faces monitored against a central database of known and suspected offenders. Responding to the police claim that the system was approximately 80 per cent accurate, a spokesperson for Liberty commented: 'The accuracy of facial mapping is very limited... What the police call an 80% success rate is what we would call a one in five chance of a mistake.' Note also that on 24 April 1995, the *Hull Daily Mail* reported that a national database of facial features was being developed by the Warwickshire police, with a view to providing jurors with statistics on the probability of suspects' facial features matching those recorded on CCTV video.

[52] In 1997 the Home Office announced that from October 1998, all new passport photographs would be digitized and stored on a central database. Davies has estimated that some 3.5 million photo images—together with additional related information, such as personal and family details—will be added to this database each year, the eventual result being the creation of a searchable archive containing details on up to 35 million people within ten years (Davies (1998), 252). At the time of writing, the Home Office had not yet begun to construct this database or attempted to collect passport photos as previously announced.

[53] In the United States, much of the video surveillance technology developed by the military for use in Vietnam was adapted for police needs following the end of the war.

CCTV the British police were keen to avoid being portrayed as a 'Big Brother' figure by civil liberties groups and other opponents of public area surveillance. Such fears eventually led the Association of Chief Police Officers (ACPO) to advise Chief Constables in 1993 to take a 'back-seat' role in the promotion of CCTV and to hold off from committing resources to the technology until the police were better able to gauge the public reaction to the introduction of cameras. As CCTV became increasingly popular with politicians and the media, however, police forces around the country quickly abandoned their 'wait-and-see' policy and began to become more actively involved in the promotion and installation of the technology. By the mid-1990s the police were leaders or active partners in CCTV schemes all over the country.

In order to understand how it was possible for CCTV to spread throughout Britain so quickly, it is necessary to consider why this technology was so popular with successive Conservative and Labour governments in Britain, and to investigate the role played by local authorities and the media in the promotion of CCTV. Public area CCTV did not emerge in a social and political vacuum, but rather at a time when politicians and policy-makers were in search of a new solution to the problem of crime and, perhaps more importantly, a way of convincing the public that they were serious about crime prevention.

1.4   Exercises in rhetoric: the politics and presentation of CCTV

Throughout the early 1990s, public area CCTV enjoyed something of a honeymoon period in Britain. Despite the fact that CCTV cameras were appearing in towns and cities all over the country, until the mid-1990s it was difficult to find anyone in Britain except for a handful of journalists, academics, and civil libertarians prepared to be openly critical of CCTV.[54] As a number of commen-

Mount Vernon, New York, is credited with developing the world's first police-operated CCTV system, consisting of two cameras mounted some 22 feet above the ground feeding video signals back to a low-light-level television system. For further details on the use of CCTV by police in the United States, see Manwaring-White (1983), 90.

[54] See D. Campbell (1995) 'Spy cameras become part of the landscape' The *Guardian* (30 Jan.), 6. Many commentators have come to regard July 1996 as a

tators have since pointed out, this lack of opposition to the spread of CCTV is somewhat surprising.[55] The technology of CCTV is hardly invisible, and given the hold that the writings of Orwell and others have had on the liberal imagination since the publication of *Nineteen Eighty-Four*, it is remarkable to think that the installation of over 300,000 public area CCTV cameras in less than ten years did not at least raise some alarm bells among politicians and the wider public.

Yet for the most part, early opposition to CCTV in Britain was muted. In contrast, across the channel in France advocates of public area CCTV were met with stiff opposition. As early as 1986, the French National Committee on Computer Data and Individual Freedom (CNIL) called on the French government to regulate the use of cameras and to provide effective safeguards against possible misuse of the technology.[56] Although the campaign took time to build momentum, by 1994 the CNIL was publicly demanding that CCTV be made subject to tight controls over the types of areas that could be placed under surveillance and how any pictures produced by the cameras could be used.[57] In June of that year, the National Committee recommended that all public area CCTV systems be subject to four basic rules: that the public must be informed of the presence of cameras in a given area; that the range of such cameras must not extend beyond the area described; that all pictures taken

significant turning point in the CCTV debate, when the Centre for Criminology and Criminal Justice at the University of Hull held a major conference entitled CCTV Surveillance and Social Control. At the conference, a number of academics, local officials, and police officers were brought together to discuss various issues raised by the growing use of public area CCTV. The collected papers from the conference can be found in Norris *et al.* (1998*b*). See also Davies (1998).

[55] Stephen Graham has noted, 'it would seem virtually everyone, apart from a few civil liberties activists, agrees that public-area CCTV is a "Good Thing"'. See Graham (1998*c*), 89, 90. For further discussion of the 'CCTV debate'—or rather, the lack of debate—see also Davies (1998), 244.

[56] As it was in Britain, public support for CCTV appeared to be extremely high in France during the early 1990s. While few seemed to regard the presence of CCTV cameras as an invasion of privacy, however, various surveys suggested that French citizens were less comfortable with the fact that the same cameras could be used to take still pictures of individuals in public places. In a survey undertaken in 1996, researchers found that 51 per cent of respondents felt that showing pictures of a person taken in a public place without consent was a serious violation of an individual's right to privacy. See Vitalis (1998), 15.

[57] ibid.

by the cameras must be destroyed within a short period of time unless they were otherwise needed as part of a police investigation; and that people must be made aware of their right to have access to the system and to see any pictures taken of them. In response to this pressure, in January 1995 the French government passed security legislation which severely restricted the spread of CCTV and made video surveillance subject to various established principles of data protection.[58] As one commentator later remarked, the legislation ensured that for the time being at least, in France '[l]e débat sur la vidéosurveillance est clos, semble-t-il'.[59]

Looking further afield, the contrast between the British and German responses to the emergence of CCTV has been even more stark. While video cameras were widely used by the German police during the early 1980s in their efforts to combat terrorism,[60] from the outset many in Germany—including the Federal Constitutional Court—were strongly opposed to the idea of cameras or similar devices also being used for more general surveillance.[61] In a land-

---

[58] Under the provisions of Loi No. 95–73 du janvier 1995 (paru au J. O. le 24 janvier 1995), surveillance is only allowed in those places where there is a particular risk of assault or theft. Furthermore, even where such a risk is held to exist, cameras can only be installed with the prior authorization of the prefect of police, subject to the advice of a departmental committee chaired by a judge. See Vitalis (1998), 15. A full text of the provisions can be found in (Jan. 1995) No. 4 l'Actualité législative Dalloz 90. For a discussion of the use of video surveillance in France and some of the effects of the legislation, see J. J. Delfour (1996) 'La vidéosurveillance et le pouvoir du voir (Du panoptisme comme modèle de société)' Lignes 27: 151.

[59] Delfour (1996). For a more general discussion of public area surveillance in France, see F. Ocqueteau and M. L. Pottier (1995a) 'Videosurveillance et gestion de l'insécurité dans un centre commercial: Les leçons de l'observation' Les Cahiers de la Sécurité Intérieure 21: 60; F. Ocquteau and M. L. Pottier (1995b) Vigilance et sécurité dans les grandes surfaces (Paris: L'Harmattan); and Tunstall (1994), 55.

[60] H. W. Sternsdorff (1983) 'Aktion "Paddy". Die Möglichkeiten der Videofahndung' in W. Meyer-Larsen (ed.) Der Orwell-Statt 1984 (Reinbek: Rowohlt), 95. For a general discussion of the use of video surveillance (Videoüberwachung) by the police in Germany—including its use as an anti-terrorism measure—see F. Sack, D. Nogala, and M. Lindenberg (1997) 'Social Control Technologies: Aspekte und Konsequenzen des Technikeinsatzes bei Instanzen strafrechtlicher Sozialkontrolle im nationalen und internationalen Kontext' Aufbau- und Kontakstudium Kriminologie 295–306.

[61] As the newspaper Die Zeit observed on 12 August 1983, the use of cameras by the police had prompted public concern about the possibility of a 'videocamera network': 'dichten Netz von Videokameras, der unser öffentliches Leben überwacht'. Quoted in A. von Münchhausen (1984) 'Die stummen Aufpasser: ein dichtes Netz von Videokameras, der unser öffentliches Leben überwacht' in K.-H. Janßen (ed.) Ihr

mark decision handed down in 1983, the Federal Constitutional Court recognized the existence of a 'right of informational self-determination' based on Article 2 of the German Constitution, which could act like a limited right of privacy and would necessarily prohibit the kind of general surveillance typically undertaken by public area CCTV schemes.[62] Two decades later, judicial and public opinion remains largely unmoved. As Britain began to embrace public area surveillance in the 1990s, the German government strengthened its data protection laws and imposed new restrictions on police surveillance practices, making it even more unlikely that widespread use of public area CCTV would become a reality in Germany.[63] For both the government and the German public, the notion that any organization, public or private, should be allowed

glücklichen Augen... (Frankfurt: Robinson), 90. According to Hempel and Töpfer, since the first public area CCTV scheme was installed in Leipzig in 1996, only about a dozen similar schemes have been established throughout the whole of Germany. See L. Hempel and E. Töpfer (2002) *Working Paper No. 1: Inception Report*, Urban eye project: On the threshold to urban Panopticon? Analysing the employment of CCTV in European cities and assessing its social and political impacts (Berlin: Centre for technology and society, Technical University Berlin), 12. On the general spread of public area CCTV in Germany, see also D. Nogala (1998) 'Social control technologies: Verwendungsgrammatiken, Systematisierung and problemfelder technisierter sozialer Kontrollarrangements' unpublished diss. (Berlin: Free University).

[62]   BVerfGE 65, 1.

[63]   As Sack *et al.* have observed, '[S]ystematischen und kontinuierlichen polizeilichen Überwachung des offtenlichen Raumes mittels Videokameras ist aber bisher in der Bundesrepublik—vielleicht nicht zuletzt wegen der datenschutzrechtlichen Problematik—nicht die Rede gewesen'. ('The systematic and continuous police surveillance of public life using video cameras—possibly because of the problems created by data protection legislation—has not yet been considered in Germany.') See Sack *et al.* (1997), 295, 304. On the legal position of video surveillance in Germany, see B. Kramer (1992) 'Videoaufnahmen und andere Eingriffe in das Allgemeine Persönlichkeitrecht auf der Grundlage des § 163 StPO' *Neue Juristische Wochenschrift* 2732 ff. For a general discussion of the law relating to electronic surveillance (*Elektronische Überwachung*) in Germany, see W. Hassemer (1992) 'Brauchen wir den "Großen Lauschangriff"?' *Deutsche Richterzeitung* (Sept.) 355. For a more specific discussion of the law relating to the use of surveillance techniques by the police in Germany, see W. Gropp (1993*a*) *Besondere Ermittlungsmaßnahmen zur Bekämpfung der Organisierten Kriminalität—Ein rechtsvergleichendes Gutachten im Auftrag des Bundesministeriums der Justiz und des Bayerischen Staatsministeriums der Justiz* (Freiburg im Briesgau: Max-Planck-Institut für ausländisches und internationales Strafrecht), 105–209. For a shortened English version of this article, see W. Gropp (1993*b*) 'Special methods of investigation for combating organised crime' *European Journal of Crime, Criminal Law and Criminal Justice* 1: 20.

to engage in the sorts of surveillance activities regularly carried out by CCTV schemes across Britain is now unthinkable.[64] Indeed, so complete has been the German rejection of public area CCTV that it is difficult to find any debate of the issue at all, either in political circles or the media.

In light of this reaction, why did CCTV have such an easy ride in Britain? It is not enough simply to explain away the British fascination with CCTV with passing references to crime rates and the financial pressures of recession. Like Britain, France and Germany were also confronted with the problem of rising crime and unsustainable police budgets during the 1980s and early 1990s, and yet both countries greeted the arrival of CCTV and the rhetoric that accompanied it with considerable caution. Cameras were never seen as a panacea in either France or Germany, or indeed in any other part of Europe.[65] Only in Britain did government and the public accept at face value claims about the CCTV's supposed benefits, many of which could only be described as extremely optimistic:

---

[64] The use of private CCTV surveillance in Germany is, however, becoming increasingly widespread. As reported in the *Berliner Zeitung* (1 Sept. 1998), for example, the housing corporation GSW currently offers its tenants the option of being able to watch their children play in surrounding playgrounds via a private closed circuit television link. See also Hempel and Töpfer (2002), 5.

[65] According to Poole, for example, in Denmark 'CCTV and other forms of visual surveillance are still a strong civil liberties issue and are seen as spying on innocent people'. See R. Poole (1991) *Safer Shopping: The Identification of Opportunities for Crime and Disorder in Covered Shopping Centres* (London: West Midlands Police and Home Office), 49. In Norway, concern over the spread of public area CCTV has led to recent amendment of the country's data protection legislation. See Privacy International (1998) *Privacy and Human Rights: An International Survey of Privacy Laws and Practices* (London: Privacy International). On the use of public area CCTV in Europe—particularly France, Germany, and Spain—see Hempel and Töpfer (2002), 9–12. For an examination of the use and regulation of CCTV in Norway and Denmark, see C. Wiecek and A. Rudinow Saetnan (2002a) '*Working paper No. 4: Restrictive? Permissive? The contradictory framing of video surveillance in Norway and Denmark*', Urban eye project: On the threshold to urban Panopticon? Analysing the employment of CCTV in European cities and assessing its social and political impacts (Berlin: Centre for technology and society, Technical University Berlin); and C. Wiecek and A. Rudinow Saetnan (2002b) '*Working paper No. 5: Geographies of visibility. Zooming in on video surveillance systems in Oslo and Copenhagen*', Urban eye project (Berlin: Centre for technology and society, Technical University Berlin).

CCTV has proved itself to be a flexible, efficient and effective means of deterring, detecting and monitoring criminal activity in a wide variety of applications. (British Security Industry Association[66])

[CCTV's] effectiveness in the prevention and detection of crime has been proved. These include places such as town centres, shopping malls and car parks. (CCTV designer and supplier[67])

CCTV is a wonderful technological supplement to the police... CCTV spots crimes, identifies law breakers and helps convict the guilty... CCTV is a real asset to communities: a great deterrent to crime and a huge reassurance to the public.[68] (Michael Howard, British Home Secretary)

This last statement is not a quotation from a security industry sales brochure, but rather an extract taken from an interview given by then Home Secretary Michael Howard in May 1995 to the trade magazine *CCTV Today*. Speaking to the *New Scientist* some months later, Howard went on to claim that cameras were 'overwhelmingly popular', while at the same time acknowledging that there was 'a shortage of good quality research on CCTV'.[69] This pattern was to be repeated throughout the mid-1990s, with the Home Secretary and various other ministers presenting CCTV as a solution to the problem of crime, while openly admitting that—for the time being at least—there was little evidence to support such claims.[70] Instead of encouraging debate, the government actively encouraged councils and local authorities to consider installing their own CCTV systems, and dismissed concerns about the possible implications for privacy and civil liberties as unwarranted. As the Conservative Home Office Minister David Maclean confidently asserted at the

---

[66] Evidence of the British Security Industry Association (BSIA) to the House of Commons Home Affairs Committee, quoted in A. Beck and A. Willis (1995) *Crime and Security: Managing the Risk to Safe Shopping* (Leicester: Perpetuity Press), 171–2.

[67] Quoted in Beck and Willis (1995), 172.

[68] M. Howard (May 1995), quoted by Norris and Armstrong (1998), 10.

[69] *New Scientist* (1996) 'Crime watch' (Jan.) 6(13): 47.

[70] The lack of evidence about the effectiveness of CCTV has been discussed by a number of commentators. See Beck and Willis (1995), 171–2; D. Skinns (1998) 'Crime reduction, diffusion and displacement: evaluating the effectiveness of CCTV' in Norris *et al.* (1998b), 175; McCahill and Norris (2002b); and R. Armitage (2002) 'To CCTV or not to CCTV? A review of current research into the effectiveness of CCTV systems in reducing crime' *NACRO Community Safety Practice Briefing* (London: NACRO).

launch of the Liverpool City Centre CCTV scheme in 1995, the technology of video surveillance was something to be welcomed, not feared: 'This is a friendly eye in the sky. There is nothing sinister about it and the innocent have nothing to fear. It will put criminals on the run and evidence will be clear to see.'[71]

As Simon Davies has observed, in the face of such enthusiastic support the 1990s were a 'difficult time for anyone wanting to challenge the rationale behind CCTV'.[72] Within the Home Office, it was generally accepted that criticism of the cameras would not be welcome, and that the Home Secretary was unlikely to 'take kindly to any "bad news" about CCTV'.[73] According to Barbara Koch, Home Office officials frequently referred to CCTV as 'Howard's little project', and were careful to emphasize the potential benefits of surveillance cameras and downplay the shortage of good quality research.[74] In a 1995 study into the use CCTV in town centres, Ben Brown of the Home Office Police Research Group drew attention to this lack of evidence, but only in so far as to note that it might 'affect the willingness of retailers to fund such schemes in the future'.[75] He made no reference to the larger question of whether such investment in CCTV should be encouraged in the first place.

CCTV also enjoyed the support of many involved with the administration of criminal justice in Britain. Speaking in 1996, the former Chief Constable of Northumbria John Stevens claimed that 'law-abiding' citizens had no reason to be afraid of CCTV, whereas criminals had 'plenty to worry about'.[76] At one point, even the judiciary seemed keen to get in on the act. Judge Dennis Clarke, passing sentence on a pair of youths for an assault caught on CCTV,

---

[71] Comments made by Home Office Minister David Maclean at the launch of the Liverpool City Centre CCTV Scheme launch, quoted in Beck and Willis (1995), 165.

[72] Davies (1998), 244.

[73] Extract from a statement by a Home Office official, quoted in B. C. M. Koch (1998) *The Politics of Crime Prevention* (Aldershot: Ashgate), 38.

[74] Koch (1998), 38.

[75] B. Brown (1995) 'CCTV in town centres: three case studies' Crime Detection and Prevention Series, Paper No. 68 (London: Police Research Group, Home Office Police Department), 1.

[76] Extract from a speech made by John Stevens, former Chief Constable of Northumbria, quoted by A. Michael, *Hansard House of Commons Debates*, 30 July 1997, col. 41.

was particularly outspoken: 'A lot of people talk nonsense about civil liberties. But CCTV is of great benefit to all of us and our civil liberties. It is a safeguard and a reassuring tool in the armoury of justice.'[77]

Despite this official enthusiasm, however, there remained little in the way of reliable evidence to suggest that CCTV was anything more than an expensive placebo for the public's fear of crime.[78] What, then, compelled the government, in apparent collusion with councils and local authorities, to wire up virtually every major town and city in England with CCTV in less than a decade? How was a country traditionally wary of anything resembling a move towards a police state persuaded to accept the need for mass surveillance? Why, alone in all of Europe, did Britain embrace CCTV?

In part, the answer to these questions can be found in the way in which thinking about crime and criminal justice has changed in Britain over the last 25 years. Although a broad range of trends and influences have contributed to the rise of CCTV—some of which will be discussed below—the impact of these predominantly sociological forces can only be understood when set against a picture of the recent political landscape. As Heal has argued, anyone seeking to understand recent changes in the British response to crime 'must put the clock back to the early 1980s'.[79] This is particularly true when trying to explain the enthusiasm shown by successive governments—both Conservative and Labour—for CCTV and public area surveillance. Viewed in this way, the rise of CCTV in Britain begins to look less like an accident and more like the inevitable consequence of a gradual but significant shift in thinking about crime and issues relating to criminal justice.

[77] Judge Dennis Clarke, quoted in M. Bunyan (1997) 'Judge angry as boy thugs go free' *Daily Telegraph* (7 June).

[78] As Ditton and Short have noted, there was plenty of 'unreliable' evidence as to the effectiveness of CCTV. See J. Ditton and E. Short (1996) 'Does CCTV affect crime?' Paper presented at the conference CCTV Surveillance and Social Control (University of Hull, 9 July 1996); and J. Ditton (1998) 'Public support for town centre CCTV schemes: myth or reality?' in Norris *et al.* (1998*b*), 221.

[79] K. Heal (1992) 'Changing perspectives on crime prevention: the role of information and structure' in D. Evans, N. R. Fyfe, and D. Herbert (eds.) *Crime, Policing and Place: Essays in Environmental Criminology* (London: Routledge), 257. See also Koch (1998), 27.

1.4.1   Crime prevention and the politicization of criminal justice

As many commentators have observed, the election of the Conservative Party in 1979 marked a decisive break with the political consensus that had dominated the development of public policy since the war, and replaced it with an ideological commitment to the principles of the New Right and a style of government based on what was later to become known as 'conviction politics'.[80] This was especially the case when it came to the formulation of criminal justice policy. As Savage has written:

Prior to the 1979 General Election 'law and order' policy... exhibited many of the features of the consensus politics of the post-war period. Indeed, so broad was the agreement over policy in this area (with the exception of perhaps support for or opposition to the reintroduction of capital punishment), that in many respects law and order was hardly a 'political' issue in the sense of falling along party-political lines.[81]

In the lead-up to the 1979 General Election, the Conservatives worked hard to make criminal justice a key election issue.[82] Arguing that, under Labour, Britain had fallen victim to rising levels of crime, growing public disorder, and civil unrest, the Conservatives enthusiastically presented themselves as the 'party for law and order'.[83] Over and over again in speeches and interviews Labour

[80] S. P. Savage (1998) 'The politics of criminal justice policy' in I. K. McKenzie (ed.) *Law, Power and Justice in England and Wales* (Westport, Conn.: Praeger Publishers), 172, 172–3.

[81] S. P. Savage (1990) 'A war on crime? Law and order policies in the 1980s' in S. P. Savage and L. Robbins (eds) *Public Policy under Thatcher* (London: Macmillan), 89. As Savage notes on the same page, however, political agreement did not necessarily mean that criminal justice policy remained static during this period, but rather that 'the major developments which did take place did so within a broad framework of consensus'.

[82] See the discussion of the lead-up to the election in M. Nash and S. P. Savage (1994) 'A criminal record? Law, order and Conservative policy' in S. P. Savage, R. Atkinson, and L. Robbins (eds.) *Public Policy in Britain* (London: Macmillan), 137.

[83] D. Downes and R. Morgan (1994) '"Hostages to fortune"? The politics of law and order in post-war Britain' in M. Maguire, R. Morgan, and R. Reiner (eds.) *The Oxford Handbook of Criminology* (Oxford: Clarendon), 183, 190–2. As Downes and Young have noted, the irony of all this is that during the post-war period, the increase in general crime rates under successive Conservative governments was on average twice that under Labour. See D. Downes and J. Young (1987) 'Crime and government' *New Society* (21 May), 55.

was painted as the party of excuses, unable to stem the tide of economic decline and industrial malaise, and with it Britain's slide into lawlessness. In an interview with the *Daily Telegraph* in March 1979, Margaret Thatcher skilfully played on public anxiety about the power of trade unions, the state of the economy, and crime, drawing them all together and presenting them as different facets of the same problem:

A Trade Union leader has advised his members to carry on picketing because they would act in such numbers that the authorities would need to use football stadiums as detention centres. That is the rule of the mob and not of law, and ought to be condemned by every institution in the land. The demand in the country will be for two things: less tax and more order.[84]

It has been argued by a number of commentators, perhaps most notably by the sociologist Stuart Hall, that this drift towards a 'get tough' approach to criminal justice had begun long before the lead-up to the 1979 General Election.[85] According to Hall, the move towards a more authoritarian, disciplinary society in Britain has been a gradual one, emerging in part as a response to the country's inability to cope with successive recessions and the need for economic restructuring. Faced with tough times, simmering class tensions, and the prospect of increased social fragmentation, strong government and the values of law and order inevitably proved to be popular with the majority of voters, particularly in what has come to be known as 'middle England'. On this analysis, the politicization of criminal justice fostered by the Conservatives in the lead-up to the 1979 General Election was just another example of a broad trend within British politics, the origins of which can be traced back to the end of the Second World War. In terms of their thinking about public policy generally—and criminal justice in particular—all of the major parties were in the process of drifting further and further

[84] The *Daily Telegraph* (28 Mar. 1979), quoted in M. Brake and C. Hale (1992) *Public Order and Private Lives: The Politics of Law and Order* (London: Routledge), 15.

[85] S. Hall (1979) *Drifting into a Law and Order Society* (London: Cobden Trust); and S. Hall (1985) 'Authoritarian populism' *New Left Review* 115, 115–24. See also M. Kettle (1980) 'The drift to law and order' *Marxism Today* (Oct.), 20; J. Lea and J. Young (1984) *What is to be Done about Law and Order?* (Harmondsworth: Penguin); J. Morison (1987) 'New strategies in the politics of law and order' *Howard Journal* 26(3): 203; and Brake and Hale (1992), 35.

to the right in an effort to establish themselves as the natural party of government. By the time Thatcher's Conservatives arrived on the scene, capturing the high ground on law and order and encouraging 'authoritarian populism' was seen as essential to any successful political campaign.[86] As Hall argues, the election of the Conservatives in 1979 did not so much represent a decisive break with the past as yet another chapter in the 'great moving right show'.

Writing in a similar vein, Martin Kettle has also claimed that there has been a drift in Britain towards the establishment of an authoritarian state, although he sees this shift as a far more recent phenomenon than Hall. According to Kettle, many of the law and order polices adopted by the Conservatives in the months following the 1979 election simply represented the continuation and development of the approach taken by the previous Labour government and, to a lesser extent, their immediate Tory predecessors.[87] What was different, however, was the power of Thatcher's rhetoric: 'People have asked me whether I am going to make the fight against crime an issue at the next General Election. No I am not going to make it an issue. It is the people of Britain who are going to make it an issue' (Conservative Party Conference, 1977).[88]

Whatever the origins of the tougher stance on law and order, the 1979 election was undoubtedly a watershed for the development of criminal justice policy in Britain. For many within the Conservative Party, victory in 1979 was seen as a triumph for this new strategy and a confirmation of the rhetorical appeal of talking tough on criminal justice. Within months of the election, the new government embarked on a wide-ranging criminal justice programme which soon began to reflect the extent to which certain key changes in policy direction were being politically and ideologically driven rather than research-led.[89]

1.4.2   In the public eye: CCTV and the Bulger case

In hindsight, the 1979 General Election was significant for the future of CCTV and public surveillance in Britain for two reasons.

[86] Hall (1985), 115–24.

[87] M. Kettle (1982) *Uprising! The Police, the People and the Riots in Britain's Cities* (London: Pan).

[88] Margaret Thatcher at the Conservative Party Conference 1977, quoted in Brake and Hale (1992), 15.

[89] Savage (1998), 172.

First and foremost, it signalled the beginning of a new and ongoing political conflict between the major parties over which could be seen as the most concerned about the problem of crime. As Britain moved into the 1980s and then the 1990s, the increasing politicization of criminal justice policy made 'silver bullet' solutions to the problem of crime all the more attractive to politicians and policymakers alike.[90] In 1984, the Home Office produced a circular that marked a dramatic realignment of British criminal justice policy, shifting the government's focus away from a commitment to 'fighting crime'—as previously outlined in the 1979 and 1983 Conservative Party Manifestos—towards broader strategies of crime prevention.[91] The effects of Home Office Circular 8/1984 have been discussed at great length in the literature of crime prevention, and its publication has since come to be regarded as something of a turning point in the development of criminal justice policy in Britain.[92] Aside from acknowledging the need to develop strategies aimed at preventing criminal behaviour, the circular also emphasized the importance of involving local authorities and other agencies in any new programme of crime prevention. Along with crime prevention, 'partnership' was the main theme of the circular:

[90] J. Bannister, N. R. Fyfe, and A. Kearnes (1998) 'Closed circuit television and the city' in Norris et al. (1998b), 21, 22. As Rutherford has noted, one of the central features of this post-war consensus was the role played by senior Home Office civil servants in the formation of criminal justice policy, with the emphasis in the Home Office being 'essentially pragmatic in orientation rather than driven by formulated principles'. See A. Rutherford (1996) *Transforming Criminal Policy: Spheres of Influence in the United States, the Netherlands and England and Wales during the 1980s* (Winchester: Waterside Press), 85.

[91] Home Office (1984) 'Crime prevention', Home Office Circular 8/1984 (London: Home Office). According to the earlier 1979 Manifesto, 'Surer detection means surer deterrence'. This theme was echoed in the 1983 Manifesto, in which increased police numbers, the provision of tougher sentencing powers, and plans to build more courtrooms and more prisons, are all facts given as evidence of the Conservative Party's commitment to the 'war against crime'. See Conservative Central Office (1979) *Conservative Manifesto 1979* (London: McCorquodale Printer Ltd.), 19; and Conservative Central Office (1983) *Conservative Manifesto 1983* (London: McCorquodale Printer Ltd.), 33–4.

[92] As Crawford puts it, circular 8/1984 has 'become a crucially symbolic milestone in the renaissance of crime prevention'. See A. Crawford (1998) *Crime Prevention and Community Safety: Politics, Policies, and Practices* (Harlow: Addison Wesley Longman Ltd.), 36.

A primary objective of the police has always been the prevention of crime. However, since some of the factors affecting crime lie outside the control or the direct influence of the police, crime prevention cannot be left to them alone. Every individual citizen and all those agencies whose policies and practices can influence the extent of crime should make their contribution. Preventing crime is a task for the whole community.[93]

According to Garland, such sentiments can also be seen as indicative of a more general shift in thinking about criminal justice in Britain.[94] Forces of late modernity—including the democratization of social and cultural life, the rise of mass media, and fundamental changes in the structure of the family—had all combined with the politics of post-welfarism to create an environment in which crime control and the empowerment of local communities had become a major concern. In linking crime prevention with community responsibility, the Conservatives had begun to embrace a 'neo-liberal' agenda and make a decisive break with the politics of the past.

At first, this reorientation of policy led to the development of a variety of government initiatives aimed at promoting the new values of prevention and partnership. The establishment of the organization Crime Concern and the Safer Cities Programme in 1988 were both early products of this change in approach.[95] By 1990 and the release of Home Office Circular 44/1990 entitled 'Crime Prevention: The Success of the Partnership Approach', the philosophy of the 1984 circular had become central to the Conservative government's criminal justice policy. Local authorities, the police, probation services, and other criminal justice agencies were encouraged to 'reconsider with others the contribution which their organisations [were] making to crime prevention'.[96]

Allied to this desire to reduce crime and improve public safety, however, was another, arguably more important concern: to promote business and encourage consumer confidence. As Gamble has noted, the Conservative government's commitment to the New Right principle of a 'free economy-strong state' meant that it was

[93] Home Office Circular 8/1984.

[94] Garland (2001), 75–102.

[95] For a discussion of the role played by Crime Concern and Safer Cities in the Conservative government's crime prevention strategy, see Crawford (1998), 37, 50–8.

[96] Home Office (1990*a*) 'Crime prevention: the success of the partnership approach', Home Office Circular 44/1990 (London: Home Office), 2.

similarly committed to ensuring that businesses and consumers were free to engage in commerce unhindered.[97] Criminal and anti-social behaviour was perceived to be a threat not only to public order and feelings of community safety, but also to the rights of businesses and 'consumer citizenship'.[98] Both the Public Order Act 1986 and the Criminal Justice and Public Order Act 1994 reflected this concern. Whereas the 1986 Act placed restrictions on marches and public assemblies in order to 'reduce the serious disruption sometimes suffered by pedestrians, business and commerce',[99] the 1994 Act created a new offence—aggravated trespass—that could potentially be used to prevent consumers from protesting outside shops.[100] Both of these factors—the desire to respond to public fears about crime on the one hand, and to protect businesses from criminal activity and 'flawed consumers' on the other[101]—made it almost inevitable that CCTV would be greeted by the Conservative government with open arms.

The initial enthusiasm—and later neglect—shown for schemes such as Neighbourhood Watch, Street Watch, and building up the special constabulary, is in large part indicative of this pragmatic approach to criminal justice policy. By the end of 1995, with government support for Street Watch waning in the face of less than spectacular results,[102] the Home Secretary Michael Howard began

[97]   A. Gamble (1988) *The Free Economy and the Strong State: The Politics of Thatcherism* (London: Macmillan), 28. See also Bannister *et al.* (1998), 30–1.

[98]   N. R. Fyfe (1995a) 'Controlling the local spaces of democracy and liberty? 1994 criminal justice legislation' *Urban Geography* 16(3): 192; N. R. Fyfe (1995b) 'Law and order policy and the spaces of citizenship in contemporary Britain' *Political Geography* 14(2): 177.

[99]   Home Office (1986) 'Review of Public Order Law' (London: HMSO), para. 4.22.

[100]   According to section 61(1) of the Criminal Justice and Public Order Act 1994, a person commits the offence of aggravated trespass if they trespass 'on land in the open air and, in relation to any lawful activity which persons are engaging in or are about to engage in on that or adjoining land in the open air, does anything which is intended by him or her to have the effect—(a) of intimidating those persons or any of them so as to deter them or any of them from engaging in that activity, or (b) of obstructing that activity, or (c) of disrupting that activity'. For a discussion of the scope of the offence, see Liberty (1995) *Defending Diversity, Defending Dissent: What's Wrong with the Criminal Justice and Public Order Act 1994* (London: National Council for Civil Liberties).

[101]   McCahill (1998), 51.

[102]   Although public support for Neighbourhood Watch was high during the early 1990s, by the late 1980s both the government and the Home Office had begun to

openly searching for a new crime prevention strategy to champion.[103] Perhaps more so than any of its predecessors, CCTV seemed to offer an almost magical solution to the problems of street crime and public disorder. The very public role played by cameras in the Bulger case had already created a groundswell of popular support for CCTV (despite the fact that the cameras had been powerless to stop Thompson and Venables from murdering their victim), and many Conservatives, Michael Howard among them, were quick to realize this. As Davies has argued, the abduction of James Bulger had suddenly thrust CCTV cameras and public surveillance into the limelight:

[I]n 1993, hard on the heels of the murder of toddler James Bulger, the symbolism that fuelled CCTV was extraordinarily powerful... Although the killers were not actually identified or apprehended as a result of this footage, the connection was irrevocably made between cameras and crime control. Put bluntly, an argument against CCTV was interpreted as an argument in favour of baby killers.[104]

In the months that followed James Bulger's death, the haunting black-and-white images of his abduction were shown repeatedly on television screens across Britain, raising CCTV's public profile even further. Keen to exploit the public mood, the Conservatives wasted little time in giving CCTV their unqualified blessing. Within less than a year, John Major had committed the government to providing considerable financial support for CCTV, enthusiastically proclaiming at the 1994 Conservative Party Conference that 'anything that helps people and hinders criminals is fine by me'.[105] Soon the

---

regard such schemes as incapable of significantly reducing levels of crime in the community. Extensive research undertaken by Bennett in 1989 and 1990 had suggested that the effectiveness of Neighbourhood Watch and other similar public surveillance schemes was extremely limited, a result which appeared to confirm the findings of a number of similar studies conducted in the United States. See T. Bennett (1990) *Evaluating Neighbourhood Watch* (Aldershot: Gower); D. P. Rosenbaum (1988) 'A critical eye on neighbourhood watch: does it reduce crime and fear?' in T. Hope and M. Shaw (eds.) *Communities and Crime Reduction* (London: HMSO), 126; and W. Skogan (1990) *Disorder and Decline* (New York: Free Press).

[103] See Koch (1998), 38.

[104] Davies (1998), 244. For an analysis of media coverage of CCTV in Britain, see McCahill and Norris (2002b), 28–49.

[105] Speech to the Conservative Party Conference, quoted in *Planning Week* (3 Mar. 1994).

Environment Minister was encouraging local authorities to consider installing their own CCTV systems, on the grounds that public area surveillance had the potential to 'bring enormous benefits to towns and cities'.[106] Indeed, such was the government's desire to promote CCTV that it quickly removed the need for councils and local authorities to obtain planning permission for new schemes, and rejected calls for licensing or any other legal regulation of the technology.[107] All of this took place without the benefit of parliamentary debate, inter-agency consultation, or even clear evidence that CCTV in fact reduced crime.[108] As the Home Secretary Michael Howard was later to admit, what mattered most was that the public wanted CCTV:

CCTV is overwhelmingly popular. People want it in their town because it makes them feel safer, reduces the fear of crime and lets them use and enjoy their high streets again. The money we are putting into CCTV is partly a response to this public support, but it is also an indication of our confidence that it is worth it . . . When the evaluations of the schemes helped by the Home Office become available I am sure they will show the same.[109]

Just as readers of the *Sun* had been able to convince the Home Secretary to increase the sentence handed down to James Bulger's killers, so too had public opinion provided a reason for the government to begin wiring up towns and cities across the country, with

---

[106] Sir Paul Beresford, quoted in *Planning Week* (13 Oct. 1994).

[107] See comments on planning regulations in Privacy International (1997*a*). In line with these changes, in part 12, section 163 of the Criminal Justice and Public Order Act 1994, the government also gave local authorities in England and Wales the power to install CCTV cameras for the purpose of making visual recordings of events occurring on any land under their control. See M. Maguire (1998) 'Restraining Big Brother? The regulation of surveillance in England and Wales' in Norris *et al.* (1998*b*), 229.

[108] At that time, only one major study of public area CCTV had been conducted in England and Wales, and this study had only considered public perceptions of the effectiveness of CCTV. See T. Honess and E. Charman (1992) 'Closed circuit television in public places: its acceptability and perceived effectiveness', Crime Prevention Unit Series, Paper 35 (London: Home Office Police Research Group).

[109] *New Scientist* (1996) 'Crime watch' (Jan.) 6(13): 47, quoted in Koch (1998), 38. Michael Howard's perception of CCTV's popularity with the public was later echoed by the chief constable of Dyfred-Powys, Raymond White, who argued in 1997 that '[w]e are now seeing a clear public demand for this technology . . . the public find CCTV systems very reassuring, second in value only to a patrolling police officer'. Quoted by A. Michael, *Hansard House of Commons Debates*, 30 July 1997, col. 41.

little regard for the long-term consequences of such a policy. What is perhaps most ironic about the rise of CCTV is that, having been championed by the Conservatives as part of an effort to appear tough on crime, the technology has also been used since by Labour as the cornerstone of a new political consensus on law and order:

There are now many areas, especially those connected with law and order, in which there is some non-partisan consensus. Apart from all being against crime, we are now also all in favour of public-private partnerships, and of making every pound of public expenditure go as far as possible. CCTV fulfils all those ideals.[110]

In 1999, for example, Jack Straw enthusiastically threw his support behind CCTV, echoing the rhetoric of the previous Home Secretary Michael Howard and displaying the same disregard for the need for thorough independent research:

The evidence is clear. In the right context, CCTV can significantly reduce crime and disorder. It is like having permanently on the beat in particular streets or areas a number of police officers with eyes in the back of their heads and an incontrovertible record of what they have seen. When used properly, CCTV can deter criminals, greatly assist the police and others in bringing offenders to justice and help to reduce people's fear of crime.[111]

It is difficult to be sure exactly what 'evidence' the Home Secretary was referring to in this speech. While considerably more is known about the effectiveness of CCTV now than in the mid-1990s when Michael Howard was making similar claims, the relationship between closed circuit surveillance and crime remains extremely under-researched. It is still the case that little is known about the effect CCTV may have on levels of violent crime, or whether the many CCTV success stories frequently recounted by MPs mask problems of displacement.[112] Aside from a handful of small and highly context-specific studies, the only major piece of

[110] Michael, *Hansard House of Commons Debates*, 30 July 1997, col. 41.

[111] J. Straw, Secretary of State for the Home Department, *Hansard House of Commons Debates*, 16 Mar. 1999.

[112] For a comprehensive overview of the CCTV evaluation literature, see B. C. Welsh and D. P. Farrington (2002) 'Crime prevention effects of closed circuit television: a systematic review', Home Office Research Study 252 (London: Development and Statistics Directorate, Home Office). Significantly, after examining a total of 22 evaluations, the authors concluded that CCTV could only be said to reduce overall crime 'to a small degree' (p. vii).

empirical research to emerge during the early 1990s was Ben Brown's paper on the operation and effectiveness of CCTV systems in Newcastle, Birmingham, and King's Lynn.[113] Based on an examination of how the police use CCTV systems to combat criminal and anti-social behaviour within a number of town centre areas, Brown's study looked at the effect of camera systems on overall crime rates for different types of offences in different town and city areas, and concluded that CCTV is generally much more effective at reducing property-related crime than it is at combating problems associated with anti-social behaviour and public order. Although the presence of cameras may help to alleviate public concerns about personal safety within city and town centres, according to the case studies featured in the paper, there is little evidence to suggest that CCTV actually acts as a significant deterrent in the case of personal crimes such as assault, particularly in large metropolitan areas. Where CCTV does appear to have an impact is in the way in which it enhances the ability of the police to respond to such disorders, both in terms of deploying officers to the scene and gathering evidence after the offence has taken place. The study also notes that even in relation to property crime, the deterrent effect of CCTV can be short-lived unless there is also a parallel increase in the risk of arrest for these offences. On the basis of these findings, Brown argues that in order to be effective in the long term, CCTV cannot be used as a lone measure:

CCTV seems to work best when it is part of a package of measures, which in this case is a general command and control strategy. With packages of measures it can be difficult to separate any individual element and point to it as a source of success, and so in this case simply installing cameras is no guarantee that crime will reduce in the long term. What is important is the way in which CCTV is used as part of an overall strategy for policing town centres.[114]

Since the publication of Brown's study in 1995, there have been few other empirical studies of the impact or effectiveness of CCTV

---

[113] Brown (1995). Some narrowly focused studies regarding CCTV include: M. R. Chatterton and S. J. Frenz (1994) 'CCTV: its role in reducing burglaries and the fear of crime in sheltered accommodation for the elderly' *Security Journal* 3(3): 133; and M. Speed, J. Burrows, and J. Bamfield (1995) *Retail Crime Costs1993/94 Survey: The Impact of Crime and the Retail Response* (London: British Retail Consortium).

[114] Brown (1995), 65.

in Britain, and what little research there is paints a confused picture. In their study of the impact of CCTV on crime rates in the Scottish town of Airdrie, for example, Jason Ditton and Emma Short found that, although crime had fallen by 21 per cent in the two years since the cameras were first introduced, during the same period the number of public order offences committed in the town centre had risen by 33 per cent, results that led them to question the 'populist' suggestion that 'CCTV works'.[115] Similarly, in his study of CCTV in Doncaster, David Skinns found that while the presence of cameras appeared to have had a positive effect on crime rates within the town centre, there was also evidence to suggest that some of this reduction had come at the expense of an increase in crime in nearby residential areas and local townships.[116] As a consequence, although the then Home Secretary Jack Straw may have been convinced that CCTV can 'significantly reduce crime and disorder', the available evidence for that proposition is weak.[117] Little is known

[115] J. Ditton and E. Short (1998a) 'Evaluating Scotland's first town centre CCTV' in Norris et al. (1998b), 155, 161. Interestingly, Ditton and Short also found that crimes of dishonesty fell to 48 per cent of their pre-CCTV level. Commenting on their results, Ditton and Short noted that overall CCTV seemed to 'have had a variable effect on the rates of different types of recorded crimes and offences', and concluded (at p. 169), 'That the response to CCTV is varied, complex, and unpredictable (rather than uniformly a simple case of predictable mono-causal crime prevention) may seem logical—particularly with the benefit of hindsight—but is nevertheless hard to establish in the face of the populist, and chiefly amateur, onslaught that CCTV "works"'.

[116] Skinns (1998). As Skinns rightly notes at p. 186, it is important to remember when attempting to evaluate the impact of CCTV on crime rates that 'establishing a connection between the introduction of CCTV and a change in the crime rate does not tell us why that reduction or increase has occurred'.

[117] In addition to the studies mentioned, an evaluation of the effectiveness of CCTV in Brighton conducted by Squires and Measor also returned results similar to those of Ditton and Short, and of Skinns: an overall fall in crime of 10 per cent accompanied by a 1 per cent rise in violent crime and evidence of displacement to surrounding residential areas. See P. Squires and L. Measor (1996) *Closed Circuit TV Surveillance and Crime Prevention in Brighton: Half Yearly Report* (Brighton: University of Brighton Health and Social Policy Research Centre); and P. Squires and L. Measor (1997) *Closed Circuit TV Surveillance and Crime Prevention in Brighton: Follow-up Analysis* (Brighton: University of Brighton Health and Social Policy Research Centre). For a general summary of most of the evaluative studies to date, see Welsh and Farrington (2002); and C. Phillips (1999) 'A review of CCTV evaluations: crime reduction effects and attitudes towards its use' in K. Painter and N. Tilley (eds.) *Surveillance of Public Space: CCTV, Street Lighting, and Crime Prevention* (Monsey, NY: Criminal Justice Press).

about how and why CCTV affects crime rates or criminal behaviour, or the extent to which displacement effects such as those uncovered by Skinns are a common result of the introduction of town centre cameras. Nonetheless, CCTV is extremely popular with politicians and policy-makers, who continue to support and invest in this technology without really knowing exactly what it does.

1.5 CCTV: why was no one watching?

There is clearly much more that could be said about the political background to the emergence of CCTV in Britain over the past decade. Yet surprisingly little has been written on the subject of public area CCTV and its place in the development of criminal justice policy during the late 1980s and early 1990s. Certainly, there is a noticeable gap in the criminological literature when it comes to the subject of open street surveillance and the politics of public safety and public policing. Crime prevention initiatives such as Neighbourhood Watch, Street Watch, and the Safer Cities project have all attracted attention from academics and researchers keen not only to assess the impact of such programmes on crime and community safety, but also to understand the reasons behind the development and promotion of these schemes by local and national government.[118] In contrast, up until very recently CCTV barely warranted a mention in most mainstream accounts of the development of crime prevention policy in Britain. Of the dozens of books and articles published on crime prevention and the development of criminal justice policy over the last ten years, barely a handful bother to mention CCTV and public surveillance at all.[119] Leaving

[118] See e.g. Bennett (1990); P. Ekblom and K. Pease (1995) 'Evaluating crime prevention' in M. Tonry and D. Farrington (eds.) *Building a Safer Society: Strategic Approaches to Crime Prevention*, Crime and Justice Series, vol. 19 (London: University of Chicago Press), 582; K. Pease (1997) 'Crime prevention' in Maguire *et al.* (1997), 659; M. Sutton (1996) 'Implementing crime prevention schemes in a multi-agency setting: aspects of process in the Safer Cities Programme', *Home Office Research Studies* (London: HMSO); and N. Tilley (1993a) 'Crime prevention and the Safer Cities story' *Howard Journal* 32(1): 40.

[119] For example, none of the following studies mention CCTV, despite their focus on contemporary issues in crime prevention: J. Bright (1997) *Turning the Tide: Crime, Community and Prevention* (London: Demos); R. V. Clarke (1995) 'Situational crime prevention' in Tonry and Farrington (1995), 91; E. Currie (1996) 'Social crime

TABLE 1.1. Crime prevention expenditure (£m)

Year	Publicity	Safer cities	Crime prevention college	Crime prevention unit	Crime concern	Crime prevention research	CCTV	Total
1993–4	5.0	6.0	0.9	0.8	0.5	0.1	0.0	13.3
1994–5	8.2	2.1	0.8	0.9	0.6	0.2	5.0	17.8
1995–6	5.6	1.0	0.8	0.9	0.5	0.2	0.0	9.0
1996–7	1.5	0.3	0.8	0.9	0.5	0.2	15.0	19.2
1997–8	1.5	0.3	0.8	0.9	0.5	0.2	15.0	19.2
1998–9	1.4	0.3	0.8	0.9	0.5	0.2	15.0	19.1

Note: These figures do not, of course, reflect levels of overall spending on CCTV throughout the 1990s. Very few—if any—local authorities have received awards from the Home Office sufficient to cover the entire cost of installing and maintaining a reasonably sized town centre CCTV system, with most covering the remaining cost with funds drawn from local businesses or the police.

Source: The Politics of Crime Prevention, Koch (1998), Ashgate.

aside the fact that CCTV should be a prime target for any criminologist interested in crime prevention, this gap in the literature is even more difficult to understand when one considers that more public money has been spent on CCTV in the past five years than on almost all other forms of crime prevention combined. As Table 1.1 shows, between 1996 and 1999, of a total of £57.5 million allocated by the Home Office to crime prevention, approximately £45 million—79 per cent of the overall budget—was spent on CCTV. Furthermore, this money was distributed to councils and local authorities on the understanding that they would be solely responsible for evaluating their own CCTV schemes once operational, with no additional funding being made available by the Home Office for local evaluations or any large-scale studies of the impact of the public area surveillance programme as a whole.[120]

prevention strategies in a market society' in J. Muncie, E. McLaughlin, and M. Langan (eds.) Criminological Perspectives: A Reader (London: Sage), 343; K. Pease (1996) 'Opportunities for crime prevention: the need for incentives' in W. Saulsbury, J. Mott, and T. Newburn (eds.) Themes in Contemporary Policing (London: Policy Studies Institute/Police Foundation), 96.

[120] Koch (1998), 50.

In short, while the government has been prepared to bankroll scores of new CCTV schemes, it apparently has no great interest in seeing whether they actually work. Here again, a contrast needs to be drawn between CCTV and the various crime prevention initiatives that preceded it. Both Safer Cities and Neighbourhood Watch have been the subjects of Home Office-funded research, not just in the early stages of each scheme but throughout the life of each programme. That successive governments—Conservative and Labour—appear to have been reticent about encouraging research into the impact of CCTV raises the question of why public area surveillance has been so popular with politicians and policy-makers.

So why was no one apparently very interested in asking this question? Why was no one in the criminological community interested—at the time at least—in asking why one of the most political of post-war Home Secretaries decided to promote CCTV so vigorously, or why his political opponents did not question the 'wiring up' of Britain? Given the general hostility shown by many criminologists to the policies pursued by the Conservatives in their last years in office, it seems odd that CCTV should have been spared the same sort of scrutiny that greeted most of the Major government's new criminal justice initiatives. As has already been mentioned, on the few occasions where the government felt compelled to justify its support for this new technology, it invariably did so by reference to largely anecdotal evidence about the effectiveness of CCTV and dubious claims about the level of public support enjoyed by open street surveillance.[121] If for no other reason, this alone should have set the alarm bells ringing or at least inspired a few articles in the *British Journal of Criminology*.

There are a number of possible explanations for this apparent lack of interest in 'the politics of CCTV'. Certainly, the amount of

---

[121] For an examination of the problems associated with measuring levels of public support for CCTV, see Ditton (1998). Note that although Ditton is right to call attention to the shortage of professional surveys of public attitudes to CCTV, a number of independent studies have suggested that public support for CCTV during this period was in fact relatively high. See Squires and Measor (1997); V. Mahalingham (1996) 'Sutton town centre public perception survey' in M. Bulos and D. Grant (eds.) *Towards a Safer Sutton? CCTV One Year On* (London: London Borough of Sutton); and T. Bennett and L. Gelsthorpe (1996) 'Public attitudes towards CCTV in public places' *Studies on Crime and Crime Prevention* 5(1): 72.

government funding made available for CCTV research during the mid-1990s played a part. At the time of the University of Hull conference in July 1996, Brown's study of the impact of public area CCTV in King's Lynn, Newcastle, and Birmingham remained the only major evaluation of this new technology. If, as was suggested earlier in this chapter, the driving force behind the expansion of CCTV has been a desire on the part of both Conservative and Labour Home Secretaries to appear sufficiently serious about the problem of crime and public order, then this would in part help to explain why there has been so little government-funded research into the impact of CCTV. From a purely political standpoint, the question of whether CCTV actually has any impact on crime is largely irrelevant provided the public continues to demand more cameras and more surveillance.

In addition, privacy advocate Simon Davies has suggested that public area surveillance was not only absent from meaningful political debate, but also absent as a larger social issue. According to Davies, technology as 'powerful and ubiquitous as [CCTV] should have excited the concerns of liberal and conservative thinkers alike many years ago'.[122] He points out that until 1996 very little was written about CCTV, either on the possible impact of cameras on crime and public order, or the reasons behind the popularity of CCTV with the government and the Home Office. Long before 1996, however, many academics were excited by the advent of CCTV, but most of them—in the beginning at least—were not lawyers, criminologists, or civil libertarians. Instead, they were sociologists and social theorists keen to explore the new technology of public surveillance through the ideas of Rule, Foucault, and Giddens. It is this fact, perhaps more than any other, that has shaped the way in which the academic *and* political communities now think about CCTV. Because CCTV initially belonged to the preserve of sociologists and urban geographers rather than criminologists or social and political historians, the issues surrounding CCTV have tended to be conceived of in terms of sociological discourse, specifically the discourse of surveillance and social control.[123] Until

[122] Davies (1998), 244.
[123] See e.g. Bannister *et al*. (1998); Graham (1998*c*); Reeve (1998*a*); N. R. Fyfe and J. Bannister (1996) 'City watching: closed circuit television surveillance in public places' *Area* 28(1): 37; D Garland (1995) 'Panopticon days: surveillance and society'

recently, what little literature was published discussed CCTV in the context of modernity and social control. More narrow but more specific and concrete criminological and political concerns have, at least until very recently, had little impact on the study of surveillance in Britain.

This book seeks to redress some of this imbalance by focusing on the most neglected area of CCTV research—the impact of CCTV on policing. For all the political rhetoric and academic speculation, almost nothing is known about how the police—one of the primary users of CCTV—have responded to the introduction and spread of this technology. Drawing on two years of field research in police stations and over 100 interviews with police officers, politicians, and local officials, this book presents the findings of an extensive study of CCTV and policing practices conducted in Britain. As the following chapters reveal, many of the findings of this research sit uncomfortably with the predictions of both supporters and opponents of CCTV alike, and shed light not only on the organization and management of the police in Britain, but also on many of the issues raised by the emergence of new surveillance technologies.

Criminal Justice Matters (20): 4; and A. von Hirsch (2000) 'The ethics of public television surveillance' in A. von Hirsch, D. Garland and A. Wakefield (eds.) *Ethical and Social Perspectives on Situational Crime Prevention* (Oxford: Hart), 59.

2

Research Methods

In many ways, working alongside police officers and CCTV operators requires a researcher to confront a number of difficult questions about the role of observer and to re-examine many of the
ethical boundaries typically set out before entering the field. Research methodology chapters often seem to suggest that—provided
researchers are armed with sufficiently well-designed observation
sheets to fill out and interview questions to ask—doing fieldwork in
police stations and CCTV control rooms is relatively straightforward and unproblematic. In light of the challenges that actually face
criminologists in the field, however, it would be misleading to give
the impression that research findings are always collected without
difficulty or that decisions about how to present data are simple and
clear-cut. In addition to describing the research methods adopted
for this study, this chapter examines a number of ethical issues
associated with studying the police, and explores some of the problems that regularly confront criminologists in the field.

2.1 The research programme

The research that forms the basis of this book was completed in
three distinct but closely related phases. The first phase, which
culminated in the production of a pilot report in January 1998,
took place between June and August 1997. The main aim of this
pilot study was to look briefly at how a number of police- and local
authority-led CCTV schemes in the Southern Region Police area
were run, and to determine how viable it would be to include each
of them in the main study.[1] In part, the decision to focus on CCTV
schemes in the Southern Region was based on a desire to include a

---

[1] In order to maintain the anonymity of the police officers, camera operators, and
local government employees involved with this research, fictitious names have been
used for all individuals, institutions, and places.

variety of different systems in the final study. As one of the largest forces in Britain, the Southern Region Police are responsible for an area that encompasses a wide range of rural and urban communities, and by making them the focus of the research, it was possible to look at the way in which the police use CCTV in a number of different contexts. In addition, the Southern Region Police were chosen because, unlike many other forces around the country, they appeared to be genuinely interested in supporting external research. Having already invested heavily in CCTV, a number of senior officers were curious to see whether the presence of cameras had actually had any effect on the policing of towns and cities within the region, and were keen for this research to go ahead.

Following discussions with the Southern Region Police, appropriate local authority representatives, and individual scheme managers, five CCTV schemes within the Southern Region Area were selected for study. Of these five schemes, four—Schemes C1, C2, C3, and C4—were managed and staffed by the relevant local authority, with the police providing varying levels of financial and technical support. In the case of the fifth scheme—Scheme P2—these positions were reversed, with the police being responsible for the day-to-day operation of the cameras and management of staff, and the local authority providing financial and managerial assistance.[2]

During the course of the pilot study, each of the five schemes was visited on numerous occasions and meetings were held with local managers, police officers, and CCTV control room staff. In these meetings, the conditions under which the main study would be carried out were discussed, and all of the parties involved were given the opportunity to express any concerns or reservations they might have about the research. In addition, managers and operators were invited to make suggestions about the design and direction of the project, and to draw attention to any potential problems that they felt might arise. These discussions served to calm and reassure a number of local managers and operators, some of whom were later to admit that they had at first been unwilling to be involved in the project for fear that they would be 'made to look bad'.

Following these discussions, formal observations were carried out in each of the five sites and preliminary, informal interviews under-

---

[2] Throughout the book the prefixes P and C are used to denote police-led and council (local authority)-led schemes respectively.

taken with CCTV operators and local officers. In total, approximately 30 hours of monitoring were observed and ten semi-structured interviews completed, and after a short period during which the results of this initial study were examined, a final report was produced in January 1998. This report was circulated throughout the Southern Region Police area and copies were sent to managers of all the schemes in the survey with a request for comments. Several of the scheme managers made useful suggestions on how best to proceed with the onsite observation work, and many were eager to be involved in the research after reading the pilot study report. Although only a few of the operators appeared to have read the pilot study, those who had were also helpful, often pointing out areas where they felt that I had misunderstood some of the practices I had observed.

Looking back over the research as a whole, the completion of this initial pilot study was significant for a variety of reasons. First and foremost, a number of key research tools were tested prior to commencement of the main study. After spending a couple of afternoons observing CCTV operators at work, I soon realized that trying to fill in complex observation sheets while in the control room was impractical due to time constraints, and also had a tendency to make operators and police officers nervous. This conclusion led to the adoption of more informal methods of recording field data and keeping observation notes. Similarly, I also came to the conclusion that a strictly non-interactive approach to observation had to be abandoned if I were to have any chance of understanding how targeting decisions were being made. In the course of the pilot study, it became apparent that attempting to code targeted surveillances according to what each incident 'seemed to be about' was unacceptably subjective. Instead, I decided that it was also important to ask operators *why* they had decided to target a particular individual or group. In part, this challenged my perceptions of what I was seeing, and also helped to develop an understanding of what the operators thought that they were doing. In these important respects, the pilot phase proved to be crucial in developing and refining the research strategy used in the main study.

Following completion of the pilot study, the second phase of the research was carried out between March 1998 and June 1999. During this 18-month period, over 200 separate visits were made to CCTV control rooms and police stations across the Southern Region, and over 1,000 hours were spent 'in the field' engaging in observation, interviewing, and data collection. In the course of this main study, approximately 330 hours were spent formally observing CCTV operators and police officers, and 95 interviews with criminal justice agents involved with CCTV were conducted. As one of the main aims of the research was to determine whether the organization and management of a CCTV scheme affected the way in which surveillance was carried out, it was important to examine a range of different police- and local authority-led schemes. Of the five sites that were included in the pilot study, four of these—Schemes C1, C2, C3, and P2—were also included in the main study, along with two additional police-led schemes—Schemes P1 and P3, making six schemes in all.[3] Although none of the schemes was operated exclusively by either the police or the relevant local authority, for the purposes of this study schemes were defined as either police- or local authority-led according to who was responsible for the day-to-day running of the scheme. A brief summary of the key characteristics of each scheme is included in Table 2.1.

TABLE 2.1. Basic scheme details

	Scheme	Location of control room	Number of cameras	Overt or covert cameras	Operators per shift	Operators	Managers
Police-led	P1	Police station	15	Covert	1	Civilian	Police
	P2	Police station	25	Overt	1	Civilian	Police
	P3	Police station	21	Covert	1	Police & Civilian	Police
Local authority-led	C1	Council office	6	Overt	1	Civilian	Civilian
	C2	Council office	35	Covert	2	Civilian	Civilian
	C3	Council office	31	Overt	2	Civilian	Civilian

[3] The decision to add one police-led scheme—Scheme P3—and to exclude Scheme C4 from the main study was made to ensure that the list of schemes included in the study contained an equal number of police- and local authority-led schemes. The specific decision to drop Scheme C4 was also influenced by the fact that the scheme itself was far less physically accessible than any of the other local authority schemes included in the pilot study.

Schemes P1, P2, C2, and C3 were all located in medium-sized country towns—with populations of between 30,000 and 70,000—where most of the activity during the day centred around High Street shops and small shopping malls located in and around the immediate town centre. For the most part, life in each of these towns appeared to move at a fairly slow pace, with many of the town centres being virtually deserted outside shopping hours and on Sundays. Although all of these towns had a number of pubs and clubs located in the town centre, only C2 could be said to have enjoyed a particularly active nightlife, and this was largely confined to Friday and Saturday evenings and the area around one particularly popular nightclub. In each of the other towns, by midnight the town centre was relatively quiet.

In contrast, Scheme P3 was situated in a much larger town with a population of just over 200,000. Instead of being confined to a central high street, activity during the day was spread evenly throughout a number of busy shopping streets and malls, while at night the town filled with people out enjoying the many restaurants, pubs, and clubs located in the town centre. Weekends were particularly busy as large groups of people from the surrounding towns and villages ventured into the centre to do their shopping, with the result that the streets were often teeming with people on Saturday and Sunday afternoons. In addition, Town P3 was also well known for its pubs and nightclubs, many of which stayed open until the early hours of the morning and attracted large numbers of young people, especially students from the local university. Unlike the smaller towns included in the study, P3 also had a major railway station situated in the heart of the town, which became a focal point for activity whenever the town played host to football games and various outdoor concerts.

Finally, the remaining scheme, C1, was located in a quiet, largely rural town with a population of less than 10,000. Although some of its more devoted residents frequently claimed that C1 had thriving nightlife, there was little evidence of this and by 6 p.m. it was unusual to find anyone in the town centre unless they were waiting for a bus to go elsewhere. In many ways, Scheme C1 stood out from the rest of the sites included in the study. While all of the other towns had experienced rising levels of crime prior to the introduction of CCTV, in contrast crime levels in C1 had remained consistently low in the years leading up to the installation of the cameras.

Public order problems were virtually unknown, and the little theft that took place in and around the town either took the form of residential burglaries or juvenile shoplifting.[4] Of all the local authority-led schemes, C1 was the only one to use local, unpaid volunteers as operators, and formal contact with the police was minimal and largely confined to irregular meetings between council members and the local beat officer.

Despite these various differences, all six of the schemes—P1, P2, P3, C1, C2, and C3—shared many essential features. All made use of near-identical camera and storage technologies, were theoretically bound by similar codes of practice, and employed the same numbers of operators on each shift. In addition, all of the schemes had been running for approximately the same length of time, namely between 12 months and two years. As a result of these similarities, it was possible to draw comparisons between schemes during the course of the observation period without having to make allowances for any fundamental differences in their basic operating methods.

After completion of the formal observation period, a number of additional site visits were conducted between July 1999 and March 2000. During this final phase of the research, preliminary findings were discussed with operators, police officers, and scheme managers, and the ongoing review of the various scheme logbooks, files, and incident sheets was completed. In addition, a number of operators and officers were re-interviewed, enabling them to clarify statements they had made during the course of the main study.[5] Having already established a good working relationship with the majority of these individuals, I found that many of their answers were much less guarded the second time around, and that they were able to shed light on a number of issues that they had been less willing to discuss earlier.

Following this final phase, a further six months was spent transcribing interviews, collating information taken from police and local authority documents, and analysing the data. Using a system

[4] Local crime figures indicated that the level of public order offences in Town C1 was well below the national or the regional average, as were most other forms of crime.

[5] Note that 're-interviews' were not counted in the final list of interviews completed. If taken into account, however, the total number of interviews conducted comes to 110.

of qualitative analysis first developed by Lofland, all of the field notes and interview transcripts were reorganized according to six categories—acts, activities, meanings, participation, relationships, and settings—and a number of key themes identified.[6] In addition, detailed case studies for each of the schemes were constructed in order to enable direct comparisons to be made among the different schemes and the practices of different operators.[7] By combining these two techniques—thematic and case-based analysis—it was possible to examine the data from a number of different perspectives and to test various hypotheses about the impact of individual and organizational differences on surveillance outcomes and general policing practices. In particular, this approach proved to be extremely helpful when it came to testing the reliability of the field notes and observations. Since each entry was eventually classified twice—once for the purposes of developing a thematic analysis and again for each case study—I was forced to re-evaluate my assessment of each observation and to ask whether my thematic classification was consistent with a more contextual view of events. As a direct consequence, by the time the formal process of analysis was over, I was not only confident that my overall impressions were consistent with the actual field data, but also that I had managed to avoid ascribing too much significance to some of the more colourful events and interactions.

2.2   Negotiating and renegotiating access

Access to the various CCTV schemes and police stations included in the study was initially arranged with the help of senior police officers at Southern Region Police Headquarters, who were happy to introduce me to local officials and police officers involved in the operation of CCTV in the region. From the outset, the police appeared to be keen for the research to go ahead. Having invested

---

[6] J. Lofland (1971) *Analysing Social Settings* (New York: Wadsworth). See also R. Burgess (1989c) 'Styles of data analysis: approaches and implications' in R. Burgess (ed.) (1989e) *Field Research: A Sourcebook and Field Manual* (London: Routledge), 235.

[7] This approach to data analysis—which rejects the practice of 'apt illustration' in favour of a case method based on examining a series of incidents involving specific individuals over a period of time—is often accredited to the Manchester School of Sociology and Social Anthropology. See M. Gluckman (1961) 'Ethnographic data in British social anthropology' *Sociological Review* 9(1): 5.

a considerable amount of time and money in the development of a number of systems throughout the region, many senior officers were of the opinion that some sort of independent evaluation needed to be done before the force committed itself to any further investment in CCTV.

Although the police were quick to grant almost unfettered access to police-led CCTV schemes and stations throughout the region, many of the local authorities involved in the research were guarded at first. In the various negotiations and meetings that preceded the pilot study, a number of local councillors and scheme managers expressed concern about the nature of the research and the possibility that they and their schemes might become the focus of criticism should the findings be published. The prospect of negative media attention was something that particularly worried one local councillor, despite the fact that he had been given an assurance that all findings would be anonymized to prevent individuals and schemes being identified. In the end, after almost six weeks of negotiations, all of the relevant local authority officials and scheme managers were finally convinced that I could be 'trusted'. Once this had been established, I received almost identical levels of access to those that had already been granted by the police—namely full access to local authority-led CCTV control rooms, CCTV operators and staff, and all files directly related to the establishment and operation of the schemes. In practice, this meant that during the course of the research I had virtually unlimited physical access to all of the schemes and CCTV control rooms involved in the study, and a remit to interview anyone either directly or indirectly associated with the use of CCTV in the region.

It is sometimes tempting to see the weeks spent negotiating and renegotiating with local officials as time that could have been used more productively. It is a mistake, however, to think that the time spent attempting to gain access is wasted. As Jupp observes:

[N]egotiating and gaining access should be considered as part of the process of collecting data. The individuals and groups to be confronted, the interests they represent, and the blocks or constraints they seek to impose on research activity provide, in their own right, important forms of data about the criminal justice system and the way in which it works.[8]

---

[8] V. Jupp (1996) *Methods of Criminological Research* (London: Routledge), 149.

As he rightly emphasizes, the process of negotiating access 'does not end when one has successfully bypassed all those who have some formal power to prevent the research taking place'.[9] This was certainly true in the case of the pilot study and, to a lesser extent, the main study. On many occasions during the course of both studies, I encountered gatekeepers who, although aware that my presence had already been sanctioned by the police and the relevant local authorities, attempted to deny me access or impede the progress of my research. In each case, the process of explaining the enterprise and attempting to gain a degree of trust had to be repeated. While in theory it would have been possible to 'pull rank'—to wave the letter of authorization and demand to see files, reports, and so on—having read of other researchers' experiences it seemed unlikely that in the long run this would be a successful strategy. In the process of renegotiation, however, a great deal was learnt about the anxieties that officers and operators had about CCTV surveillance and their reservations about being involved with it. Much of the reticence encountered appeared to stem from an anxiety that they would be wrongly associated with 'Big Brother' or from more tangible fears about their own job security. It is also important to recognize that operators and police officers working closely with CCTV often find themselves not only guarding the systems from outsiders, but from unwanted insider attention as well. As one operator put it, at times he not only had to 'protect' the system from intrusions by the public, but from the police as well: 'I mean, obviously you've got a lot of information in here, you've got your tapes and things . . . and it's not just an open door to everybody. You have to have a certain amount, like a barrier you might say, to stop [the police] just coming in willy-nilly' (Operator A, Scheme P2).

As a consequence, as the research proceeded, I came to realize that I faced a variety of gatekeepers who not only had an interest in keeping me out, but also in keeping out those who were—nominally at least—their partners. Fortunately, over time this initial suspicion seemed to recede and many of those who had previously been sceptical about the project became more interested in its progress. This change in attitude was probably due to a number of related factors. Of crucial importance was the help given by a number of

[9] Jupp (1996), 149.

senior police officers. In addition, a great deal of potential conflict was avoided by holding to a simple rule: be as open as possible. At all stages I made it clear that I was happy to discuss my progress and the direction of the research with the officers and CCTV operators involved, and to listen to any criticisms or concerns they might have. This openness brought a number of benefits. Although I never acquired the status of a 'trusted insider', being as open and honest as possible helped to alleviate any concerns that I was in some way out to simply 'rubbish' CCTV or to create problems for CCTV staff and their colleagues. In addition, it also meant that people were more comfortable drawing my attention to concerns they had about the research and making suggestions about how it could be strengthened. Of course not all of the comments and suggestions made by the CCTV operators and police officers were equally useful, but they constantly forced me to re-evaluate how the research was developing. In particular, much productive thinking about the ethics and value of field research can be traced back to comments made by operators during the first few months of the research.

2.3   Data collection

Although the traditional—and frankly not entirely helpful—divide between quantitative and qualitative research has been gradually eroded, there is still considerable controversy surrounding the usefulness of participant and non-participant observation research. For this study, an ethnographic approach based primarily on observation and informal interviewing of subjects was employed.[10] Given that part of my concern was to understand the processes of CCTV surveillance and the way in which operators and officers see their work, it was essential to determine how they defined themselves and

---

[10] As Hammersley has noted, the term ethnography is not clearly defined in common usage, and there is some disagreement about what sorts of methods do and do not fall within its scope. Hammersley himself offers the following definition and justification for it: 'I shall use the term "ethnography" in a wide sense that is largely synonymous with "qualitative method". This has become an increasingly common usage, and it is justified to some extent by the fact that there is little agreement over competing narrower definitions of the term.' See M. Hammersley (1998) *Reading Ethnographic Research: A Critical Guide* (Harlow: Addison Wesley Longman Ltd.), 1.

attributed meaning to their work. As Simon Holdaway noted in his insider study of the British police, ethnography's methodological commitment to the value of empathy and the importance of understanding actors within their specific context makes it particularly well suited to studying the police.[11]

The desire to emulate the ethnographic methods of social and cultural anthropologists is, however, inherently problematic for researchers who wish to study subcultures or working groups like the police. There is a fundamental tension between using methods drawn from classic ethnography—which demand a complete and comprehensive examination of a given subject group—and the narrower desire of criminologists who wish to understand how certain institutions and the people within them deal with the specific problems of crime. Unlike anthropologists, who ideally live with their subjects for long periods of time and observe all aspects of their daily lives, when criminologists set out to examine a group like the police, most accept that their field of study will be limited to observing individuals 'on the job'.

This inherent tension should not, however, lead us to abandon the use of ethnographic methods altogether. Ethnography's commitment to naturalism and the study of group behaviour in everyday contexts is something that any good field researcher should seek to emulate. It is important to be clear, however, that when we undertake field research in criminology, we use ethnographic methods rather than practise ethnography. Field research—particularly if it is based on non-participant observation—is a blunt tool that can provide only a snapshot of the lives of those under study. If we admit this, it then becomes clear that something more is needed to ensure that an accurate picture of our subject is being obtained. One of the 'defences' most frequently used by field researchers when fending off accusations of subjectivity is the claim that objectivity was assured by looking at multiple sources of data and cross-verifying key findings against them.[12] Accordingly, it is now

[11] S. Holdaway (1983) *Inside the British Police* (Oxford: Blackwell), 4.

[12] One of the most common forms of cross-verification is 'data triangulation'. Data-source triangulation involves the comparison of data relating to the same phenomenon but deriving from different phases of the fieldwork, different points in the temporal cycles occurring in the setting, or...the accounts of different participants (including the ethnographer's) involved in the setting. M. Hammersley and P. Atkinson (1983) *Ethnography: Principles in Practice* (London: Tavistock), 198.

common practice for non-participant observers to conduct interviews or engage in detailed document analysis in an effort to confirm the conclusions drawn from their own observations.[13] Certainly, this was one of the key reasons behind my own decision to go beyond simply spending time observing police officers and CCTV operators. While data triangulation is an extremely useful technique, it does not in and of itself ensure that the context in which the data are being collected is sufficiently broad. By choosing to look only at the behaviour of a subject within a limited setting— for example, the activities of police officers in a police station or CCTV operators in a CCTV control room—we necessarily exclude any examination of their behaviour in other contexts as would be required for the development of a true ethnography of that group's working culture. Observing how individuals behave outside the work environment may provide crucial insights that enable us to better understand how they perform 'on the job'.[14]

In the current case, I realized early on that in order to have any chance of gaining a sense of the factors that influenced their decision-making, I needed to spend time with officers and operators in other, less formal settings. This conclusion led me to broaden my field of observation. In addition to the programme of formal non-participant observation and collecting basic demographic data about each subject—age, educational background, work history, and so on—I also began to spend more time socializing with subjects outside their immediate work environment, frequently having lunch with police officers away from the station, or going for drinks with CCTV operators after work. Although the time spent attempting to expand the ethnographic base of the research did not necessarily produce any great insights, it did increase my trust in the project as a whole. Seeing operators or officers behave in certain

---

[13] Over time there have been various suggestions as to how best to go about the task of verifying social research data. In particular, Burgess refers to techniques such as 'combined operations', 'triangulation', and 'mixed strategies.' See Burgess (1989*e*), ch. 1.

[14] As Fielding and Fielding point out, using different methods of information gathering can in fact increase the chance of error: 'We should recognise that the multi-operational approach implies a good deal more than merely a piling on of instruments'. See N. G. Fielding and J. L. Fielding (1986) *Linking Data*, Sage University Paper series on Qualitative Research Methods, vol. 4 (Newbury Park, Calif.: Sage), 31.

ways or express certain opinions that were consistent with those that I had already observed in the work setting gave me greater confidence in the conclusions that I was beginning to draw from my formal observations and interviews.

Throughout the course of the research, however, I was careful not to assume that I had in any sense become a 'trusted insider'. I have always been sceptical of methodology chapters in which the author—after detailing the various challenges that had confronted him or her—claims to have been in some way accepted by the police. In light of what has been written about the police and police working cultures, it seems unlikely that they would admit a researcher into their 'world' within a few short months. As Robert Reiner notes: 'Even with observational work there is a problem of whether the researcher has the trust of the subjects of the research, and how their behaviour is likely to be modified by the presence of the researcher. Trust is unlikely to ever be complete'.[15]

It is virtually impossible for any researcher—except perhaps the truly covert participant observer like Holdaway—ever to become a police 'insider'.[16] Rather, there are degrees of acceptance, and although most of those with whom I worked over the 16 months were friendly and helpful, I suspect that many of the officers and operators observed and interviewed remained suspicious of me right up to the end of the project. Whether this suspicion affected their answers to questions or their willingness to be honest with me during the course of the research is difficult to judge. Accepting from the outset that I was never going to be regarded as an 'insider', however, saved me from falling into the trap of believing everything I was told, and ensured that I worked hard to maintain a good working relationship with the police wherever possible. In the end, adopting this approach—and being honest about the challenges faced—greatly improved the quality and reliability of the data collected.

2.3.1 Observation and field notes

During the period of the main study, over 330 hours of formal observation were carried out, which amounted to approximately

---

[15] R. Reiner (2000) 'Police research' in R. D. King and E. Wincup (eds.) *Doing Research on Crime and Justice* (Oxford: Oxford University Press), 205, 219.

[16] See Holdaway (1983).

55 hours of observation at each of the six sites. In addition, each site was visited on average at least 25 times for the purposes of interviews and documentary analysis, during which time many more hours of informal observation of operator and police working practices were carried out. In the course of the formal observation, all days of the week were covered, and an effort was made to include equal numbers of morning and afternoon shifts. As the pilot study had revealed that very little tended to happen in any of the towns after dark except at weekends, during the main study most night-time observation work was confined to Friday and Saturday nights. Although covering all shifts on all days for each of the schemes would have been preferable, this would have meant spending at least 1,008 hours engaged in formal observation, which was simply not feasible.[17] In deciding which shifts to cover, I attempted to include an equal number of 'quiet' and 'busy' shifts in order to ensure that I was not just covering those times of the day when the operators were most likely to be engaged in active surveillance.[18] Watching what operators and police officers did while they were bored was, in fact, often as interesting and revealing as watching them when they were following targets or looking for known offenders.

For each of the sites studied, two sets of field notes were kept—substantive field notes and methodological field notes.[19] In the substantive notes, the primary focus was on recording the main observations, conversations, and informal interviews that arose out of the time spent in the various CCTV control rooms, local authority offices, and police stations included in the study. In addition, systematic notes were kept for each 'target' observed, and of any comments made by operators or officers relating to those targets.

---

[17] The figure of 1,008 hours is arrived at by multiplying the number of shifts per day by the number of days per week by the number of schemes included in the main study.

[18] I was also aware of the danger of diminishing returns, and after the completion of the pilot study I had come to the conclusion that my time would be better spent conducting interviews and undertaking a full review of documents rather than attempting to cover every possible day and shift combination for every scheme.

[19] This division is recommended in R. Burgess (1989a) 'Keeping field notes' in Burgess (1989e), 191.

In contrast, the methodological field notes were used to record details about the circumstances in which the data were collected and personal impressions of situations and subjects. These notes included comments about the apparent reliability of subjects, the atmosphere in the control room, and others' reactions to my presence as a researcher. They also included many comments that were made off the record. Early in the research, operators or police officers were occasionally happy to answer informal questions provided their answers were 'off the record'. In each case, I made a point of recording these comments in my methodology notes to ensure that they were not confused with those that could more properly be referred to as forming part of the substantive research. In the process of data analysis, such comments were isolated and a decision made about whether to include them or not in the final report. In some cases, because of the obvious agitation of the subject, I gave an assurance that their comments would not be used in any way, and in the following chapters I have adhered to these assurances. In other cases, where the request that the comments be off the record was made more as a reflex or an aside, the substance if not the form of the statement has been treated as part of the substantive data. Again, how a researcher chooses to deal with such instances is a question of personal and professional ethics. For the purpose of the current study, I decided to treat each case on its own merits while trying to remain within the broad ethical constraints that I had set for myself at the outset of the project.

It is important to point out that I made no effort to conceal the fact that I was taking these notes, and as such my observations were recorded either at the time of or immediately after the events took place. Given that most of my subjects were already wary of my presence, I was concerned not to give them any further reasons for being suspicious, either by pretending that I was not recording what they were doing or by sneaking around the police station or control room. Understandably, individuals whose work revolves around surveillance, including CCTV operators, tend to be guarded about their own work and their observations about the work of others. Over time, however, most of the subjects became used to my fairly constant scribbling, and they frequently seemed to forget about me or to some extent took my presence for granted, in much the same way that interview subjects often appear to forget they are being taped after the first few minutes of a recorded interview.

In addition to substantive and methodological notes, I also kept a daily fieldwork diary in which I recorded my general feelings and impressions as to how the work was proceeding. These notes later served to put the substantive notes in an overall context and also helped to remind me of the various problems faced when collecting the data. In this second sense, they helped to keep the process of data analysis honest: it is harder to gloss over methodological problems or simple failures when you are faced with a written record of them.

2.3.2   Interviewing

In the course of the research period, a total of 95 interviews were conducted. Of these, 50 were with police officers ranging from the rank of constable to Chief Inspector and Assistant Chief Constable, the remaining 45 being with civilian operators, scheme managers, and local officials. In order to give each individual the opportunity to explain themselves fully, a semi-structured interview format was followed. One of the key justifications for the use of semi-structured interviewing is that it allows subjects to speak freely and at length using their own concepts and terminology. As such, a semi-structured interview format is in keeping with the desire for naturalism that lies at the heart of any attempt to follow an essentially ethnographic approach to one's subject.[20] As the interviews were tape-recorded and transcribed verbatim, the individual respondent's methods of describing and explaining their behaviour was preserved. By the end of the research period, the interview data consisted of approximately 40 hours of taped interviews, which once transcribed ran to over 900 typed pages.

At all stages, the nature and purpose of the research was explained to those officers and operators observed or interviewed, and all were asked directly whether they had any concerns about being involved in the study. Where appropriate, the names of people interviewed and places visited in the course of this research have been anonymized. Given the sensitive nature of police surveillance, it is not surprising that many of the operators expressed concern about taking part. In many of the schemes under study a serious breach of the codes of practice could lead to dismissal, and so

---

[20]   See Burgess (1989e); and M. Brenner, J. Brown, and D. Canter (eds.) (1985) *The Research Interview: Uses and Approaches* (London: Academic Press).

operators were understandably guarded when questioned about their own or their colleagues' conduct. This was an issue that was to arise repeatedly during the course of the research. Additionally, many of the civilian operators—and some of the police operators—seemed uncomfortable talking about the role of the police in the operation of CCTV. In part, this reticence may have stemmed from the desire of operators to maintain good relations with the police or their local authority employers, but it may also be indicative of a general reluctance to expose themselves to outside scrutiny.

All of this said, most interview subjects accepted my assurances of anonymity and gave honest answers to the questions asked. As a rule of thumb, I tried to avoid interviewing operators unless I had already spent time with them on a previous shift, during which I discussed the aims of research with them. Most operators, once the project had been explained to them, seemed genuinely interested, and many expressed the opinion that 'it was about time somebody had a look at CCTV'. Many of the operators interviewed appeared to have thought quite deeply about many of the ethical and social issues associated with public area surveillance and their role in the process. This is not to say that they all necessarily behaved in ways consistent with the views they expressed in interviews and conversation, but it did serve constantly to remind me not to underestimate the extent to which many of the operators were conscious of what they were doing and of the difficult decisions they were frequently forced to make.

In addition to these formal, semi-structured interviews, I also had frequent opportunities to speak with operators and officers while 'on the job'. Although none of these conversations was tape-recorded, near-contemporaneous notes were almost always made. These conversations were in many cases initiated by the subjects themselves, and frequently focused on various complaints they had about the operation or management of the system. One common complaint to emerge from operators in the course of the research was that many of them felt undervalued and ignored by management and the police, and my presence may have provided some of them with an opportunity to speak about their work and express certain frustrations. Field researchers frequently find themselves in the position of having to act as a 'confessor', with interview subjects often seeing them as sympathetic to their concerns. Being placed in this position can be awkward, but in the current case listening to such complaints was valuable, if only because it helped to break down barriers between myself and a number of the operators. In addition, since I was interested in the interactions between the operators and the police, these conversations frequently provided me with the opportunity to ask very specific, predetermined questions about how the schemes were organized, managed, and run without appearing to be too curious or calculating. In this way, I was often able to fill in 'gaps' from the formal interviews and open lines of inquiry that would have been more difficult to pursue using more formal interview techniques.

2.3.3   Documentary analysis

In addition to being granted physical access to the schemes and the opportunity to interview operators, officers, and local officials, during the course of both the pilot study and the main study I was allowed to examine documents relating to the establishment, organization, and daily running of each of the six schemes. These documents included initial feasibility and planning studies, records of local authority and police meetings and agreements, codes of practice and procedural manuals, and all files kept in the control rooms themselves. Although many of these individual documents were not particularly detailed or enlightening, taken together and used in combination with the interview data they proved to be extremely helpful in enabling me to construct a picture of how each scheme had been set up and the role played by the police in their development.

Of all of the documents made available during the research period, the most valuable—at least in terms of the field research— were the scheme logbooks. Typically, the logbooks recorded a brief description of every major incident observed by the operators, as well as a note of whether the police or anyone else in the town centre had been involved. Using these logbooks, it was possible not only to get a sense of the type of surveillance being regularly carried out in each of the schemes, but also to compare my own accounts of the various incidents I had observed with those recorded by the operators themselves. Perhaps unsurprisingly, on many occasions there were significant differences between my field notes and the relevant logbook entries, differences that helped to shed light not only on the attitudes of individual operators, but also on the objectivity of my own observation.

2.4   The ethics of covert research

Verifying data obtained in the course of observation or interviewing presents a difficult problem for any researcher. No matter how much effort is taken to 'blend in' or establish relations of trust, field researchers working within criminal justice agencies are likely to be regarded by many of their subjects as 'outsiders'. This is particularly so in the case of the police, who have become notorious for their secrecy and unwillingness to expose themselves or their working culture to external scrutiny. How this might influence the behaviour of officers or CCTV operators is extremely difficult to determine, so much so that the 'researcher effect' is regarded by many as an inescapable fact of qualitative fieldwork: 'Ultimately there is no way of knowing for certain whether what the police do in front of observers, or what they say to interviewers, is intended to present an acceptable face to outsiders'.[21]

Although at no point during the course of either the pilot study or the main study was covert research deliberately undertaken, there were many occasions when opportunities to gather information covertly presented themselves. On those occasions, I frequently found myself reflecting on the issue of covert observation and on the ethical boundaries I had set for my own research. The ethics of covert research is a topic rarely discussed in most criminological studies, despite the fact that the question of whether to go beyond the bounds of one's own adopted research standards or guidelines is one that must confront nearly all field researchers at some point.[22] In many methodology chapters, the issue is conveniently swept aside. Claims such as 'all research was conducted in strict accordance with the ethical guidelines set down by the British Sociological Association (BSA) Statement of Ethical Practice' sound particularly unconvincing after over a year in the field, during which time I was confronted with a range of ethical issues that were barely covered by

---

[21] Reiner (2000), 220.

[22] Some of the general issues surrounding the use of covert observation as it relates to the role of the participant observer are discussed briefly in R. Burgess (1989b) 'Some role problems in field research' in Burgess (1989e) 46. Here, Burgess also refers to an interesting exchange between Homan and Bulmer about the ethics of covert research which deals with many of the central questions relating to issues of consent and expectations of personal privacy. See R. Homan (1980) 'The ethics of covert methods' *British Journal of Sociology* 31(1): 46, and the critical reply from G. Bulmer (1980) in the same issue.

these or similar sets of guidelines.[23] Finding myself alone in one CCTV control room at 4 a.m. while an operator took a cigarette break, on one occasion I was tempted to look around for the 'greatest hits' tape that I suspected was hidden somewhere in the room.[24] Although I managed to resist the temptation, would succumbing have been a breach of the ethical standards I had committed myself to at the start of the project? Undoubtedly yes, but the situation raises the more difficult question of whether I was wrong to commit myself to such standards in the first place.

Similarly, there were moments when it would have been extremely easy to have passed myself off as an 'insider', if only temporarily. The number of times I was mistaken for a camera technician or—even more remarkably—a plain-clothes police officer was surprising to say the least, and on each occasion I was presented with the dilemma of deciding at what stage in the conversation I should point out that a mistake had been made. Certainly, there were many occasions on which I considered letting a conversation run on just a little longer before revealing myself. Similarly, there were times when I was tempted to 'mistakenly' leave my tape-recorder on after an interview had finished, or to 'accidentally' walk in on a surveillance operation I knew I was not supposed to see. Although in each case I adhered to my initial decision to reject covert methods, these situations helped me to understand that untangling the ethics of covert research is not just about the decision of whether to use hidden microphones or cameras—it is also about deciding how one deals with the vagaries of field research and the inevitable 'opportunities' that necessarily arise.

As Holdaway notes, it is not enough to dismiss covert research within criminology as being vaguely unethical. Reasons need to be given as to why such an approach is not appropriate to the given circumstances, rather than simply brushing the issue aside on the grounds that such methods are self-evidently wrong or dishonest.

---

[23]   British Sociological Association (1992) 'Statement of ethical practice' *Sociology* 26: 703.

[24]   In many schemes, it is alleged that operators—often in direct contravention of Codes of Practice and the Data Protection Act—keep a compilation tape of their favourite incidents. During the course of the research, I was shown one such tape at Scheme P2, and was made aware of the existence of similar tapes at Schemes P3 and C3.

This is particularly true when the subject of observation is the police:

[T]he case for covert research is strengthened by the central and powerful situation of the police within our social structure. The police are said to be accountable to the rule of law, a constitutional constraint which restricts their right to privacy but which they can neutralize by maintaining a protective occupational culture. When an institution is over-protective, its members restrict the right to privacy that they possess. It is important that they be researched.[25]

Holdaway's argument seems particularly pertinent when applied to the subject of police surveillance. Given that many members of the public are unaware that they are being watched by CCTV cameras or that—on some level at least—their privacy is being infringed, it seems appropriate to consider whether and to what extent the police or local authorities undertaking such surveillance can themselves have a legitimate expectation of privacy. Should CCTV operators who breach codes of practice have a right to expect that a researcher will not make use of 'off the record' conversations to draw attention to this? Does a police officer have a legitimate complaint against a researcher who, in going beyond the ambit of their ethical guidelines to use covert observation methods, becomes aware of an attempt by the police to tamper with evidence?

In failing to acknowledge that these issues exist—and that as researchers we are regularly confronted with them—criminologists leave themselves open to accusations of double standards. If we are to criticize the police for their apparent failure to deal with certain key ethical issues or their failure to meet certain standards of behaviour, we must at the same time acknowledge that we are also faced with difficult ethical choices. Thus, we need to confront the fact that qualitative research necessarily involves making judgements about how far one is prepared to go in order to develop a 'true picture' of whatever it is one is studying. By avoiding this question, and by failing to acknowledge the problems inherent in participant observation, we make it easier for the police and others to dismiss important research as 'too good to be true' or as an overly subjective reconstruction of the facts.

[25] Holdaway (1983), 5.

2.5   Conclusion

Given that this book is about surveillance, many of the issues raised in this chapter have a particular resonance that goes beyond any general discussion of ethnographic and criminological research methods. Throughout the course of the research I found myself asking questions about the ethics of overt and covert observation which were not dissimilar from the questions that confront many CCTV operators and police officers on a daily basis. Having faced the question of whether to use information obtained—either purposefully or inadvertently—in contravention of the ethical standards I had adopted at the beginning of my research, I could not help feeling at times a certain empathy for those operators who frequently found themselves in similar positions. In this sense, public surveillance and non-participant observation have much in common. On the one hand, both present the observer with highly fluid situations in which the boundaries of ethical conduct are not always clear. The question of whether to listen in on a private conversation between research subjects in the hope of gaining 'useful' information does seem similar to the question of whether to follow an individual with a camera in the 'hope' that they may commit an offence. In both instances, the researcher and the operator have to decide which is more important—the privacy of the 'subject' or the purpose of observation.

More significantly, however, public area surveillance and field research—at least as it is practised via non-participant observation in criminology—both represent highly mediated forms of observation. In each instance, the aim is to observe one particular aspect of the life of the subject. In my case, I was concerned with looking at how the police, both as individuals and as a group, look at the world through the medium of CCTV. In their case, officers and operators were concerned with looking at the members of the public in terms of their propensity to commit offences. Just as video monitors may provide operators and officers with a distorted view of the outside world—a world divided solely into offenders and non-offenders—there is an equal danger that by seeking to understand one aspect of a complex working culture through the use of observation, field diaries, and interviews, all we are left with is a distorted picture of the 'inside world' of CCTV.

By choosing to take an open and flexible approach to my field research, I have done my best to avoid this danger as far as possible. During the course of my research, many of the operators, scheme managers, and police officers featured in this study played a vital role in helping to ensure that the account presented in the following chapters is based on more than hours of completely detached observation or answers to rigid interview questions. In my effort to explore some of the limits of field research as ethnography, I adopted a research strategy that not only constantly forced me to re-evaluate my role as an observer, but also gave my subjects the opportunity to explain what they were attempting to do as well as what they actually did. As a consequence, I was able to look at CCTV from a range of different perspectives and gain a unique insight into the role of the police in the development of public area surveillance in Britain.

3
Playing 'Little Brother'

The purpose of this chapter is to examine how CCTV came to be installed in each of the six towns included in this study, and to understand the role played by the police in the decision-making processes that led to the establishment of these schemes. It has already been argued in Chapter 1 that the rapid expansion in CCTV during the early 1990s was in part the result of a campaign by central government to encourage the use of video surveillance by town and city councils. This drive was successful largely owing to both the willingness of local government to become involved in the problem of local crime prevention and the desire of councils to take advantage of the funds made available through the CCTV Challenge Competition.[1] At a national level, however, the promotion of CCTV was marked by a lack of consultation with the police. Neither the Association of Chief Police Officers (ACPO) nor the Police Federation were involved in the development of Home Office policy regarding the use of CCTV or formally consulted about the possible impact of this technology on the policing of crime. As we shall see in this chapter, this is a pattern that has been repeated at the local government level as well.

In the course of the research period, a range of local authority representatives, scheme managers, and senior police officers were questioned about the decision to install CCTV cameras in their area. They were asked to describe the various stages that preceded the adoption of CCTV, and how decisions relating to the financing,

---

[1] In 1995, the Home Office distributed over £5 m. to 106 town centre CCTV schemes as part of the first round of the Home Office CCTV Challenge Competition. Between 1995 and 1998, there were an additional three rounds in the competition, resulting in the allocation of an additional £31 m. for the establishment of new schemes and the upgrading of existing public area CCTV systems. For a more detailed analysis of the CCTV Challenge Competition, see McCahill and Norris (2002*b*), 14.

management, and design of the schemes were finally reached. In addition, access was gained to central police files that documented the preliminary negotiations that took place between the police and local authorities regarding the level of police involvement in CCTV around the region. These files contained basic minutes of all formal meetings between the police and local representatives in each of the six towns included in the study, as well as notes of early designs and funding proposals for 'partnership schemes' between the police and local authorities.

3.1 Getting involved: the police

Although it is difficult to establish exactly when the Southern Region Police first became aware of CCTV, it is likely that senior management within the force began considering the prospect of cameras being installed in selected town centres from as early as 1990. By the late 1980s, the favourable publicity received by London's 'Ring of Steel' and by smaller schemes in towns such as King's Lynn meant that many city councils and local authorities within the region had started to contemplate installing their own systems. Nationally, police authorities around the country were under considerable pressure to respond to the apparent public demand for this new technology, and within the Southern Region there was an expectation—among local councillors, members of the business community, and certain sections of the public—that when CCTV finally did arrive, it would have the full support of the police.

In responding to this pressure, however, the Southern Region Police followed the 'wait and see' approach adopted by many other forces around the country.[2] Publicly, senior officers welcomed the efforts of local authorities to bring CCTV to their towns, while privately they held back from actually committing police funds or resources to the new technology. As a consequence of this early reticence, the first scheme to go live in the region did so without any financial or operational backing from the police. Although senior officers regularly referred to 'force policy' when discussing police involvement with CCTV, no formal guidelines regarding the role of CCTV within the overall policing strategy for the region had

---

[2] See Ch. 1, Sect. 1.3.

yet been devised. Instead, each individual town force was left to decide—within a broad framework of 'limited involvement' laid down by senior management—just how far it was prepared to go in supporting any local initiative, either financially or in terms of management and logistical support. In practice, this meant that early negotiations regarding the installation of CCTV were influenced by the particular relations between the police and the local council in any given town, and to a lesser extent by the personalities of the individual officers and councillors involved.

There are a number of factors that contributed to this early reticence on the part of the police. Like many other forces in Britain, the Southern Region Police had been using covert surveillance cameras since the early 1970s and as such already had some experience with CCTV, albeit on a much smaller scale than was being proposed by central and local government. As a number of officers noted in the course of the study, from the outset senior police within the force were acutely aware of many of the legal and technical issues associated with the use of surveillance cameras. In the absence of guidance from the government about how CCTV was to be regulated, senior management were understandably hesitant to commit resources to the new technology until it was clear how the cameras were to be used and what constraints might be placed upon them. There was little point, as far as the police were concerned, in embracing CCTV if it later turned out that legal restrictions would prevent them from using cameras for anything other than monitoring traffic or reducing the incidence of shoplifting.

Another, more mundane, explanation for this initial antipathy towards CCTV was the lack of available resources. Officers within the Southern Region Police were quick to realize that no matter how advanced the camera system, CCTV surveillance was going to be labour intensive, both in terms of providing operators to monitor the cameras and other staff to 'interrogate tapes'. Having reached this conclusion, senior management were reluctant to allow CCTV—regardless of whether it was to be run by the police or the local authority—into already crowded police stations. As one senior officer noted, the concern was that the police would eventually be overwhelmed by the demands of CCTV, both in terms of the monopolization of police time and police space: 'We were going to end up with our patrol room walls covered with CCTV monitors, all coming into police stations, which we couldn't afford to do either in terms of resources to watch them or space etc. etc.' (Chief Inspector A, Police Headquarters).

As will be discussed later in this chapter, the issue of resources had a major impact on the types of partnership agreements that were eventually struck between the police and local government in the Southern Region. In the early days of collaboration, the police were happy to enter into arrangements with local authorities in which they shared some of the staff costs, on the understanding that they did not need to give up space in their stations or sacrifice trained officers to the scheme. As various partnerships proved themselves to be successful, however, the police began to consider the possibility of closer links between themselves and the already-established local authority schemes, as well as the prospect of operating their own systems without outside assistance.

Leaving aside questions of resources and concerns about the usefulness of CCTV, perhaps the most significant influence on the initial police response to public area surveillance—both in the Southern Region and throughout the country—was the desire to avoid being seen as the driving force behind the spread of CCTV. Fears that the police risked being cast in the role of 'Big Brother' had already led the Association of Chief Police Officers (ACPO) to advise chief constables to hold back from taking a leading role in the promotion of CCTV or committing resources to new schemes, despite the fact that CCTV had already received a great deal of favourable attention both in the media and in Parliament.[3] As has already been noted in Chapter 1, the sudden arrival of CCTV in the early 1990s was marked by a lack of both critical debate and credible research on the subject of CCTV and its potential effect on problems of crime and public order. Consequently, by 1993 the Southern Region Police found itself in the difficult position of having to decide how to approach the issue of CCTV with few serious research studies to refer to and little idea about the potential pitfalls of this new technology. As one officer observed, the police were concerned about a possible public backlash, even though the

---

[3] Although this position did not form part of ACPO's stated public policy in relation to CCTV, according to senior officers in the course of this study, an ACPO memo was distributed to chief constables in early 1993 advising them to hold back from making a strong commitment to CCTV. A copy of this memo was not obtainable from either ACPO or the Southern Region Police.

government and many local councillors appeared convinced of the benefits of CCTV:

There were lots of assumptions being made really at that point, and there were very few systems, very few town centre public systems that were existing that we could actually go and do research on...We didn't want it [CCTV] to be seen as a police initiative because we were very conscious of the Big Brother syndrome, and the privacy issues and the police state and so on and so forth. And we didn't want it to become that. We wanted it to become a community issue. (Chief Inspector A, Police Headquarters)

At a force level, these general concerns were soon translated into a policy of 'limited involvement'. Taking the ACPO guidelines as their starting point, the Southern Region force decided to adopt a wait-and-see approach, making it clear to local authorities that while they could offer limited financial and logistic support for existing schemes, they were not prepared to provide space within police stations for new CCTV control rooms. New schemes needed to operate independently of the police and under the control of the local authorities that funded them. While they were prepared to benefit from public area CCTV and support local initiatives, the police were determined to avoid responsibility for them. According to one Southern Region officer, the attitude of the time was that: 'CCTV is a wonderful thing and it was very effective and it was developing rapidly and the police service really ought be encouraging it—with the proviso being that although we should encourage and form partnerships we shouldn't take a leading role' (Police Manager A, Scheme P2).

Given that the police have traditionally greeted new technologies with caution, the approach taken by the Southern Region force hardly seems surprising. As Ackroyd et al. have noted, because the police rely on the state for resources and serve as its 'agent and protector', they have tended to be extremely sensitive to social and political factors when making decisions about whether to change existing practices or embrace new technology.[4] Technology is rarely judged in isolation, and as far as the police are concerned, the potential benefits of each new innovation must be weighed against

---

[4] S. Ackroyd, R. Harper, J. A. Hughes, D. Shapiro, and K. Soothill (1992) *New Technology and Practical Police Work: The Social Context of Technical Innovation* (Buckingham: Open University Press), 13.

the need to maintain good relations with both the public and the government.

Looked at from an another perspective, the initial police response to CCTV—both at the regional and national level—simply reflected the inherent conservatism of the police as an organization. According to Peter Manning, the police differ from other organizations in ways that tend to amplify their conservative tendencies.[5] Because the police represent a very traditional form of work organization—legitimized in part by charisma and in part by the idea of rational bureaucracy—and are clearly associated with the central values of society and state authority, they are inevitably resistant to dramatic change.[6] In addition, many lower-ranking officers are resistant to technological changes that may diminish the importance of certain core police tasks—such as foot patrol and beat policing.[7] Faced with the rapid spread of CCTV, the initial reaction of both ACPO and the Southern Region to the technology of public surveillance was thus a predictable one.

Although the attitude of the police towards CCTV was to change over time, their reluctance to endorse fully the use of public area surveillance during the early 1990s ensured that local authorities retained and strengthened their early hold over the application of the technology within the region. Put simply, by taking a cautious approach at a time of rapid expansion in the use of CCTV, senior police management effectively surrendered control of the technology—control that was later extremely difficult for them to regain.

3.2   Getting involved: the local authorities

Across the Southern Region, the initial response of local government to the arrival of CCTV was extremely positive. According to their own accounts, councillors and local officials in each of the six towns included in the study had begun to consider the potential benefits of CCTV from late 1993 onwards, and by the end of 1994 three of them—P2, C1, and C2—had begun to take tentative steps towards installing their own systems. As a consequence of this enthusiasm, at the same time as the Southern Region Police were deciding on the best approach to take regarding CCTV, a number of

[5] Manning (1992), 354.   [6] ibid.
[7] Ackroyd et al. (1992), 86.

councils had already started raising funds and testing levels of public support (typically in that order). Although local authorities may not have believed all of the rhetoric that accompanied the arrival of CCTV, they were certainly far less suspicious of the new technology than the police. As such, on the whole they moved more quickly to integrate CCTV into their thinking about issues of crime and town centre management.

It is tempting to put this lack of suspicion down to ignorance on the part of council members and their advisers—ignorance of the issues surrounding public area surveillance and ignorance of the technical limits of CCTV. More charitably, however, it is possible that these local authorities were simply following the national trend. Given the hype that surrounded CCTV during the 'early years', many councils simply fell victim to the 'supply-side rhetoric' of politicians and Home Office civil servants.[8] In other words, local interest in CCTV emerged as a direct response to the growing desire of central government to shift responsibility for crime control and crime prevention away from the state and to local and non-state agencies. As Graham has noted, for example, by the mid-1990s the pressure on local authorities to join with the government in promoting CCTV was intense, with cameras being touted by ministers as the 'magic bullet' that could end the battle against local crime:

In public spaces, CCTV cameras [were] being seen as a new and cost-effective part of the local policy 'tool kit' for dealing with a range of urban problems—cutting crime, reviving consumer and business confidence in town centres, and underpinning the economic 'competitiveness' of urban areas in the UK.[9]

During this time, public area CCTV was also beginning to gain the support of the growing town centre management (TCM) movement within local government. Having emerged as a response to the fall in consumer spending during the late 1980s and early 1990s, the TCM movement had already started to influence the formation of

[8] See Graham (1998c).

[9] ibid. Typical of the comments being made by ministers at this time was that of Sir Paul Beresford, the Environment Minister, who encouraged local councils to consider the issue of crime prevention and CCTV when drawing up development plans, claiming that 'CCTV can bring enormous benefits to towns and cities'. Quoted in *Planning Week* (13 Oct. 1994), cited by Graham (1998c), at 91. On the influence of these 'supply-side' pressures on local government, see also McCahill (1998).

local government policy by the time CCTV arrived on the scene, and its proponents saw cameras as yet another way of reviving consumer confidence and increasing the 'feel-good' factor in town and city centres.[10] As Reeve has noted, in the minds of many town centre managers and local councillors, it was clear that 'Aside from acting as a possible disincentive to criminal activity, CCTV [could] be interpreted as being employed to enhance a particular view of a town centre as a safe environment for those staying within the standards determined by the agencies controlling its use'.[11]

Both of these factors—supply-side rhetoric and the TCM movement—had a clear influence on the attitudes of local authorities within the Southern Region. In towns like C3 and P3, for example, the incidence of shoplifting and public disorder had been on the increase for a number of years, and councillors were under considerable pressure from the public and local businesses to be seen to be doing something about crime. In contrast, in Town C2—where town centre crime was less of a problem—CCTV arrived at a time when the issue of commercial revitalization was high on the local agenda. Indeed, the overall picture that emerges from interviews with officials and local councillors across all six towns suggests that commercial concerns were in fact the most influential. While there were a small number of elected representatives who did believe that CCTV would drastically reduce the level of local crime, the majority were not so naïve. In fact, many clearly appreciated that CCTV was unlikely to live up to the promises of the security industry or the optimism of certain Home Office ministers. Most councillors in the region were convinced, however, that cameras were extremely popular with the public, and that CCTV would help to bring people back to town and city centres. As one official noted, the key concern was not with the actual level of crime in the town, but rather with the public perception of crime:

Our crime wasn't very high compared to say London or a major city. It was high for a small market town, and it was going up at 10 per cent a year. Shoplifting had gone up by 90 per cent in the past twelve months. Also, just

[10] Norris and Armstrong (1999*b*), 39. See also A. Reeve (1996) 'The private realm of the managed town centre' *Urban design international* 1(1):61; and N.R. Fyfe and J. Bannister (1996) 'City watching: Closed circuit television surveillance in public places' *Area* 28(1): 37.
[11] Reeve (1998*a*), 81.

before we actually engaged our security consultants, our community safety manager undertook a local attitude survey to find out what the public's perceptions of the problems were and also what the view on CCTV was. I can't remember precisely, but the fear of crime was very high. An awful lot of people said they just wouldn't come into the town after eight o'clock on certain evenings. (Local Councillor C, Town C2)

Although researchers such as Ditton have since called into question the reliability of the public attitude surveys carried out by the Home Office and others during this time, many local politicians took these surveys seriously and concluded that the public were largely in favour of CCTV.[12] Given that money was being made available for CCTV via the Challenge Competition and that the public appeared to be in favour of the cameras, many councillors felt something of an obligation at least to consider the possibility of installing CCTV. As one official in Town C3 noted, during the heady days of the first and second Challenge rounds, even surveys which did not specifically set out to address public attitudes towards CCTV were soon reinterpreted to provide a justification for councils to go ahead with initial feasibility studies and applications for funding:

The survey wasn't aimed at CCTV—it was aimed at the public's perception of crime in the town and the sort of things they would like to see addressed. I think it was a very high proportion who had a very severe fear of crime, and on the question 'What would your view be on CCTV?' I think something like 90 per cent supported it . . . So although I wouldn't say that gave us public support, at least we knew there wouldn't be a big outcry against it. (Local Official M, Town C3)

In short, as far as local government was concerned, the time was right for CCTV. Although publicly local councillors talked of the need to involve the police in CCTV and the importance of local partnerships, the reality was that by the mid-1990s they were already committed to going ahead with installing cameras with or without the support of the police. The public wanted CCTV, and even if cameras did not end up reducing crime, the other benefits— for local businesses and the community at large—seemed clear. All

---

[12] Ditton (1998). As Jason Ditton and Emma Short have noted, there was plenty of 'unreliable' evidence as to the effectiveness of CCTV. See also Ditton and Short (1996); Honess and Charman (1992).

that remained was finding the money, the staff, and somewhere to put the control room.

3.3 Pilot schemes and changing police attitudes

By the end of 1995, two town centre CCTV schemes had already 'gone live' in the Southern Region, with three more due to come online within the following year. All of these schemes were the result of local government initiatives, and in each case the cameras were paid for by the relevant councils in conjunction with local businesses. Although the police had not been excluded from the planning process entirely, their policy of 'limited involvement' ensured that they had exercised little influence over questions of scheme design or camera positioning. As a consequence, the Southern Region Police soon found themselves in the position of having to work with schemes that had not been designed with police procedures or priorities in mind.

This was a problem that had already begun to confront other forces around the country. Although it is possible to point to some notable exceptions—Newcastle and King's Lynn being two of the most obvious—by the beginning of 1996 the majority of CCTV schemes throughout Britain were in the hands of local authorities.[13] In many towns and cities, therefore, the police found themselves being treated as but one of a number of potential end-users or 'customers' of the system, along with emergency services, the local business community, and of course the public. As has already been noted in Chapter 1, the fact that local authorities were able to install and operate CCTV systems without formally needing to involve the police says volumes about the failure of central government to regulate the spread of CCTV. It is important, however, to recognize that the police were also to blame for the situation as it existed in the mid-1990s. Based on an examination of their early policy pronouncements, ACPO and the Police Association appear not only to have underestimated just how important CCTV would become, but also to have assumed that local authorities would be obliged to take account of their needs in the planning and implementation of their systems.

---

[13] See Brown (1995).

Having encountered this problem, the response of the Southern Region force was a pragmatic one. Towards the end of 1995, police in Town P2 were approached by the local council with a proposal for the establishment of a jointly run CCTV scheme. Management of the scheme was to be shared equally between the police and the authority, the control room being located in the local police station with civilian staff provided by the council. After lengthy negotiation, senior management within the force decided to lend their support to the proposed partnership, on the understanding that the new scheme was to be treated as a 'pilot' and that existing policy regarding police involvement with CCTV was to remain unchanged. As many of the officers involved with the planning and implementation of the proposed system noted during interviews, the step was a significant one and one that the police were determined to 'get right'.

As will be discussed in greater detail in Chapter 5, from the police perspective the P2 system proved to be highly successful, so much so that the scheme was to become the model upon which subsequent partnership agreements in other towns were based. Although the police did not undertake a formal survey of public opinion, at both the local and regional level officers appeared convinced that the cameras had been well received and that there was little chance of them being associated with the notion of 'Big Brother'. This meant that by the end of 1996 senior managers within the Southern Region Force were ready to abandon their policy of 'limited involvement' in favour of a more proactive role in use of public area CCTV:

The Chief Constable's management team decided that the pilot scheme had been successful and that in any future locations we would offer similar facilities . . . that we would go into partnership with a local authority, we would offer accommodation in a police building, we would offer to manage the system, we would offer to recruit, select, and train staff, we would offer to manage it once it was up and running. And we would obviously offer my 'expertise' in the consultation process leading up to the implementation. And all of that was seen as Southern Region Police's contribution to a CCTV system. (Chief Inspector A, Police Headquarters)

Thus, after almost three years of CCTV in the Southern Region, local police were finally in a position to play an active part in the use of CCTV in their towns. That said, much of the initiative had been lost. Just as the police saw the P2 partnership as providing a blueprint for future schemes in the region, many councillors were already looking to local authority-run schemes in towns such as C1 and C3 for their inspiration. As will be discussed in the next section, these different visions of the role of CCTV were to come into conflict as the police and local authorities moved into a new phase of partnership and cooperation.

3.4   Becoming partners

One of the key aims of this study was to look at how decisions about the installation of CCTV cameras are made, and the factors that influence system design and overall management. Because of the relatively high levels of autonomy given to police forces and local authorities in Britain, historically the relationship between the two has been complex. This is no more so than when it comes to the management of 'joint ventures' into local crime prevention such as public area CCTV.[14] In each of the schemes included in the study—regardless of whether they were police- or local authority-led—the issue of day-to-day management and the coordination of police and local authority objectives was one that necessarily confronted both scheme planners and managers alike.

In many ways, the experience of the police and local authority managers in Town C2 was typical of the jointly run schemes included in the study. Handed a mandate by the local council to install a town-centre, public-area CCTV system, the managers were immediately faced with the problem of having to decide on the type of system to adopt, how it should be managed, and who should have responsibility for overseeing the various aspects of its operation. By their own admission, neither the council nor the police manager in joint charge of the system had any previous experience of working with CCTV, and thus both faced the daunting prospect of having to become familiar not only with the various legal and administrative problems involved with public area surveillance, but also with complex technical issues relating to control room design, camera specifications, camera locations, and recording procedures. Like so

---

[14] On the topic of multi-agency partnerships (specifically between the police and local authorities) and their impact on local crime prevention initiatives, see: Crawford (1998); and A. Crawford (1997) *The Local Governance of Crime* (Oxford: Oxford University Press).

many managers before them, they soon discovered that there was little available in the way of professional literature on the subject of CCTV installation or management.[15] They therefore decided to go on a 'fact-finding tour' of other schemes:

We had to go on a steep learning curve to actually find out how CCTV is used. We visited loads of other places, and one of the things that did come home was that we had less money than anyone else, so we were on a very, very strict budget. But the police and the council officers here were very keen, so we had to come up with a solution for the manning of the scheme. (Police Manager, Scheme C2)

In addition to examining the set-up of cameras and the management arrangements in a range of other schemes, both managers also visited a number of CCTV control rooms with a view to constructing a picture of best practice that could be incorporated into their codes of practice and procedural manuals. As the police manager remarked, this was not a straightforward process:

We visited many other areas and places that have CCTV. We've also taken a good quantity of codes of practice and tried to get the best practice of everything that we were going to do—all the systems, finding out what pitfalls there were... Of course, there are so many different systems, that what might work for... I don't know... Town C3 or wherever... it might not work here. (Police Manager, Scheme C2)

Having made a substantial financial commitment to the scheme, the police were keen to play a role in the initial design of the system and in its ongoing management once they had become involved. Even after the management and staffing arrangements were agreed upon, it became clear, in various interviews and informal discussions with the local officer responsible for police liaison with the scheme, that the level of input and commitment on the part of the police was something that remained open to discussion and

---

[15] The Home Office has recently taken a significant step towards rectifying this situation with the publication of a CCTV implementation and practice guide. Produced by the Scarman Centre National CCTV Evaluation Team, the guide contains information and recommendations for local crime and disorder reduction partnerships (CDRPs) on such matters as project management, engagement of stakeholders, identification of costs and resources, and the design and technology of CCT schemes. See Home Office (2003) 'National evaluation of CCTV: early findings on scheme implementation and effective practice guide', Home Office Development and Practice Report (London: HMSO).

renegotiation. Given that the police had made a substantial contribution to the cost of staffing the system, there was a feeling that they should have greater access to the system and be able to communicate with the operators directly via a police radio: 'When it actually came down to the managing of it, there was a bit of a problem. In short, a cynic could say that the police are paying up to 50 per cent of the wages for all these people here, so we should have a police radio in here' (Police Manager, Scheme C2).

Ironically, both managers had to accept from the outset that various decisions about the placement of cameras and the overall design of the system had already been made by the council. In the case of Town C2, despite the fact that local crime figures compiled by the police clearly showed that the vast majority of criminal offences were being committed outside the town centre—with the highest concentration located in a number of 'problem estates'—the council nevertheless decided to concentrate its resources on the high street and its immediate surrounds. As the police officer in charge of CCTV ruefully remarked in interview, this decision had as much to do with responding to public misconceptions as it did to any genuine commitment to reduce overall crime levels in and around the town:

So the figures actually didn't justify that within the surveillance area we should have cameras there [in the town centre]. There are other places within the town that ought to, but the council did a survey, and people's *perception* of crime in the town—the fear of crime—actually got the council to actually put in a town system. (Local Authority Manager, Scheme C2)

This was a picture that was repeated across the majority of the schemes included in the study. With the possible exceptions of Towns C3 and P3—both of which had struggled in previous years to overcome relatively serious problems relating to public order and drugs—the initial decision to install CCTV in the other towns appeared to have had as much to do with the vagaries of local politics as it did with any serious commitment to tackling local crime. This fact was not lost on the police, and, as has already been mentioned, their desire to avoid being drawn into exercises in public reassurance had in part influenced the early decision of a senior management within the force to offer only limited technical and staff support for CCTV in the region.

As in all of the jointly run schemes included in the study, decisions about camera positions in Town C2 were determined according to three main concerns. The first and most important of these was to ensure that all of the town centre 'hot-spots' were adequately covered. Secondly, in addition to the High Street itself, adjoining streets—particularly those containing large numbers of pubs, night-clubs, and take-away food vendors—were included in the initial scheme design. Once these key areas had been identified, the final concern was to ensure that the cameras were positioned in such a way so as to eliminate as far as was practicable the existence of 'blind spots'. Although the police helped to identify the 'key areas' in Town C2, decisions about where the cameras should be positioned were ultimately made by the local council, as they were in the other local council-led towns. While they may have been partners in schemes like Scheme C2, the police were in reality frequently shut out of crucial stages in the design process. As will be discussed in the following chapters, as time went on, such lack of cooperation and coordination was seriously to undermine working relations between the police and local authorities when it came to managing the CCTV schemes.

3.5 Tensions and concerns

As has already been noted, in all the schemes included in the study the initiative to install CCTV in the town centre came from the relevant local authority. In each case, it was only after some in-principle decision to adopt CCTV had been made that the police were approached, either with an offer of partnership or joint management or simply to inform them of the decision. Although in the case of Scheme C2, for example, the police were privy to early discussions about the possibility of installing CCTV, at no stage did they have a 'deciding vote' in the matter. In fact, one of the things that soon became clear after speaking with local councillors was the desire of the various authorities to be credited with 'bringing CCTV to their town'. Without exception, every councillor interviewed appeared to view CCTV as a means by which local government could play a more active and autonomous role in the fight against crime in their area and demonstrate their commitment to improving public confidence and safety.

Looking past the rhetoric, however, it also appears that one of the reasons why some of the local authorities did not involve the police from the very outset was because of their desire to prevent the system 'falling into police hands'. While to some extent this fear reflected a belief that the police would inevitably attempt to monopolize the cameras and the operators, it was also indicative of a realization on the part of the local authorities that CCTV could—if used 'properly'—fulfil a variety of other, non-crime-related, functions. In this sense, local councils were quick to recognize both the potential of public area CCTV and the need for them to manage it as a local government resource. For town centre planners, then, CCTV was not just a tool for crime prevention but an aid to traffic management and the coordination of community services as well. This desire on the part of local authorities to expand the ambit of CCTV was one of the major sources of tension between the council planners and managers and the police. In Scheme C2 where the police were joint financiers, for example, this led to an ongoing dispute over the allocation of operator time and camera positioning which continued well after the initial planning and installation of the system. Although the police and local authority representatives eventually managed to develop what appeared to be a good working relationship, it became clear in a number of interviews that the prioritization of CCTV resources was still an unresolved issue, despite the fact that the scheme had been up and running for almost two years.

In addition to the strain created by these attempts by local authorities to maintain ultimate control over scheme resources, tension also arose over their desire to ensure that the needs of specific businesses were adequately accounted for. As has already been touched upon, one of the problems that typically confronts local authorities and police forces interested in installing public area CCTV is how best to involve town centre businesses in the process of planning and operation. Aside from the fact that many CCTV schemes—at least in the early stages of their development—rely upon the financial support of town centre retailers and other businesses, most CCTV managers also recognize the importance of ensuring that these groups are actively working with the scheme so as to ensure its effectiveness in preventing crime. Decisions concerning alarms, lighting, and overall architectural design all affect the security of a business, and consequently the extent to which that business requires additional protection from public area CCTV. Ensuring that local retailers take responsibility for the security of their premises and do not fall into the trap of relying only on CCTV to protect themselves is a key concern for managers, as is ensuring that future buildings and shopping centres do not inhibit the operation of the system but rather enhance the overall level of security in the town centre. This was a point taken up by the local authority manager of Scheme C2 when commenting on plans for a new retail development in the town centre:

> We want to design security into the place if we can. It's a lot less traumatic for the town if you do that, and it's a lot easier to get it right if you're trying to design it in. I don't know whether or not we'll be able to influence the architectural design, but we may be able to add the security features as part of the project. (Local Authority Manager, Scheme C2)

While the police in towns like P1 and C2 were clearly aware of these issues, in the initial planning stages it was apparent that police officers often had difficulty accepting that there were other 'key customers' for the system. Returning to the example of Town C2, there was little doubt that the police saw themselves as having a greater claim over the resources of the system than either the council or local businesses, despite the fact that the majority of the funding came from these two groups. For the police, the question of who really 'owned' the system had little if any bearing on the more central issue of how it should be used. What mattered most to the police was that they should be the *primary* user of CCTV, and as a consequence their needs should take priority when it came to questions of design and operation: 'But who will be the scheme's biggest customer? It's the police. So the police need to have a major input into the design of it and the development and management of it' (Police Manager, Scheme C2).

Differences also emerged between the police and local authorities when it came to the question of whether to use covert or 'hidden' cameras in the town centre. As has already been discussed in Chapter 1, despite the fact that there is some evidence to suggest that overt CCTV cameras may have a deterrent effect on certain forms or crime—most obviously shoplifting and car theft—many local authorities across Britain have favoured the use of covert cameras in the belief that this will increase the likelihood of apprehending and successfully prosecuting offenders. For example, officials in

Town C2 decided to use covert cameras because they believed that this would make it more difficult for potential offenders to evade notice and therefore prosecution.

Yeah, well, they [the covert cameras] were chosen deliberately because the town centre is a conservation area, and we thought that by using domed cameras, not only would you fit the technology into the conservation area in a sympathetic way, but you also are using cameras that are less easy for the criminal to avoid. A conventional camera, you can see which way it's pointing. Wait until it moves, and then carry on doing whatever. These ones you can't tell whether you're being observed or not. But they're not meant to be covert cameras; they're just meant to be discreet. That's the word— discreet. (Local Authority Manager, Scheme C2)

In contrast, the police in Town C2 (as well as Town C3) expressed the view during the planning stage that overt cameras would en- hance the general deterrent effect of the system. In both Towns C2 and C3, however, local authority officials and town councillors prevailed on the grounds that the overriding concern was to catch rather than simply deter criminals. From comments made in a number of informal conversations with these local authority repre- sentatives, it became increasingly clear that this preference for apprehension over prevention stemmed from a belief that the public would only continue to support CCTV if they could 'see results'. As a consequence, ensuring that CCTV brought about an increase in arrest rates was a key concern for elected representatives, despite the fact that the police in both towns felt that the use of overt cameras was likely to have a greater impact on actual levels of crime. Covert cameras were eventually installed in both town centres, although as will be discussed in Chapter 7, this decision was to have few implications for either arrest rates or the allocation of police resources.

3.6   Conclusion

Understanding how it was that the police became involved in the use of CCTV and the extent to which they influenced the overall design and organization of the schemes included in this study is an essential precursor to understanding current police surveillance practices and attitudes to CCTV. Looking at the existing level of police involve- ment in town centre CCTV systems across the Southern Region, it is tempting to assume that the police were one of the driving forces behind the spread of CCTV. What is clear, however, is that the current situation emerged almost independently of the police, and their involvement came only after many crucial decisions had already been made. In short, although they were to become one of the major users of CCTV in the area, the police played a relatively minor role in determining the shape of CCTV surveillance in the region.

The experience of the Southern Region Police also casts doubt over whether it is right to characterize police use of public area CCTV as part of a larger 'responsibilization' strategy in Britain.[16] As noted in Chapter 1, a number of commentators have argued that the popularity of technologies like CCTV is best understood in terms of a recent 'neo-liberal' approach to criminal justice, which is primarily concerned with the local governance of crime and the empowerment of non-state agencies.[17] According to Mike McCahill, the spread of CCTV is part of a trend towards shifting responsibility for crime control away from the state and the police to local governments and the community: 'Thus, from the perspective of the police, CCTV systems provide a means of devolving responsibility for, and shifting the costs of, crime prevention, while at the same time allowing them to retain a coordinating role which enables them to develop new structures of information exchange'.[18]

Rather than shifting responsibility and retaining a coordinating role, however, the police in the Southern Region instead surrendered initial control over public area CCTV and then struggled to become more involved once the systems proved to be a 'success'. In short, the devolvement of authority and the process of responsibilization—at least as far as the police and CCTV were concerned—was neither straightforward nor satisfactory.

By all accounts, the experience of the Southern Region police has been fairly typical of forces across the country. Many other regional police forces were also caught largely unprepared by the emergence

[16] For a discussion of the idea of 'responsibilization', see: P. O'Malley (1996) 'Post-Keynesian policing' *Economy and Society* 25(2): 137–55; and P. O'Malley (1992) 'Risk, power, and crime prevention' *Economy and Society* 21(3): 252–75.

[17] See e.g. Garland (2001); and Stenson and Sullivan (2001).

[18] M. McCahill (2002) *The Surveillance Web: The Rise of Visual Surveillance in an English City* (Cullompton, Devon: Willan Publishing), 193.

of CCTV, and as a result, their responses to the formulation of policy regarding the use of CCTV have also been haphazard. What the example of the Southern Region Police indicates is that this general failure may be the result of lack of foresight on the part of the police rather than the product of any deliberate strategy. In contrast, local authorities appear to have had a much clearer vision of the potential of CCTV from the very beginning, a fact that has enabled them to exert a far greater influence over the shape and direction of CCTV surveillance in Britain than the police. This being the case, it is perhaps ironic that the police have recently found themselves the focus of civil liberties groups and privacy advocates, while the local authorities have come to be seen as the silent and less-influential partners in the process. Far from assuming the role of 'Big Brother', in the early days of CCTV the police had instead to be content with playing the part of the younger sibling. This is a point that will be discussed in greater detail at the end of this book, but as we shall see in the next three chapters, the inability of the police to shake off the role of 'Little Brother' was to have a considerable impact on the operation and regulation of CCTV, both in the Southern Region and in many other schemes across Britain.

4

Going by the Codes

This chapter examines the regulation of public area surveillance in Britain and the impact that this regulatory framework has had on the development and use of CCTV throughout the Southern Region. Despite the fact that successive governments have committed millions of pounds to promoting and supporting CCTV over the past decade, to date central government has been reluctant to impose legal restraints on the use of this technology by the police and local authorities. As a consequence, the task of deciding what constitutes a legitimate use of CCTV and the limits that should be placed on public area surveillance has fallen to local officials and police officers. As a result, there are often marked differences in the regulation and working practices of CCTV schemes across Britain.

In the Southern Region, the police were forced to confront the problem of regulation at an early stage. Although initially hesitant to become involved with public area CCTV, the police began entering into successive partnership arrangements and soon found themselves faced with the same difficult questions, namely who should be responsible for the development of regulations and codes of practice? Furthermore, what sorts of restrictions should be placed on the use of CCTV in the region? As we shall see in this chapter, the failure of the police to take these questions sufficiently seriously created problems for the operation of each of these systems, and perhaps more importantly, placed even greater strains on the relationship between them and their local authority partners. Just as a lack of foresight had left the police playing the role of junior partner to local authorities in many schemes across the region, lack of foresight also marred subsequent attempts by the police to ensure that these schemes were regulated according to police needs and were pursuing goals that reflected police priorities.[1]

[1] Sections of this chapter are taken from Goold (2002b). The author is grateful to the editors of *Criminal Justice Ethics* for their permission to reproduce this material.

4.1   Regulating CCTV: the national picture

At present there is no formal legal regulation of public area CCTV in Britain. As a consequence, it is possible for any local authority or police force, regardless of whether they have specific planning approval, to install and operate a CCTV system in almost any public place, including town centres and residential areas.[2] This situation stands in stark contrast to the position in most other European countries and Western democracies, in which the use of public area CCTV is either expressly prohibited or extensively regulated.[3] Chapter 1 has already identified some of the reasons behind the rapid expansion in the use of CCTV in Britain over the past decade, including belief by central and local government in the largely unproved benefits of this new technology. There can be little doubt that the spread of CCTV has been assisted by a reluctance on the part of the government and the courts to impose any formal legal constraints on the use of public area surveillance. In light of recent changes to the Data Protection Act and the incorporation of the European Convention on Human Rights, however, the legality of public area CCTV is likely to be tested in the near future.

4.1.1   The right to privacy at common law and the Human Rights Act

Leaving aside possible political explanations, the current lack of regulation is not surprising given that English law has traditionally failed to recognize the existence of any general right to privacy, either in private spaces such as the home or in the public sphere. In the absence of a written constitution that sets out the rights to be

---

[2] See: The Town and Country Planning (General Permitted Development) Order 1995, Part 33 (SI 1995 No. 418); and The Town and Country Planning (General Permitted Development) (Scotland) Amendment Order 1996, Part 25 (SI 1996 No. 1266 (s. 124)). For a discussion of the effects of these amendments, see Fay (1998), 317–18; and Davies (1996a), 187. The majority of public area CCTV schemes in operation in Britain derive their legal authority from section 163 of the Criminal Justice and Public Order Act 1994 and section 17 of the Crime and Disorder Act 1998.

[3] In France, for example, under the provisions of Loi No. 95–73 du janvier 1995 (paru au J.O. le 24 janvier 1995), camera surveillance is only permitted in public places in the event that a particular risk of assault or theft can be established. In addition, assuming that such a risk is held to exist, cameras can then only be installed with the prior authorization of the prefect of police, subject to the advice of a departmental committee chaired by a judge. See also Chapter 1, Sect. 1.4.

enjoyed by citizens, the courts in Britain have drawn on a variety of different sources in their efforts to develop a notion of privacy, in each case extending the scope of the existing law by way of analogy and implication.[4] The main weakness of this approach to the protection of rights is that it makes it extremely difficult to assert that a 'new' right exists, or that such a right is 'fundamental' under the existing law. This problem is further exacerbated when the right in question is one as difficult to define as privacy. As David Feldman has noted, 'The problem is that the right to privacy is controversial. The very breadth of the idea, and its tendency to merge with the idea of liberty itself, produces a lack of definition which weakens its force in moral and political discourse'.[5]

As a consequence, the laws of trespass, nuisance, breach of copyright, and defamation have all been used at various times by the courts in Britain in an effort to provide individuals with limited protection against unwanted intrusions into their 'private lives'.[6] The very fact that such a disparate set of torts has been enlisted in the cause of privacy has meant, however, that it is difficult to discern a set of general principles which might be used to provide the basis for the establishment of an independent right to privacy at common law.

Even assuming that the courts were willing to recognize the existence of a general right to privacy in domestic law, it is particularly difficult to envisage how such a right might operate in public spaces.[7] While many would argue that we should have

---

[4] E. Short and C. de Than (1998) *Civil Liberties: Legal Principles of Individual Freedom* (London: Sweet & Maxwell), 363.

[5] D. Feldman (1994) 'Secrecy, dignity or autonomy? Views of privacy as a civil liberty' *Current Legal Problems* 47(2): 41. See also arguments by Ronald Dworkin concerning the problems inherent in the relationship between privacy and liberty: R. Dworkin (1977) *Taking Rights Seriously* (London: Duckworth), 266–78. I have discussed this issue in greater detail in Goold (2002b).

[6] See in particular *Bernstein v Skyview and General Ltd* [1978] 1 QB 479 (regarding aerial photographs and trespass to land); *Khorasandijan v Bush* [1993] QB 727 (private nuisance); *The Lady Anne Tennant v Associated Newspapers Group Ltd* [1979] 5 FSR 298 (breach of copyright); and *Kaye v Robertson* [1991] FSR 62.

[7] D. Feldman (1997) 'Privacy-related rights and their social value' in P. Birks (ed.) *Privacy and Loyalty* (Oxford: Clarendon Press), 15. See also Feldman (1994). In this second piece (at p. 53), Feldman neatly summarizes the complexity of the problem: 'At one time I thought that the fact that one chose to do things in public automatically negated any claim to privacy rights in respect of them. Now, however, I think that the position is more complicated.'

some expectation of privacy when we stand in the street, go shopping, or walk through a park, determining the limits of such an
expectation—and identifying the interests that are harmed by the
absence of privacy protections in such circumstances—is problematic. How, for example, is being watched by a CCTV camera
different from being watched by a stranger at a bus stop or, for
that matter, by a police officer standing on a street corner? Is one
somehow more intrusive than the other, and if so how should the
law discriminate between such situations?

To date, the position regarding the protection of individual privacy in public spaces has been largely unaffected by the incorporation of the European Convention of Human Rights into domestic
law.[8] Although the Convention recognizes a citizen's right to 'respect for his private and family life, his home and his correspondence', it is unclear as to whether this right gives rise to any
expectation of privacy in public places.[9] One of the few cases in
which the Court has had the opportunity to consider this issue was
in 1996 in *Friedl v Austria*.[10] In *Friedl*, the applicant complained of
being photographed by the police while taking part in a public
demonstration in Vienna, claiming that this constituted an interference with his right to enjoy a private life under the provisions of
Article 8 of the Convention. According to the applicant's submis-
sions, the taking of his photograph, the establishing of his identity,
and the recording of his personal data, as well as the storing of this
material, all represented a violation of his right to privacy under the
article. Further, the applicant claimed that the absence of redress for
this interference constituted a breach of his rights under Article 13
of the Convention, which guarantees 'an effective remedy before a
national authority'.[11]

---

[8] Human Rights Act 1998.

[9] European Convention on Human Rights, Article 8: Right to Respect of Privacy
states that '(1) Everyone has the right to respect for his private and family life, his
home and his correspondence; (2) There shall be no interference by a public authority
with the exercise of this right except such as is in accordance with the law and is
necessary in a democratic society in the interests of national security, public safety or
the economic well-being of the country, for the prevention of disorder or crime, for
the protection of health or morals, or the protection of the rights and freedoms of
others'.

[10] European Court of Human Rights, *Friedl v Austria* (1996) 21 EHRR 83.

[11] Article 13 of the Convention provides that 'Everyone whose rights and freedoms as set forth in [the] Convention are violated shall have an effective remedy

In dismissing the case, the Court noted that although previous case-law of the Convention held that the storing and release of information relating to an individual's private life in a secret police register was an interference under Article 8, in those cases the information in question had been obtained as a result of some interference with the individual's private—as opposed to public—life.[12] As a consequence, the Court was unwilling to extend the protections afforded under Article 8 to include information obtained about the individual while engaged in activities in a public space.[13] Significantly, however, in reaching its decision in *Friedl* the Court went on to consider the question of what could be held to constitute the boundaries of an individual's 'private life' for the purpose of the Convention. Referring to a number of past decisions, the Court observed that the notion of 'private life' was 'not limited to an "inner circle" in which the individual may live his own personal life as he chooses and exclude therefrom entirely the outside world not encompassed within this circle'.[14] On the strength of this, the Court went on to conclude that Article 8 could provide 'to a certain degree the right to establish and develop relationships with other human beings and the outside world', although no such right appeared to have been violated as regards the applicant in *Friedl*.[15]

before a national authority notwithstanding that the violation has been committed by persons acting in an official capacity'. In *Friedl*, the Court concluded in a vote of 14 to nine that there had been no violation of Article 13 as regards the complaint about the taking of photographs and their retention. See European Court of Human Rights, *Friedl v Austria* (1996) 21 EHRR 83.

[12] European Court of Human Rights, *Leander v Sweden* (1987) 9 EHRR 433, judgment of 26 Mar. 1987, p. 22 § 48.

[13] Paragraph 49 of the decision reads, 'For the purpose of delimiting the scope of the protection afforded by Article 8 of the Convention against arbitrary interference by public authorities, the Court has attached importance to the questions whether the taking of photographs amounted to an intrusion into the individual's privacy, whether it related to private matters or public incidents, and whether the material thus obtained was envisaged for a limited use or was likely to be made available to the general public'. *Friedl v Austria* (1996) 21 EHRR 83. The Court goes on to cite the decision in application no. 5877/72, decision of 12 Oct. 1972, Yearbook, vol. 16, 328 in support of this conclusion.

[14] See, in particular, European Court of Human Rights cases *Niemietz v Germany* (1993) 16 EHRR 97 and *Brüggemann and Scheuten v Germany* (1981) 3 EHRR 244.

[15] A similar approach has been taken by courts in the United States. Despite declaring in *Katz v United States* (1967) 389 US 347 that the Fourth Amendment 'protects people not places', since the late 1960s the Supreme Court has been highly

This conclusion has been taken by some academic commentators and civil liberties groups to suggest that the Court is likely to be sympathetic to future claims based on an appeal to a general expectation of privacy in public places. In their report to the House of Lords Select Committee on Science and Technology, for example, the group Justice claimed on the basis of *Friedl* that the 'European Commission of Human Rights has affirmed that privacy rights may, in certain circumstances, be asserted in public places'.[16] This interpretation is perhaps optimistic. Aside from the fact that the Court in *Friedl* appears to have been more concerned with the possibility of a very limited expansion of the private sphere rather than any consideration of the more difficult question of what constitutes a public space, the concept of an 'inner circle' is not one that has been taken up or expanded upon by the Court in subsequent decisions. For example, although the Court acknowledged in *Peck v United Kingdom* that meaningful distinctions can be drawn between different types of public activities and circumstances, there was no suggestion that the Council in question was wrong to engage in the general surveillance of individuals in public, only that it could not assume that *all* types of public surveillance were equally acceptable.[17] In

resistant to the idea that privacy rights can be extended to streets or other public places. The Court has also repeatedly refused to consider any suggestion that public area video surveillance should be regarded as a form of police search, a view that has been consistently endorsed by the lower courts. See Q. Burrows (1997) 'Scowl because you're on candid camera: privacy and video surveillance' *Valparaiso University Law Review* 31: 1083; K. Gormley (1992) 'One hundred years of privacy' *Wisconsin Law Review* 1345; J. M. Granholm (1987) 'Video surveillance on public streets: the constitutionality of invisible citizen searches' *Detroit Law Review* 64: 694; and G. C. Robb (1980) 'Police use of CCTV surveillance: constitutional implications and proposed regulations' *University of Michigan Journal of Law Reform* 13: 582.

[16] The additional claim that this is 'especially so in relation to the exercise of other rights, such as the right to freedom of expression and assembly, when the use of CCTV cameras may have a "chilling" effect' is also difficult to sustain on the basis of the decision in *Friedl* alone. See Justice (1997) 'Digital images as evidence: report to the House of Lords Select Committee on Science and Technology' (London: Justice), 9.

[17] See e.g. the recent decision of the European Court of Human Rights in *Peck v United Kingdom* (2003) ECHR Application No. 44647/98. Although in this case the Court held that Brentwood Borough Council had interfered with the applicant's right to respect for his private life under Article 8 (by releasing CCTV images of his arrest to the media), the interference was held to be in accordance with the law as the

addition, while the Court may have touched on the issue of privacy rights in public spaces, its primary concern was with the fact that the pictures taken of the plaintiff were disclosed, and not that they were taken in the first place. In any event, as Article 8 only requires signatories to the Convention to 'respect' an individual's private life, it still remains for Parliament and the domestic courts to be persuaded to interpret this in such a way as to give rise to a general right of privacy.[18]

4.1.2 Rules of evidence and the Data Protection Act

Although there is no recognized or general right to privacy that could be used as a basis for the regulation of public area surveillance in Britain, existing rules of evidence relating to the use of video footage in court have provided some basic guidance for the police and other operators of public area CCTV schemes in relation to the handling and storage of CCTV recordings. Traditionally, English law has not recognized a difference between photographic evidence and other forms of evidence such as eye-witness accounts, with the Court of Appeal in *R v Maqsud Ali* acknowledging in 1966 that 'for many years now photographs have been admissible in evidence on proof that they are relevant to the issues of the case'.[19] Subsequent cases—such as *R v Fowden and White*—have held that there is no substantive difference between a video film and a photograph in

disclosure of the footage was for a legitimate aim, namely public safety. On the issue of privacy rights in public spaces, it is important to note that while the Court in *Peck* acknowledged that meaningful distinctions can be drawn between different types of public activities and circumstances, given the very specific and unusual facts of this case it remains to be seen whether it will have any impact on the general legality of CCTV schemes in Britain or the operation of Article 8 of the Convention.

[18] As Feldman has noted, the term 'respect' was used by the drafters of the Convention in an effort to avoid creating a 'far-reaching right to privacy, honour, and reputation as had been recognised under the Universal Declaration of Human Rights, Article 12, which included a right to legal protection against interferences'. See Feldman (1997), 29. Article 12 of the Declaration states that: 'No one shall be subjected to arbitrary interference with his privacy, family, home or correspondence, nor to attacks upon his honour and reputation. Everyone has the right to the protection of the law against such interference or attacks.' See also J. E. S. Fawcett (1987) *The Application of the European Convention on Human Rights*, 2nd edn. (Oxford: Clarendon), 211: 'What began in the Teitgen proposals as "inviolability", and became "immunity from arbitrary interference", then protection from governmental interference [immixtions gouvernementales], ended tamely as "respect"'.

[19] [1966] 1 QB 688.

terms of their value as real evidence, and as a consequence there is nothing in principle to prevent the use of video evidence obtained from CCTV cameras from being presented in court.[20] Although there is some debate as to the admissibility of digital images, the issue turns more on resolving questions of authentication rather than on any substantive issue about the admissibility of video evidence in general.[21] In any event, given that video footage is generally admissible, since the earliest days of CCTV in Britain, scheme managers have been aware of the need to be able to demonstrate that video footage is both authentic and has not been tampered with.

In addition, recent changes to the data protection laws regarding the collection and storage of personal information on video have led many managers of public area CCTV systems to reconsider their previous working practices. Enacted in response to the EU Data Protection Directive 1998, the Data Protection Act 1998 came into force on 1 March 2000, and requires all bodies engaged in the collection and storage of personal information to comply with eight key data protection principles.[22] Section 1(1) of the Act defines 'personal information as:

[D]ata which relate to a living individual who can be identified (a) from those data, or (b) from those data and other information which is in the possession of, or is likely to come into the possession of, the data controller, and includes any expression of opinion about the individual and any

---

[20] [1982] Crim LR 588. It is important to note, however, the possible exception created by *R v Cook (Christopher)* [1987] 1 QB 417, in which the court held that photographic evidence is best considered to be in an evidential category all of its own: '[t]he photograph, the sketch and the photofit are in a class of evidence of their own to which neither the rule against hearsay nor the rule against the admission of an earlier consistent statement applies'.

[21] See P. Plowden, M. Stockdale, and D. Elliot (1997) 'New techniques and new devices: video evidence and the criminal courts' *New Law Journal* (4 Apr.), 502. The digital recording and storage of CCTV images has become increasingly prevalent in the last two years, particularly as the reliability of this technology improves and the cost falls. From the point of view of scheme management, the use of digital storage methods does away with the need to keep actual videotapes and enables a scheme to record footage on computer disk or CD ROMs instead.

[22] Although the Act became law in March 2000, provision was made within the legislation for two 'transition periods' to give existing schemes additional time to adjust to the new rules. As a result, established schemes were not required to comply with the legislation until 24 October 2001.

indication of the intentions of the data controller or any other person in respect of the individual.

As the images produced by public area CCTV cameras constitute 'personal data' under the Act, most town and city centre CCTV schemes now fall within the ambit of the new provisions.[23] The Act also stipulates that all CCTV systems that undertake surveillance in areas to which the public have 'largely free and unrestricted access' must be registered with the Information Commissioner, and must comply with various provisions and general principles of the Act.[24]

In practice, however, compliance with many of these provisions is not particularly onerous. Under the legislation, for example, all recording and storage equipment—such as video recorders, tapes, and multiplexers—must be housed in a secured room or cabinet, and a system of logbooks and tape management must be established. In addition, signs indicating that CCTV is in operation must be posted in and around the area under surveillance so that members of the public are aware that their activities are being monitored. Significantly, however, the Act says nothing about how surveillance should be carried out, or how operators and managers should determine whom to follow and for how long. Public area surveillance is deemed to be lawful under the Act provided that it is carried out for a purpose which is in the public interest, which according to section 29 includes surveillance aimed at preventing

[23] Note that according to the Codes of Practice published by the office of the Information Commissioner (formerly the Data Protection Commissioner) in July 2000, the provisions of the Data Protection Act 1998 are not intended to cover: targeted and intrusive surveillance (which is regulated by the Regulation of Investigatory Powers Act 2000); surveillance carried out by employers to ensure employees comply with the terms of their contract of employment; home security equipment (exempt under the provisions of s. 36 of the Data Protection Act 1998); or cameras used for the purpose of journalism. For a short summary of the main provisions of the CCTV Codes of Practice (available on the Information Commissioner's website at http://www.dataprotection.gov.uk/dpr/dpdoc.nsf), see McCahill and Norris (2002b), 52–4.

[24] The central aim of the Act is to ensure that personal data is processed fairly and lawfully. Under the Act, this broad aim gives rise to a number of key data protection principles, namely that: (1) data shall be processed for one or more lawful purposes and not further processed for incompatible purposes; (2) data shall be adequate, relevant and not excessive; (3) data shall be accurate and where necessary kept up to date; (4) data shall not be kept for longer than is necessary; and (5) data shall be processed in accordance with rights of data subjects under the Data Protection Act 1998.

and detecting crime, apprehending and prosecuting of offenders, or public safety.[25] As a consequence, although in theory it would be possible to challenge the legality of a town centre scheme on the basis that it was being operated in a manner contrary to the public interest, in practice this would prove to be extremely difficult to establish given the broad definition of public interest set out in the Act.[26]

4.1.3   Informal regulation: codes of practice

In addition to the Data Protection Act and the various common law rules of evidence, there are a variety of informal controls that limit the use of public area CCTV in Britain. Chief among these are the written codes of practice that are now widely used by the police, local authorities, and private operators of CCTV. Typically, these codes lay down guidelines for the daily operation of the schemes, and cover matters such as staffing, tape handling and storage procedures, security and access to the scheme, and the control and operation of the cameras. Some codes may also include a statement of the purpose and objectives of the scheme, as well as a set of 'rules' designed to protect the public against unwarranted or intrusive surveillance.

As Clive Norris and Gary Armstrong have pointed out, it is difficult to generalize about these codes given that they vary considerably between schemes and between different police and local authority areas.[27] This may be, as they suggest, a consequence of

---

[25] According to section 29(1) of the Act: 'Personal data processed for any of the following purposes—(a) the prevention or detection of crime, (b) the apprehension or prosecution of offenders, or (c) the assessment or collection of any tax or duty or of any imposition of a similar nature, are exempt from the first data protection principle (except to the extent to which it requires compliance with the conditions in Schedules 2 and 3) and section 7 in any case to the extent to which the application of those provisions to the data would be likely to prejudice any of the matters mentioned in this subsection'.

[26] Although the Information Commissioner published a set of guidelines and standards in July 2001 in an attempt to clarify how the Data Protection Act 1998 applies to public area surveillance systems, as McCahill and Norris have observed, it is still too early to determine how the provisions of the Act will affect the operation of CCTV schemes in Britain. Given the limited resources available to the Data Protection Registrar, however, it seems unlikely that many schemes operating in violation of the Act will be identified or prosecuted. See McCahill and Norris (2002b), 51–4.

[27] Norris and G Armstrong (1999b), 100.

the fact that there is as yet no nationally agreed standard as to the minimum content of such codes or their status in law. Commenting on the findings of a comprehensive survey of CCTV codes of practice carried out for the Local Government Information Unit (LGIU) in 1995, Bulos and Sarno observed that the codes varied considerably in terms of their content, style, and length.[28] Significantly, they also noted that the great majority of them were primarily concerned with 'operational questions' and issues relating to the use of video footage as evidence:

A detailed analysis of the codes allowed clear identification of the core concerns of the parties operating CCTV systems. These concerns included the need for proper and secure video storage, retrieval and use of tapes, with particular attention being paid to the way in which video material could be used for evidential purposes. Almost as evident was the idiosyncratic and partial way in which other matters such as accountability, provision of information, monitoring and evaluation were addressed.[29]

More disturbingly, however, Bulos and Sarno also found that very few of the codes surveyed contained detailed rules relating to the actual operation of the cameras. Questions such as what might constitute 'suspicious behaviour' were rarely addressed, so that such matters were left to the discretion of individual operators.[30] In addition, only a few of the codes attempted to provide guidance as to the criteria that might provide the basis for tracking an individual or engaging in prolonged surveillance: 'Few codes specify the basis on which tracking should occur or what kind of limitation should be placed on the time a camera is trained on a single person or group in the expectation of an incident occurring'.[31]

There are a number of possible explanations for the emphasis in the codes on technical and operational matters, at the cost of larger,

[28] M. Bulos and C. Sarno (1996) *Codes of Practice and Public Closed Circuit Television Systems* (London: Local Government Information Unit), 17.

[29] Bulos and Sarno (1996), 17.

[30] Bulos and Sarno also noted that these issues were rarely discussed during the training of operators: 'The most neglected area of training consists of how to identify suspicious behaviour, when to track individuals or groups and when to take close-up views of incidents or people. This was either assumed to be self-evident or common sense. The informality of these procedures leaves unexamined the predispositions of operators to consider some people or types as more likely to commit crime than others.' Bulos and Sarno (1996), 24.

[31] ibid.

more fundamental questions of ethics and privacy. The most obvious is that questions of accountability and individual privacy were not perceived as being especially important by the police and local authorities when public area CCTV first came into operation in the mid-1990s. As a number of commentators have observed, in the early years of CCTV, codes of practice were not a 'high priority', and as a consequence when scheme managers did produce such documents they only did so in an effort to clarify their own individual working arrangements and operation practices.[32] As has already been discussed in Chapter 1, during this period the central concern of most local authorities (and some police forces) appeared to be with raising funds, resolving technical problems, and convincing their constituents of the benefits of this new technology.

Another explanation for the lack of privacy protections included in the codes surveyed by the LGIU may lie with the fact that there is no obvious or simple answer to the question of how best to provide such protections. As already noted, it is unclear as to how any meaningful legal right to privacy might operate in public spaces, and as such it is perhaps understandable that in the early days of public area CCTV the police and local authorities chose to shy away from the issue when drafting their codes of practice.[33] The lack of central government regulation may also have contributed to this reluctance, with scheme managers being left to confront issues of accountability and public privacy with little or no external guidance.

Irrespective of the possible explanations, it is important to remember that the LGIU survey is now over seven years old, and there has since been some progress towards greater uniformity in the informal regulation of CCTV. In recent years, efforts have been made by the Home Office and various CCTV user groups to provide some sort of guidance as to best practice. The publication of *A Watching Brief: A Code of Practice for CCTV* by the Local Government Information Unit in 1996—a year after Bulos and Sarno had completed their study—appears to have had a significant impact on the use of codes and the degree of uniformity of these documents.[34] As a case in point, the Model Code of Practice written

---

[32] Ansell (1998).   [33] See: von Hirsch (2000) and Goold (2002b).
[34] H. Kitchen (1996) *A Watching Brief: A Code of Practice for CCTV* (London: Local Government Information Unit).

by the police and made available to all of the schemes in the Southern Region was based on the LGIU model, a fact that led to a high level of conformity—at least on paper—between the six different schemes in terms of certain key procedures. Although the LGIU code was a relatively short document that did not address many of the specific concerns raised by Bulos and Sarno, it nevertheless provided the police, local authorities, and scheme managers with a starting point for their own thinking about how matters of scheme security and the handling of tapes could be improved and how the operation of CCTV could be made more transparent to the public.[35]

Roughly contemporaneous with the writing of the LGIU Code, the Home Office initiated a national CCTV Challenge Competition, which also did much to encourage the widespread adoption of codes by the police and local authorities.[36] Statements from the Home Office and the Competition literature made it clear that bids not accompanied by draft codes of practice would fail. Given that the vast majority of CCTV users currently operating public area schemes in Britain have entered the Challenge Competition at least once, it follows that at least the same number of schemes now have codes of practice—in draft form if nothing else.

This is a conclusion that is supported by the research available on the use of codes of practice. All of the respondents in John Ansell's 1998 survey of scheme managers, for example, claimed to be operating their systems in accordance with a written code of practice, and had nominated an individual employee of the scheme to ensure compliance with the code.[37] Significantly, however, over 80 per cent of the respondents also claimed to have written their own codes. As Ansell notes, this could mean that each of the 65 schemes included in his survey were operating according to 65 different sets of rules and procedures. Although this seems unlikely, Ansell's point does highlight the fact that the absence of national guidelines has led to a

---

[35] A similar model code of practice was also published in the United States in 2000 by the International Association of Police Chiefs (IACP) in conjunction with the US Security Industry Association (SIA). A copy of the CCTV for Public Safety and Community Guideline document can be found at http//www.securitygateway/com/E/E3_1.html.

[36] For a more detailed discussion of the CCTV Challenge Competition, see: McCahill and Norris (2002b), 12–14; and McCahill (2002), 21–2.

[37] Ansell (1998), 47–8.

situation in which the use of public area CCTV is far from uniform. Furthermore, only 32 per cent of the schemes in Ansell's study had reviewed their codes since their inception, a figure which would suggest that once a CCTV scheme is operational there is little pressure on managers to ensure that the rules and guidelines adopted are 'working', or that they are reviewed regularly to take account of changing needs or conditions. If Ansell's figure is representative, the need to ensure that there is some form of uniform regulation or that some standard code of practice be made available becomes even more apparent: since schemes do not appear to alter their practice guidelines in the light of experience, then it is important that they get these guidelines 'right' at the outset.

The ongoing work of civil liberties groups such as Liberty and Privacy International also appears to have had a considerable impact on the thinking and priorities of the police and local authorities regarding the use of CCTV and the need for regulation. Although—as was noted in Chapter 2—some of these groups have on occasion been prone to exaggeration when describing the capabilities of CCTV, they have nevertheless been instrumental in drawing the attention of politicians and the public to the need for greater control and regulation of this technology.[38] In particular, these groups have been highly critical of the use of informal codes of practice. In a statement released by Privacy International in February 1996, for example, the surveillance watchdog group questioned the effectiveness of such controls: 'The current legal situation is that visual surveillance largely escapes the cover of law. The Home Office has issued a Code of Conduct, and various authorities have their own codes. These documents in many instances are worthless'.[39]

In a similar statement, a leaflet distributed jointly by a variety of civil liberties groups in early 1997 also raised serious concerns

---

[38] In addition to raising the general public awareness of CCTV, some of the groups have also taken steps to assist in the regulation of these systems. See, for example, Liberty's submission to the Data Protection Registrar's consultation on the draft Code of Practice for CCTV (available at http://www.liberty-human-rights.org.uk/).

[39] Statement from Privacy International, February 1996, quoted in Davies (1998), 247. The statement also goes on to claim (without any specific reference to the research literature) that '[m]any CCTV system operators routinely exercise their prejudices to discriminate against race, age, class or sexual preference'. See further discussion of this issue in Ch. 6.

about the fact that 'anyone can set up a CCTV system', and that there was no effective formal or informal regulation of this new technology. Again, the use of codes of practice was singled out as being wholly inadequate, particularly when it came to protection of individual privacy: 'There is no licensing system. There is no government agency to provide oversight... The Home Office has issued a Code of Conduct, and some local authorities have their own codes, but these documents are weak and unenforceable, and offer the public no rights or protections'.[40]

As was noted in Chapter 1, after a period of relative quiet during the mid-1990s, calls from civil liberties groups for reform and regulation increased dramatically in terms of their frequency and urgency. Although there is nothing in the research literature to indicate that such statements have had any direct impact on the thinking of the police and local authorities about regulation, there is a great deal of anecdotal evidence to this effect.[41] As will be discussed in the following chapters, many of the operators, managers, and police officers interviewed in the course of this study were concerned about the possibility of being seen as playing the part of 'Big Brother' by the public and the media. More specifically, many also expressed reservations about the effectiveness of existing codes and the problems created by the general lack of regulation. Having gained considerable kudos from the publicity surrounding the involvement of CCTV in the Bulger case, many within the CCTV industry appear to be aware that a similarly high profile, but this time a negative portrayal of CCTV, could do considerable damage to the popularity of the technology. This is a point that has been addressed directly by the National CCTV Users Group: 'Most publicity has been in favour of CCTV, particularly following the sad case of young Master Bulger. However this will not always be the situation. There is bound to be some negative publicity

---

[40] Privacy International (1997a) quoted in Davies (1998), 248.

[41] As Ansell notes, 'Events such as the one day conference CCTV, Surveillance and Social Control hosted by the Centre for Criminology and Criminal Justice at the University of Hull, in July 1996 did much to raise awareness of the "other side" of CCTV—genuine concerns and dangers associated with the blanket coverage of our towns and cities by technological surveillance'. See Ansell (1998), 46, and also the various papers that resulted from the conference as published in Norris et al. (1998b).

which will lead to a clamour for legislation to regulate the CCTV industry'.[42]

Established in 1996, the foundation of the National CCTV Users Group marked a significant development in the organization and coordination of CCTV at a national level.[43] Aside from providing a mechanism for the exchange of information and experience about CCTV practice, the group also provides guidance regarding questions of best practice and training, as well as a forum for managers and operators to discuss the potential impact of legislation such as the Data Protection Act and the Human Rights Act.[44] For example, in response to growing public and media concerns over the lack of CCTV regulation, the User Group established in early 1997 a Standards Committee which was composed of User Group members, and police and local authority representatives. Although concerns have since been expressed about the independence of the group and its connections with the security industry, the Users Group has been proactive in promoting the development of a more regulated and standardized approach to the use of public area CCTV, providing model codes of practice and encouraging managers to re-examine their existing operator training methods.

4.2 The local picture: the regulation of CCTV in the southern region

As discussed in the previous chapter, by the time the police had finally decided to become an active partner in the operation and management of public area CCTV in the Southern Region, many key decisions about the design and organization of schemes in the area had already been made. Significantly, none of the local authorities in the area had given any serious thought to questions of how

---

[42] Comment by Malcom Wood, Finance Director of Optimum Security Services and founding member of the User Group, writing in its association magazine. See *Vision: The Magazine of the CCTV User Group* (autumn 1997), 2–3.

[43] The User Group was established in September 1996, with support and funding from the private security company Optimum Risk Management. According to Malcom Wood, the Finance Director of Optimum Security Services Ltd., the Group was formed in response to the need for a central body which could help devise and promote standards of best practice. See *Vision: The Magazine of the CCTV User Group* (autumn 1997), 2–3.

[44] See ibid, 11.

CCTV should be regulated before committing themselves to instal-ling cameras in their town and city centres. Based on comments made by a number of senior police officers, however, it is clear that the police recognized the importance of ensuring that the schemes were subject to some form of regulation, and that guidelines covering matters of security and tape handling were in place well before any of the schemes actually 'went live'. As one chief inspector noted, the police were especially concerned to ensure that the images produced by the cameras would be admissible as evidence in court. This meant that, at the very least, procedures needed to be in place to prevent tapes being tampered with or the cameras being used for anything other than legal surveillance.

As a consequence, from the outset the police took the initiative regarding the development of codes of practice and regulations for new schemes within the region. A Model Code of Practice was produced and distributed throughout the Southern Region and—after negotiations with relevant local authorities—was used as the basis for the regulation of all police-led and some local authority-led CCTV schemes in the area (including Schemes P1, P2, P3, and C2). Yet despite the fact that the police were attempting to make certain that CCTV was 'properly regulated', as the next section demon-strates, the Model Code provided little in the way of concrete guidance for either operators or managers, or a set of rules that would ensure that the schemes would be suitably accountable or operated in accordance with the law. Instead, the police were in-strumental in entrenching a regulatory framework that was not only ill-defined and ill-thought-out, but one which would later exacer-bate existing tensions between the police and their local authority partners.

4.2.1 Going by the code

Each of the six schemes included in the main study operated according to their own code of practice. In four of the schemes—P1, P2, P3, and C2—the local code had been adapted without substantial change from the Model Code of Practice produced by the Southern Region Police and distributed free to all of the CCTV schemes in the area.[45] Scheme C3—which was operated and

---

[45] The Model Code of Practice was drafted by a senior police officer with specific responsibility for overseeing the use of CCTV within the police area, and was based

maintained by a private security firm on behalf of the local council—used its own code, while Scheme C1 made use of a code produced by members of the local authority and based on the Home Office Guidelines. A copy of the relevant code was typically kept in the viewing suite of each of the schemes, and was (in theory at least) available for public inspection. In some of the schemes—notably schemes P1, P2, P3, and C2—each of the operators had been given their own copies of the code and additional copies were held by the police and the relevant local authority.

All six of the codes reviewed share many of the basic features identified by Bulos and Sarno. None of the codes exceeded 20 pages in length, and all six could reasonably be described as being brief and lacking in detail. Sections relating to staffing, control of the cameras, system access, and security were each less than two pages in length, and consisted primarily of statements of general principle rather than amounting to a detailed commitment to a defined procedure or set of working rules. In the Model Code and the codes derived directly from it, for example, the section on public access reads as follows: 'Public access to the room will be prohibited except for lawful, proper and sufficient reasons and only with the personal authority of the scheme manager. Any such visits will be conducted and recorded in accordance with the procedural manual.'

Aside from the fact that the codes are silent as to what might constitute 'lawful, proper and sufficient' reasons, the section provides little in the way of a guarantee of accountability given that the question of whether or not to grant access ultimately remains the decision of the individual scheme manager. Furthermore, although the code refers to the Model Procedural Manual, this supplementary document simply repeats the wording of the original section and adds little additional guidance as to how questions of access are to be determined: 'No visit will comprise more than six people and

on the national model code of practice published by the Local Government Information Unit. See Kitchen (1996). In addition to the Model Code of Practice, the police also made available a Model Procedural Manual. This manual duplicates and expands upon key sections of the code of practice (such as those relating to access and system security), and also includes a set of appendices which contain—among other things—extracts from the Police and Criminal Evidence Act 1984, the Criminal Procedures and Investigation Act 1996, and model 'Record of Occurrences' and 'Tape Tracking' sheets.

will only take place with the prior knowledge of the CCTV operator. Visitors will always be accompanied by the police or local authority liaison officer, or someone nominated by them who is not a CCTV operator.'

This lack of detail and definition regarding core procedures is a pattern that is repeated throughout all of the codes reviewed for the study. This is especially true of those sections relating to the operation of the cameras and the protection of individual privacy. All of the codes, either in their preface or in the main body of the text, make reference to the importance of safeguarding the individual from unwarranted or illegal surveillance. In addition, they recognize the need for the police and their partners to be mindful of the rights of the individual and reiterate the importance of being seen to be open and accountable, typically in a form adapted directly from the preface to the Model Code:

Despite the rapid growth of schemes there remains a dearth of statutory regulation governing the use of open street surveillance cameras. And yet if, as users, owners and managers of such schemes, we are to command the respect and support of the general public, the schemes must not only be used with the utmost probity at all times, they must be used in a manner which stands up to scrutiny and is accountable to the very people it is aiming to protect.

Leaving aside the fact that there is no mention of the rights or legitimate expectations of those individuals or groups who may be the subjects of surveillance—they are, presumably, not among those whom the schemes are 'aiming to protect'—the question of what constitutes 'utmost probity' is not one that is addressed in either the Model Code or the procedural manual. In fact, in the section relating to the control and operation of the cameras, the phrase is simply repeated, with broad references being made to the objectives of the scheme and the importance of respecting private property.[46] This

---

[46] The actual text of general principles as contained in 'Section 7—Control and Operation of the Cameras' is as follows: 'The operators of the cameras will act with utmost probity at all times. Every use of the cameras will accord with the purpose and key objectives of the scheme and shall comply with these codes of practice. Cameras will not be used to look into private property. "Privacy zones" may be programmed into the system as required in order to ensure that the interior of any private property within range of the scheme is not surveyed by the cameras.' Of course, the use of 'privacy zones' is not without difficulties, as the default settings and camera restrictions are easily overcome by operators who are familiar with the system.

finding echoes some of the concerns previously expressed by Norris and Armstrong, who found that many codes of practices contained 'fine sounding rhetoric' about the importance of individual privacy, but provided little in the way of actual protection against intrusive or unwanted surveillance. For example, in one of the schemes examined by Norris and Armstrong, the code of practice stated that the system 'must pay due account to the rights of privacy enjoyed by every member of society and no use shall compromise this fundamental right'.[47] As they note, given that the law does not recognize privacy as a fundamental right, the section is 'ultimately hollow'.

In addition, the codes were also unclear as to how operators' practice would be policed or what should happen in the event of a complaint. Some guidance was, however, given by the Model Procedural Manual, which states that in the event of a complaint operators may be called upon to justify their surveillance decisions:

Camera operators should beware of exercising prejudices which may lead to complaints of the scheme being used for purposes other than those for which it is intended. The operators may be required to justify their interest in, or recording of, any particular individual, group of individuals or property at any time by virtue of the audit of the scheme or by the scheme manager.[48]

This section assumes, of course, that the general public is aware of the fact that they are being watched, and that they have sufficient access to the scheme to be able to determine what sort of surveillance they have been subjected to. In any event, none of the schemes

[47] Norris and Armstrong (1999b), 101. As Norris and Armstrong go on to note, the section in question is not, at any rate, intended to provide any protection for individuals in public places (although read on its own it is easy to interpret it as such), a fact which is confirmed by the second half of the statement: 'Persons operating the system will not use the cameras to focus through windows of premises and wherever possible such opportunities will be prevented by mechanical or physical stops restricting camera movement. The restriction is intended to preserve the privacy of the public and enhance the integrity of the system.' Similar statements appeared in the codes examined in the course of the current study as well, such as the following taken from the code of practice for Scheme C3: 'Misuse of the System: The purpose of the cameras is to provide surveillance of public areas only. Wherever possible, the cameras will be sited and configured to view just public areas and not overlook private dwellings or other areas where privacy is expected . . .'.

[48] Model Procedural Manual, Section 3—Control and Operation of the Cameras: Guiding Principles.

examined during the research had a set of procedures in place which made possible or encouraged public feedback and complaints.

Of course, all of this is somewhat ironic given that one of the main reasons why the Southern Region Police were initially hesitant to become involved with public area CCTV was because of a fear that they might seem to be stepping into the role of 'Big Brother'. Having been handed a perfect opportunity to develop a set of well-defined and effective regulations that would help to shield them from accusations of intrusiveness and unaccountability, the police instead produced a document that seems almost designed to provoke civil libertarians or members of the public concerned about privacy. Similar problems also arose in the substantive sections of the Model Code and the various scheme codes that are based upon it. In Schemes P1, P2, C2, and P3, the following general principles—taken directly from the Model Code—had been reproduced at the beginning of each code as part of a 'statement of purpose and principles':

II   General Principles

The CCTV scheme will be operated fairly, within the law, and only for the purposes for which it was established or which are subsequently agreed in accordance with these codes of practice.

The scheme will be operated with due regard to the privacy of the individual.

The public interest in the operation of the scheme will be recognised by ensuring the security and integrity of operational procedures.

Participation in the scheme by any local organisation or public authority assumes an agreement by all participants to comply fully with these codes and to be accountable under these codes of practice. (Model Codes of Practice (1997) Statement of Purposes and Principles: General Principles, p. 6)

As was the case in the codes examined by Norris and Armstrong, there is no reference as to what is meant by the phrase 'due regard for the privacy of the individual', or indeed any indication of the sorts of surveillance activities that would be considered to be unfair or outside the law. Of particular interest here is the third paragraph, which makes explicit the assumption that the public interest is best served by ensuring that the system is secure rather than by regulating the type of surveillance that is undertaken by the operators. This assumption—that the privacy of the individual is not infringed by the collection of information about them but instead by the unauthorized use or release of that information—is, of course, highly questionable and one which has been considered by the courts.[49] Likewise, many of the police officers interviewed, in contrast to many of the operators and managers of the systems, viewed this assumption as highly problematic.

Returning to the general statement quoted above, the particular wording of the first paragraph is also problematic. Taken alone, it would suggest that each of the schemes in question is managed and operated according to an identifiable and circumscribed set of aims and objectives, which presumably exists to help operators to decide what sorts of activities warrant their attention. Unfortunately, none of the codes of practice that include this statement made clear what these purposes or objectives might be. As such, the paragraph is an empty one, providing nothing in the way of guidance as to the sorts of surveillance that can legitimately be carried out by the operators. In contrast, the code of practice used by Scheme C3 does contain an explicit statement of the aims and objectives of the scheme, which are listed as follows:

- To deter crime;
- To assist the detection of crime;
- To reduce the fear of crime;
- To improve public protection;
- To improve the safety and security of residents, visitors and the business community who use the facilities within the town;
- To facilitate the apprehension and prosecution of offenders in both crime and public order offences;
- To discourage anti-social behaviour including alcohol and drug-related issues;
- To deter vandalism;
- To assist the Council in monitoring and managing its assets and areas of responsibility;
- To enhance generally the environment and thereby improve the enjoyment of the town centres' facilities by all who use them.

Clearly, the inclusion of this list of objectives in Scheme C3's code of practice represents an improvement over the other CCTV schemes examined during the research. None the less, it suffers

---

[49] See e.g. the decision of the European Court of Human Rights in *Peck v United Kingdom* (2003) ECHR Application No. 44647/98.

from many of the same problems identified above in relation to the codes for Schemes P1, P2, C2, and P3. Neither 'public protection' nor 'anti-social behaviour' is defined, and no guidance is available in the code as to what is meant by the 'safety and security of residents'. Given the lack of restrictions on surveillance activities in the rest of the code, it is possible for individual operators to regard this list as providing them with a justification for targeting 'undesirables' or known offenders for almost any reason. Perhaps more importantly, however, the list also sets up a number of basic tensions, in terms of both the aims and the organization of the scheme. It is unclear from the code, for example, just how much of an operator's time should be spent monitoring traffic or taking down the licence plates of illegally parked cars as opposed to assisting the police in the apprehension and prosecution of offenders. Potentially conflicting aims such as these raise fundamental questions about the ownership and prioritization of CCTV resources and operator time.[50] When confronting a choice between pursuing goals that reflect police priorities or those more in line with local authority concerns, operators may make decisions based on factors such as who pays their wages or which organization directly manages the system, rather than by reference to any coherent set of principles. Worse yet, when faced with scheme objectives that are inconsistent or unclear, operators may feel obliged to make decisions based on their own personal beliefs about what is important, effective, and efficient.

By failing adequately to define the aims of each scheme and neglecting to address questions of competing priorities when developing the Model Code, the Southern Region Police missed a crucial opportunity to reclaim some of the control they had surrendered to local authorities at the design and planning stages. Indeed, the Model Code in effect added to already existing tensions between themselves and their local authority partners. While it is possible

---

[50] Such tensions are even more pronounced in the code of practice for Scheme C4, which was one of the schemes included in the pilot study. The above list is not only reproduced verbatim in the introduction to the Code, but with the additional requirement that the system be used to 'assist the Council in monitoring and managing its assets and areas of responsibility'. Again, nowhere in the Code is there any direction as to what sorts of surveillance are required to assist in this monitoring or management, nor is there any indication of what the assets and areas of responsibility might be.

that the police did not anticipate many of the organizational and managerial problems that were to emerge once various schemes came online, the minutes of early meetings held between senior officers and local officials prove otherwise. In Towns P2, P3, and C2 at least, issues relating to scheme resources and the prioritization of scheme goals were frequently discussed, yet notably few references were ever made to the need for these issues to be covered by the codes of practice.

Such oversight suggests that the police simply did not regard the codes of practice as providing anything more than loose guidelines for the general operation of the systems. Once cameras were installed and the systems were running, however, the codes of practice took on the status of binding—and exhaustive—documents, with the effect that the police then found it extremely difficult to change or standardize the working practices of operators and managers.

Coordinating scheme resources and objectives was not the only key organizational issue that failed to be adequately covered by the codes of practice developed in the towns included in the study. The police and their local authority partners also faced the question of CCTV camera control. Despite the fact that primary control of the cameras was the responsibility of the operators in the CCTV control room, in four of the six schemes included in the study—P1, P2, P3, and C2—a separate facility existed for external monitoring and control of the system. Depending on the particular management arrangements, this external monitoring and control was either undertaken by regular police officers (PCs) at a local station, or alternatively by police control room operators at a central station or at the force headquarters. In practice, this arrangement made it possible for the police not only to receive images from the system via an external monitor, but also to take control of the cameras themselves and engage in their own surveillance and targeting. In the case of Scheme P2, for example, where the system also monitored cameras in a neighbouring town (not included in the study), although the CCTV control room was housed in Town P2's police station, the police in the neighbouring town also had the ability to take control of the cameras. This arrangement led to a number of conflicts between the operators at the main CCTV control room and their police counterparts in the neighbouring town. Operators frequently complained that cameras were being moved from their positions without consultation, and that the police often took control of the cameras in the middle of a target either for their own independent purposes or to take control of the surveillance themselves. Leaving aside the organizational problems that such a situation creates, there is also the question of ensuring that those engaging in the external operation of the cameras are aware of and are bound by the same codes of practice.

According to the Model Code developed by the Southern Region police, it is the responsibility of the manager of the secondary site to ensure that all users and partners comply with the provisions of the code:

III   Secondary Control

When secondary control or monitoring of cameras is being undertaken from a location outside of the CCTV monitoring room, the manager of that secondary site is responsible for ensuring compliance with these codes in total and at all times, but especially will ensure this section is fully understood and complied with.

Although this section is clear in terms of the allocation of responsibility, there was little evidence to suggest that this safeguard was operating effectively. None of the secondary sites examined during the research had appointed a manager who was responsible for ensuring that the codes were complied with, and there was no system in place that made it possible for operators working from the central control room to register any complaints or concerns. Given that all of these secondary sites were located in police stations and were open to the police, this absence of accountability and control may reflect some of the deeper organizational divisions between the police and the owners and managers of the CCTV system. Clearly, system security is an issue that goes beyond simply ensuring that tapes are handled correctly or that access to the central control room is closely regulated. Under the existing codes of practice, however, there is nothing to prevent 'outside' users of the system from compromising its integrity and using the cameras for purposes not covered by the codes or envisaged by the owners of the scheme.

4.3   Conclusion

As this chapter has demonstrated, none of the CCTV schemes in the six towns examined during the course of this study was subject to well-established or effective systems of control and regulation. Theoretically then, there was nothing to stop the police, as the primary enforcer of local law and order, from making extensive use of the cameras, and actively shaping the objectives and priorities of each scheme. In practice, however, the absence of defined goals and regulations has meant that the personal working relationships between individual operators and police officers are crucial in determining the ways in which CCTV is actually used in the Southern Region. An examination of these relationships forms the basis of the next chapter.

5
Working Together?

Central to the working of any public area CCTV scheme are those responsible for the daily operation of the system—the operators. Regardless of how technically advanced the scheme or the number of CCTV cameras in use, it is the operators who determine who is watched, how long they are watched, and what—if anything—happens next. How these decisions are made and the extent to which they reflect police values and priorities inevitably have an impact on both the way in which CCTV is received by individual police officers, and whether the introduction of cameras affects local police practices and strategies.

This chapter examines the relationship between the police and CCTV operators in each of the six schemes. In particular, it considers whether operators working in police-led schemes were more likely to be accepted by local police officers than operators at local authority-led schemes, and whether this resulted in those operators being more sympathetic to police concerns. Before turning to a consideration of what CCTV operators and police officers thought of each other, however, it is important to consider the background and training of operators at each of the police- and local authority-led schemes before they were put 'behind the cameras'.

5.1 Background and recruitment of operators

In the course of the research, basic information about the educational and employment history of each of the 30 operators interviewed was collected, along with details relating to their age, gender, marital status, and ethnic background. By far the overwhelming majority of operators (22) in five of the six schemes—P1, P2, P3, C1, and C2—were married white men in their late forties or early fifties, with little or no experience of CCTV or security work prior to taking up their current positions. Although

Scheme P3 was initially staffed by police officers, by the time the main study was under way, these officers were in the process of being replaced by civilian operators, all of whom conformed to the general operator profile also found in Schemes C1, C2, P1, and P2.[1] With one exception, all of the operators interviewed at these five schemes had left full-time education at age 16 and had taken non-professional positions in retailing or manufacturing, some reaching middle management or similar positions.[2] Significantly, most confessed that they had become CCTV operators either because they had been forced to leave their previous employment and had been unable to find work in a similar field, or because they were 'semi-retired' and were looking for some form of shift-work to supplement their household income. As a consequence, with the exception of those operators at Scheme C3, very few of the operators interviewed in these schemes could be said to have 'chosen' a career in CCTV.[3]

In many ways, Jim at Scheme C2 was typical of the operators interviewed at these five schemes. Having worked as a manager in a local factory for over 25 years, he had been made redundant in his early fifties and spent almost a year searching for a similar job in the area before finally deciding to become a CCTV operator. By his own admission, Jim had never envisioned working in security, and although he enjoyed aspects of the position, he did not feel entirely comfortable with his new career even after spending over a year on

[1] Note that in the first year and a half of its operation, Scheme P3 was manned by four police officers, all of whom were PCs with experience in the local area. At the end of this period (and within the first three months of the main study), the scheme then moved over to civilian operators, partly in an effort to reduce staffing costs and partly because of a shortage of operational police officers. Of the three civilians employed, one had previously worked as a shop security guard, while the remaining two had no prior experience of working either in the security industry or with CCTV cameras.

[2] The one exception was an operator at Scheme C2, who had a bachelors degree from the University of Cambridge.

[3] Norris and Armstrong (1999b) come to a similar conclusion: 'In view of the pay and conditions it is hardly surprising that few had chosen to become a CCTV operative as a vocation, most had been forced into security work after a period of unemployment due to redundancy, ill heath or disability' (p. 103). In the case of Scheme P2, all of the operators were suffering from some form of minor physical disability which had forced them to leave their previous job, and had been contracted out to the CCTV scheme by the employment agency Remploy because the work did not require a high degree of physical mobility.

the job. Similarly, Bob at Scheme P2—who had worked as a computer salesman before having to resign due to a back problem—became a CCTV operator because it was one of the few jobs he could find which allowed him to 'sit down all day' and didn't require any previous experience. Like Jim, Bob also confessed to feeling a certain frustration at being unable to find something better paid or more suited to his interests.

In Scheme C3, however, the situation was somewhat different. Run by a national security company on behalf of the local council, Scheme C3 was staffed with operators who had either been employed previously as camera operators elsewhere, or had worked in close association with CCTV as in-store security guards. Although slightly younger than the study average—all five of the operators interviewed at Scheme C3 were either in their late twenties or early thirties—all five were white, male, and had educational and social backgrounds similar to those at other schemes. None had progressed beyond GCSEs or their equivalent, and none had acquired any form of non-vocational qualification since leaving school. None the less, in contrast with many of the other operators interviewed during the course of the main study, all of the CCTV operators working at Scheme C3 appeared to have made a conscious decision to work in the security sector. As a consequence, all of them regarded their current positions as their 'real work' as opposed to something that they were doing until something better came along. According to the head operator Robby, working in the security industry was a 'vocation' for him and his colleagues. After working as a doorman in a local club and then as a shop security officer, Robby had joined the security firm in his late twenties in order to 'make something of himself' and to build a more stable career in the industry. He received his basic training in the use of CCTV cameras from the firm, and had worked as an operator in a number of major department stores for almost three years before being posted to the C3 scheme. For Robby, working in a local authority CCTV scheme was a step up, in terms of both pay and responsibility. Like the other operators at C3—and unlike many of those working in the other schemes included in the study—he claimed to be happy with his position and in no rush to change jobs.

What is apparent from this survey of operators at each of the six schemes is that the clear majority shared similar social and educational backgrounds, regardless of whether they worked at police- or local authority-led schemes. That these similarities should exist is hardly surprising in light of the difficulties faced by scheme managers looking to recruit civilian CCTV operators. Despite the fact that the number of public area CCTV schemes in Britain has grown dramatically in recent years, by the late 1990s the industry was still a relatively new employer and experienced CCTV operators were in short supply. In addition, the problem of finding qualified or suitable persons to operate the cameras was in part exacerbated by the lack of guidance on recruitment provided to managers by the Model Code of Practice or its local equivalents:

Each candidate will be subjected to a full security vetting. They will be expected to supply two references and, during interview, their commitment to, and understanding of, total confidentiality will be thoroughly tested. All newly appointed operators will undergo a six month probationary period at the conclusion of which their contract may be terminated without explanation by either side.[4]

Although there is no nationally accredited body for the vetting and training of CCTV operators, various efforts have been made by the police and others to ensure that operators are subjected to some sort of security screening before being allowed to commence employment. In 1996, the British Standards Authority issued Standard 7858, entitled Code of Practice for Security Screening of Personnel Employed in a Security Environment, which recommended that all employees working in the security industry should be subjected to a comprehensive background screening which would look at— among other things—character references, career history, educational background, as well as verification of place of residence, date, and place of birth. Despite the fact that the Standard has been available for use by CCTV scheme managers for over four years, however, there is evidence to suggest that it has not been widely adopted. In Ansell's postal survey of some 69 CCTV schemes across Britain carried out in 1998, for example, less than half were found to have subjected their operators to the level of screening recommended by the British Standard. This would suggest that the Standards have had a limited impact on the employment decisions

---

[4] Model Procedural Manual, sect. 2, p. 7: 'Staffing of the Monitoring Room: Selection and Recruitment'.

of managers or, by implication, on the security arrangements adopted by the majority of CCTV users.[5]

In the current case, as a number of scheme managers noted during interviews, the vague and ill-defined list of 'requirements' set out in the Model Code was not very helpful when it came to making recruitment decisions, and was virtually ignored by those responsible for the hiring of operators. During the course of the research, a series of operators' recruitment interviews were observed at Scheme C2. Chaired by the scheme manager (a local authority employee), the selection panel consisted of the manager, a police representative (a local inspector), a member of the local authority's human resources division, and one of the more senior CCTV operators. Although conducted in a structured and professional manner, it was clear that the interviewers were not following their own code of practice guidelines regarding recruitment and that they were each working according to a set of personal criteria. While there were no questions aimed at testing the candidate's commitment to confidentiality—something specifically mentioned in the guidelines—the scheme manager was instead only interested in testing the candidates' powers of observation and judgement, while the police inspector appeared to be most concerned with determining whether the candidate already possessed certain operational skills, such as radio proficiency.

Although a number of local officials at Schemes P1, P2, P3, and C2 claimed that their operators had been selected according to the 'strict criteria' laid down in the codes, in reality the recruitment process at these schemes was often haphazard. As the manager of Scheme C2 noted, the problem was also compounded by the lack of 'firm guidance coming down from central government' as to what constituted sufficient qualifications for potential operators.[6] Based

---

[5] Ansell (1998), 44–50.

[6] To some extent, the lack of sufficient guidance as to recruitment and selection of CCTV operators has since been recognized by the Home Office. In 1998, two reports arising out of a four-year study undertaken by the Police Scientific and Development Branch of the Home Office were published in an effort to provide some help to public CCTV scheme mangers. The first, *Recruitment and Selection of CCTV Operators*, aims to 'provide guidance for the police service and local authorities on the selection and recruitment of CCTV operators'. The second, *Training Practices for CCTV Operators*, focuses on 'the training requirements of operators who monitor public areas such as town centres and have a high level of interaction with police staff and procedures'. Both works are cited and discussed briefly by Ansell in his study of the

on the comments of managers at each of these four schemes it appears to be case that many operators were recruited simply because they came across to those interviewing them as 'reliable', 'attentive', and 'hard-working'. Faced with a shortage of qualified applicants and little guidance as to appropriate selection criteria, it is not surprising that the majority of operators were broadly similar in terms of their age, gender, and social background.

5.2   Operator training

At a national level, ensuring that CCTV operators are suitably trained has been a stated priority of central and local government for some years. In 1996, the Local Government Information Unit (LGIU) published *A Watching Brief: A Code of Practice for CCTV*, in which the importance of providing initial and ongoing training for CCTV operators was stressed, as was the need for recruitment based on recognized qualifications. Significantly, and despite the fact that much of the pro-CCTV rhetoric which has emerged from the Home Office makes little mention of the human aspect of this technology, the LGIU was at pains to stress the central role played by camera operators and the importance of training:

To meet high standards of operation employees must be qualified or capable of being trained to the necessary level on appointment. Training is the most important element in planning for and maintaining a CCTV scheme. Research done for the preparation of this code of practice shows that many owners are struggling with difficulties associated with training staff, or expect staff to learn on the job, on the basis that the skills needed are self-evident.[7]

The statement then goes on to note that while this training may be offered by the police or by suppliers in the immediate future, the expectation is that all operators will eventually hold a National Vocational Qualification (NVQ) in CCTV operation. At the time when the 'Watching Brief' was published in early 1996, this NVQ

human aspects of public area CCTV. See Ansell (1998), 29; C. Diffley and E. Wallace (1998*a*) CCTV: *Making it Work. Training Practices for CCTV Operators* (St Albans: Home Office Police Scientific Development Branch); C. Diffley and E. Wallace (1998*b*) CCTV: *Making it Work—Recruiting and Selection of CCTV Operators* (St Albans: Home Office Police Scientific Development Branch).

[7] Kitchen (1996).

was allegedly under development and was expected to be introduced within the year. Seven years on, details of the NVQ curriculum have yet to be released and there is little to suggest that these
will be made available in the near future.[8] Furthermore, although
the security industry has developed its own series of NVQs, a
number of scheme managers in Ansell's study of CCTV schemes
pointed out that these remain geared to the needs of the private
sector and therefore do not directly address many of the particular
requirements of local government or the police, nor do they deal
directly with the specific skills required of CCTV operators.[9]
Scheme managers across the country have therefore been forced to
either develop their own training programmes, or ignore the issue of
training altogether and assume that operators will acquire whatever
skills they require 'on the job'.

In each of the six schemes included in this study all CCTV
operators were, in principle, required to undergo independent or

---

[8] According to the specifics of Kitchen's *Watching Brief* (1996), 'A National
Vocational Qualification (NVQ) will eventually be part of a larger qualification for
control room operatives, but it will be possible to take the different units separately'.
The *Brief* later goes on to claim that, once established, the 'NVQ standards can be
used as the framework for a training programme; as the basis for a job description; as
a method of appraisal; and, as a nationally recognised qualification. The code of
practice could form part of the NVQ, underpinning knowledge required for each
operator.' To date, the NVQ curriculum has not been released, none of the parts of
the 'larger qualification' mentioned in the *Brief* have been established, and there has
been no published guidance for local authorities as to how to integrate existing codes
of practice with the NVQ should they eventually become available. Reading further
into the *Watching Brief*, there is also the suggestion that schemes will be able to
maintain their own training procedures even after the establishment of the NVQs,
without giving any indication of the effect this might have on the status of the NVQ:
'In the meantime many individual local authority owners have set up their own
training programmes, or share training with other local authorities. This will continue to be relevant in parallel with the use of NVQs and should include the provision
of training on issues such as monitoring the safety of members of the public, and
privacy in residential areas.'

[9] As one manager put it, 'I've started to look at outside agencies now... but I've
found more and more it's towards the security guard. CCTV operators are something
unique, I haven't seen a training package yet that has cottoned on to that.' Quoted in
Ansell (1998), 59. Note that these NVQs were developed and are currently regulated
by the Security Industry Training Organisation (SITO). Although some of the NVQs
offered by the SITO do include training in the use of CCTV, at present there is no
course available which is dedicated to the training of CCTV operators, either for
private or public sector employment.

on-the-job training as a condition of continuing employment, regardless of whether they were police or local authority employees. Typically, this requirement was set out in each scheme's code of practice, and in those schemes where the Model Code or a version of it had been adopted, the requirement was stated as follows:

Each operator will be offered full training in the use of each item of equipment together with training in all social and legal issues. They will undertake ongoing training on a regular basis. Operators will be encouraged to work towards formal qualification and certification of their skills and abilities with a recognised body.[10]

At the local authority schemes, the training of CCTV operators was the sole responsibility of the scheme manager, who in the case of Schemes C1 and C2 was an employee of the local authority, and in Scheme C3 a security company employee. In contrast, at Schemes P1, P2, and P3 operators were trained by local police officers with the assistance of a Chief Inspector located at Southern Region Police Headquarters. Comments made by operators at both Type P and Type C schemes, however, indicated that the training received by each group was remarkably similar, both in terms of what the training did cover and what it did not. Virtually none of the operators at either type of scheme had positive things to say about their training, with many describing it as woefully inadequate. While all of the operators interviewed claimed that they had been given instruction in how to operate the cameras and basic administrative tasks such as tape handling and incident recording, most complained that they had received little or no training in radio procedures or on how to deal with more complex issues relating to targeting and privacy. Perhaps even more significantly, none of the operators (including those working at the police-led schemes) had received any instruction in basic police operational, arrest, or charging procedures. As one operator put it, for the most part the initial training had concentrated on 'technical' matters at the expense of providing operators with an understanding of the scheme's objectives or of the constraints they were required to work under: 'I mean, when we came here we sort of sat down with the [other] operators and they said "Well if you press this button you get a new camera on the screen" and things like that . . . Not much else though.

[10] Model Procedural Manual, sect. 2: 'Staffing of the Monitoring Room', p. 7.

We should get more background to the whole system.' (Operator B, Scheme P1).

Predictably, this lack of comprehensive training was viewed as being less egregious by operators working in Scheme C3, in part because all of these operators had already received some security training prior to taking up their positions in the CCTV control room. For operators in Schemes P1, P2, P3, C1, and C2, however, the perceived failure of scheme managers to provide anything more than basic operational guidance was seen as a serious problem. According to operators, it compromised their ability to operate the system effectively and develop professional relationships with police officers and other CCTV 'customers'. As the following field-note extract reveals, a lack of confidence when operating a police radio was, for many operators, a particular source of embarrassment and one that was frequently attributed to a lack of proper training:

FIELD-NOTE EXTRACT: SCHEME C2 (2/89/1.45. p.m.). While making a casual sweep of the town centre, Operator B spots two individuals smoking what he believes to be cannabis in a park just off the High Street. Given that the operators had recently been told by the scheme managers to keep an eye out for drugs in the town centre, the operator immediately attempts to radio the police control room to report the incident in progress. After fumbling with the radio for about 20 seconds, he finally manages to operate it and nervously begins to send a message to the control room. Before he has managed to complete the message, however, he fumbles with the radio again and is cut off. Another attempt at contacting the control room is made, but once contact is established the operator forgets to identify himself and is asked to repeat the message by the police operator. Eventually the full message is delivered, with the operator forgetting to sign off at the end. The operator sighs and looks extremely frustrated. 'I wish I knew how to work this properly,' he remarks, 'it's just embarrassing making mistakes.'

In many respects, these findings mirror those of previous studies of operator training in Britain. In their 1996 report for the Local Government Information Unit, Bulos and Sarno noted that, while many codes of practices set out broad requirements for the training of operators, very few laid down specific guidelines as to the minimum length or content of such training. In addition, they found that the level and quality of training provided for camera operators varied considerably across schemes throughout England and Wales.

Significantly, they also found that, where training was undertaken, little attention had been paid to issues of operator targeting or individual privacy:

The most neglected area of training consists of how to identify suspicious behaviour, when to track individuals or groups and when to take close-up views of incidents or people. This was either assumed to be self-evident or common sense. The informality of these procedures leaves unexamined the predispositions of operators to consider some people or types as more likely to commit crimes than others... [11]

These are points that have since been echoed by Ansell in his study of the 'human elements' of CCTV. One of the primary objectives of Ansell's 1998 study was to establish the level of training undertaken by operators and managers.[12] Although he found that over 93 per cent of the schemes included in the survey had instituted some form of initial training programme for operators, interviews with individual operators revealed that 'the depth of training was shallow and its specificity towards CCTV operatives was often questionable'.[13] In many cases, for example, training was provided informally and 'on the job', most often by other, more experienced, operators. Although Ansell notes that this type of training can be effective in terms of the transfer of basic skills, he also cites research by the Home Office Police Scientific Development Branch which concluded that this approach to CCTV training can also 'lead to poor operator performance by... operators learning bad habits, poor delivery and lack of structure and evaluation'.[14] In other cases, comments from the operators themselves revealed that although training had been provided—as had been claimed by the police or local authority manager in charge—it was often little more than perfunctory.[15] One of the operators interviewed by Ansell

[11] Bulos and Sarno (1996), 24.

[12] Ansell (1998), 50.

[13] ibid., 59. Ansell's research did not, however, attempt to examine the method of training delivery in detail, with Ansell himself admitting that 'the actual detail of the training, its length and suitability was never the subject of the enquiry at this stage and lends itself to more detailed research in its own right' (p. 51).

[14] Diffley and Wallace (1998b), 12, cited in Ansell (1998), 58.

[15] The issue of ongoing training is also touched upon in Ansell's survey questionnaire. Despite finding that some 93 per cent of schemes provided initial training for their operators, only 46 per cent felt it was necessary to offer continuity training. As Ansell observes, this figure 'causes one to wonder how operators keep up with

complained that 'they showed us how to use a radio—that was it', while another had difficulty even remembering whether training had taken place at all: 'Not that I can recollect. I mean when [the manager] had the time, he sort of tried to keep us up to date with what was going on.'[16]

Significantly, nearly all of the scheme managers interviewed by Ansell appeared to be acutely aware of the need for better training and were frustrated by their inability to provide it, as a result either of a lack of available funds or a shortage of accredited training schemes. For many, the problem was compounded by the fact that once a scheme was established, the presumption was that it could be left to run itself without any need for further investment in the 'human element' of the system. As one manager admitted, convincing local authorities of the need for ongoing training was extremely difficult in the face of intense competition for limited resources and funding within the organization: 'To be honest they received very little—no formal training at all. All I got was "who's going to pay for it?" On the CPA [Criminal Procedures and Investigations Act 1996] I asked for training for the CCTV staff and I got the same answer, "yes you can have it, it will cost you £500 per person".'[17]

changes in procedures and policies which may be caused by the Codes of Practice being reviewed, new legislation, case-law, etc.' See Ansell (1998), 50. Ansell also expresses similar concerns in relation to the training of managers, with even fewer (30 per cent) receiving any form of continuity training, despite the fact that in nearly all cases it is the scheme manager who is directly responsible for ensuring that the scheme is operating in compliance with new regulations and legislation. In light of the potential impact of the incorporation of the European Convention on Human Rights and changes to the Data Protection Act, this inability to respond to new legal demands and restrictions on surveillance is likely to become an even more obvious source of concern for civil libertarians already disturbed by the failure of the CCTV industry to develop a coherent and acceptable approach to questions of personal privacy and the processing of confidential information.

[16] Quoted in Ansell (1998), 59.

[17] Quoted in Ansell (1998), 59–60. Despite their dissatisfaction with existing training procedures, none of the managers interviewed was prepared to concede that this may have had a negative effect on scheme effectiveness. This somewhat paradoxical finding is not discussed in any detail by Ansell, and he offers no clear explanation for it, aside from suggesting that this apparent contradiction may be explained by the fact that the objectives of most schemes are stated so broadly as to make it almost impossible for any system to actually fail. Even if crime rates do not fall as the result of the introduction of CCTV cameras, most scheme 'mission statements' cite reducing the fear of crime and improving public safety as prime objectives, both of which are notoriously difficult to measure.

This was a point frequently echoed by scheme managers in the current study as well, with managers at local authority-led schemes in particular expressing dismay at the lack of funds made available for the training of operators. Irrespective of whether the training of CCTV operators was in fact less well funded at these schemes, it is clear that operators at both local authority- and police-led schemes ended up receiving similar levels of instruction and training. Given that nearly all of the operators shared similar social and educational backgrounds, even after they had received their basic training there was little to distinguish between those working in police-led as opposed to local authority-led schemes. Despite their similarities in background, recruitment, and training, however, Type P and Type C operators went on to form very different working relationships with the police, as the next two sections demonstrate.

5.3 What operators thought of the police

In the course of the field research, all of the CCTV operators observed were asked to describe and comment on the nature of their working relationship with the police. As might be expected, the most positive responses came from operators working in police-led schemes. Without exception, these operators were glowing in their praise for the police and generally pleased with the extent to which they had been accepted by individual officers and senior management. In the course of conversation, operators in these schemes frequently referred to police constables (PCs) and town centre officers as 'open' and 'friendly', and in interview all of them described their working relationship with the police as positive and professional. Where concerns were raised—either in relation to police manning levels or slow response times—responsibility for these problems was invariably attributed to either the failure of central government to provide sufficient funding for the police or the inadequacies of senior management (police or local authority), and never attributed to individual officers or local managers.

In contrast, operators in the local authority-led schemes were less generous in their comments about the police. Although only one operator went so far as to describe his relationship with the police as 'poor', nearly all the others felt that there was room for improvement in terms of their dealings with either individual officers or the police in general. Typically, CCTV operators at local authority-led schemes spoke of feeling unappreciated, and complained that many officers appeared to be unaware of the nature of their job or the conditions under which they worked. In Scheme C2, for example, a number of operators commented on the fact that few PCs bothered to come to the CCTV control room except to collect tapes that had previously been prepared for use in evidence. According to these operators, this lack of regular contact made it difficult for them to pass on what they regarded as valuable intelligence or to improve their understanding of police working procedures. Similar criticisms were also directed at police control room staff. As one operator at Scheme C2 observed, very few of the police radio operators were familiar with the workings of the CCTV system or the mechanics of camera operation, a fact that often led to confusion and miscommunication. Operators at Type C schemes also spoke of feeling uncomfortable when using the police radio or giving direct instructions to officers in the town centre, a situation they attributed to the lack of regular, personal contact between them and the police.

There are a number of possible explanations for these different accounts of the working relationships between operators and police officers. From the responses of operators in the Type P schemes, it is clear that they regarded the development of close relations with individual police officers as highly important, both to the effective working of the system and to their own sense of professional self-worth and job satisfaction. Given that in each of the Type P schemes the CCTV control room was located either in the police station itself or some other police-owned building (such as the town centre police offices in Scheme P1), it was relatively easy for operators to cultivate these types of relationships with their police colleagues. Perhaps more importantly, the close proximity between the CCTV operators and the police in schemes of Type P also increased the likelihood that operators would receive feedback about jobs in which they had been either directly or indirectly involved. Indeed, when describing their relationship with the police, operators in all of the Type P schemes identified positive feedback as being essential to the creation of good working relations, even if this amounted to little more than an officer saying 'thank you' to operators on the completion of a job:

We're constantly getting police officers coming in and saying 'Thanks ever so much'. Every time a big incident happens, you know, there's a lot of conversation between us and the police control room. The control room always acknowledges that you've helped with the incident and say 'Thanks for your help'. And even the police officers on the street, they'll sort of, like, say to the control room pass on our thanks to the operators. (Operator B, Scheme P1)

In the Type C schemes, where face-to-face contact between CCTV operators and the police was far less frequent, operators rarely received feedback directly from ordinary PCs or town centre officers. Instead, operators were forced to rely on their local authority line managers for information, both about their own performance and the outcome of jobs with which they had been involved. As the local managers were themselves often poorly informed, their inability to provide operators with feedback *vis-à-vis* their working relations with the police often added to the operators' sense of frustration and isolation. Significantly, the majority of operators in the Type C schemes blamed the police for this lack of contact, either on the basis that it was 'their responsibility' to make full use of the system, or because it was somehow 'their fault' that the CCTV control room had not been housed in the local police station in the first place.

In addition to problems created by the lack of contact between Type C operators and the police, differences in the employment status of operators across schemes may also in part explain why those working at Type P schemes enjoyed better relationships with the police. According to operators in Schemes P1 and P3, one of the major reasons why they enjoyed good relations with the police was because they—like the local PCs and town centre officers—were also police employees, subject to police supervision and police disciplinary procedures. As one operator put it, the fact that CCTV operators and police officers at these schemes were all 'on the same side' meant that officers could be confident that the operators were not only doing a good job and were being well managed, but also that they were looking out for officers' interests and well-being while on patrol. Similarly, another operator drew attention to the fact that as they had all been 'security checked' by the police prior to recruitment, local officers knew that they could be trusted and relied upon, and that this made them more comfortable with them as individuals and with the policing role played by the scheme.

Significantly, the view that the police respond more positively to CCTV operators who are also police employees was also shared by operators at local authority-led schemes. As noted in Chapter 3, operators in all of the Type C schemes were employed by the local authority, either directly or through employment agencies such as Remploy or, in the case of Scheme C3, as part of a contract with a national security firm.[18] Although the police made a contribution to staffing costs in each of these schemes, the operators were supervised by local authority managers and subject to the disciplinary procedures of the particular local authority. Operators working in Type C schemes frequently commented that they felt that the police would 'take them more seriously' if they were police employees rather than local authority employees, and that the fact that the scheme received some of its funding from the police as local partners made little practical difference to how they were viewed by local officers. Operators were also of the opinion that officers would be more inclined to visit the control room and share information with them if they were police employees. Again, this belief appeared to be based on the assumption that the police only had confidence in their 'own kind', and that they treated outsiders with a degree of reserve and mistrust.

This view of the importance of employment status to police–operator relations was also shared by CCTV operators at Scheme P2. Unlike their colleagues at Schemes P1 and P3, these operators were not police employees but rather were hired by the local council through Remploy. As a consequence, all of these operators found themselves working within the local police station and alongside police officers, despite the fact that they themselves were not police employees. Although these operators—like their counterparts in the other police-led scheme—spoke of enjoying good relations with the police, they were nevertheless unanimous in maintaining that their working relationship with the police would be better if they were police employees. This opinion was not, however, based

[18] According to its mission statement, Remploy exists to provide 'productive employment in a supported environment for severely disabled people who are seeking work, within the Government's Supported Employment Programme'. In practice, this means that Remploy acts as an employment agency for disabled workers, providing them with job advice and helping to place them in suitable employment. Importantly, because Remploy is subsidized by the government, it is able to contract out workers at a lower than market cost to employers. As a consequence, scheme managers at Schemes P2 and C2 had lower staff overheads than other schemes because operator salaries were in part subsidized by Remploy.

on the belief that as police employees they would automatically be accorded greater respect or taken more seriously by local officers. Indeed, all the operators interviewed at Scheme P2 felt that they had already developed an excellent rapport with station PCs and senior officers, and were confident that they were seen as a valuable part of the overall policing strategy for the town. Instead, what was important for these operators was the issue of management. In the course of the three-year history of the scheme, a succession of seven different police managers had been assigned to oversee the operation of the CCTV system, a situation which the operators believed would not have been allowed to occur had they been police employees and the system wholly police-run.

As a final point, it is important to note that insufficient training in general police procedures and working practices was cited by all of the operators—regardless of whether they worked at a local authority- or a police-led scheme—as a major stumbling block to the development of good relations with the police. As discussed in the next section, many police officers complained about the inability of certain CCTV operators to communicate quickly and effectively using the police radio, and of the tendency to call in 'jobs' that the police felt did not warrant their attention. Tellingly, many of the operators interviewed at both the local authority- and police-led schemes appeared to be aware of these issues, and expressed the belief that the problems could be alleviated by training and subsequent understanding of police working practices and priorities. In one instance, an operator at Scheme C2 spoke glowingly of a fortnight spent working in the local station while waiting to be moved to a new CCTV control room. For him, it was a unique opportunity to see 'the police point of view':

When we were changing from one site to the next, we had a week and a bit, nearly two weeks' training over at the police station, and that did really help an awful lot. I thought that was very very good. It was something like that I was looking for from the beginning...We had the aims of the council, you know, their mission statement, and we got the police point of view as well. And you put the two together...you'd have a more dynamic attitude to carrying on the task if you were trained properly from the beginning and know precisely what you stand for, and the reason why the thing is there. It's not just a job, you're actually doing something. (Operator A, Scheme C2)

Warming to his subject, the same operator went on to express the opinion—which was later echoed by others working at the scheme—that gaining a better understanding of what it was that the police expected of the system had helped him to improve his own performance as an operator and his relationship with the police officers. This realization, he concluded however, could have been achieved much earlier had his initial training covered the 'police aspect' of public area CCTV:

> If you get a proper training course . . . and when we came here the first thing we had was a sort of induction course which spelt out what the council stood for, and that, that's fine . . . and then you marry that with the police aspect and change in the attitude of criminals, the changes in policing and community policing which is not just out to catch people but their role is also to try to help the community, to keep them away from being criminal or indulging in criminal acts. And, you know, the two together, it's quite, quite interesting. (Operator A, Scheme C2)

The lack of structured and ongoing training also led to other, less obvious, difficulties in terms of the relationships between both Type P and Type C operators and the police. Many of the police officers working directly with the CCTV schemes revealed themselves to be unfamiliar with the technology, with operators frequently reporting that officers had wholly unrealistic expectations of what could be done with the cameras or by a single operator acting alone in the control room. Common misunderstandings included the belief that tracking a moving suspect was a relatively simple task, and officers would express their frustration when an operator lost sight of a target in the process of switching between cameras. Similarly, a lack of familiarity with the CCTV control room layout and camera controls led some officers to believe that the coordination of cameras and radio communications was also a straightforward task. This frequently led to frustration with operators who appeared to be slow in responding to calls from officers on the street or the police control room while an incident was unfolding. As one operator from Scheme P1 noted, this lack of understanding on the part of the police often strained otherwise good relations, a problem that could be resolved by making the police more aware of the operational and technological constraints facing the CCTV schemes:

We have a pretty good relationship. Obviously when it comes to the heat of the moment, I don't think they really appreciate how it was quite difficult for us to operate the cameras as well as try and talk to them and transmit the information to them at the same time, so they can get a bit impatient. We need to train them in how to use the actual cameras, the keyboards, and then they'll know. (Operator M, Scheme P1)

What is perhaps telling about these various findings is that the two factors identified by operators as having the greatest influence on the development of good working relationships with the police—the physical location of the control room and their employment status within the scheme—were both wholly outside their control. As a consequence, operators who had difficulties in dealing with the police frequently rationalized the problems by referring to systemic problems of physical organization or management. Significantly, these operators were often unresponsive to personal or professional criticism. This was particularly the case in Type C schemes, where complaints from the police were likely to be conveyed to operators by a local authority manager. According to these operators, if their relations with the police were at times strained, it was the fault either of the police or problems within the organization and management of the system. Unfortunately, this was not a view that was widely shared by the police.

5.4 What the police thought of operators

As was the case with operators, the responses of police officers to the issue of working relations varied considerably according to the type of CCTV scheme in operation. By far and away the most positive responses were received from officers working in association with police-led schemes. CCTV control room staff from these schemes were variously described as 'professional', 'hard-working', and 'extremely helpful', and many officers spoke of having developed effective working relationships with individual operators. Significantly, in all three Type P schemes included in the study, the location of the CCTV control room on police premises was cited by officers as of central importance to the development of these good relations. As one officer noted, all the CCTV operators were well known around the station, and the CCTV control room was generally regarded by officers of all ranks as a good place to 'drop in for coffee or a cup of tea' when there was little going on in the station.

What criticism there was of operators tended to stem from the belief that they created extra work for officers, particularly town centre PCs and police control room staff.[19] Invariably, however, complaints along these lines tended to be light-hearted and constructive in tone, with many officers acknowledging the difficult position in which the operators frequently found themselves:

It's a tricky balance for the operators to strike because, certainly from their point of view, they don't know how busy we are in here other than by listening to radio communications. Sometimes it may be that they've got something really good on the screen, and they're anxious to bring it to our attention, and we've got everyone answering phones, or we're trying to cover other jobs and we haven't got anyone to spare...I think if anyone has problems, it's them having problems with us, not being able to respond to them as quickly as they'd like, because we can't find the resources. (Police Control Room Sergeant A, Station P3)

Significantly, officers working in conjunction with Type P schemes seemed relatively untroubled by the fact that the cameras were being operated by civilians and not police officers, and tended to be more concerned about the employment status of operators. Although some of the police officers working in these areas maintained that a civilian operator could never be as effective as his police counterpart, the clear majority felt any differences that might exist simply came down to the training and experience of the particular individuals concerned. In fact, a number of officers went so far as to argue that civilian operators might be more effective because they came to the job with a greater enthusiasm than did the average PC or town centre officer:

What was really impressive about the operators when they started was their keenness to do the job, to pick up offenders...They went in there and did a damn good job and took a lot of personal pride in 'Who was on before me? How many people...? What events have you dealt with? And what events am I going to deal with?' They were very keen. (Police Constable A, Station P3)

It is interesting to note that officers in Station P2 shared the opinion of operators at the scheme that the working relationships

---

[19] The question of whether the introduction of CCTV did lead to an increase in the workload of local officers in any of the six towns included in the study is considered in Chapter 7.

between the police and CCTV staff would have been even better had the operators been police employees. This opinion was not, however, based on the assumption that the scheme would necessarily be better managed if it were entirely under police control. Instead, officers appeared to believe that the CCTV operators would feel more comfortable in their dealings with the police and police support staff if they were on the same payroll and shared similar employment-related benefits. Despite the fact that the scheme had had a series of police managers over its operational life, few officers felt that this lack of continuity had affected the day-to-day working relations between the police and the operators.

In the areas where Type C schemes operated, the police officers interviewed were considerably less enthusiastic about their working relationships with CCTV operators. Although few officers went so far as to describe operators as incompetent, it was clear that local PCs and town centre officers soon developed opinions about the reliability and effectiveness of particular operators, and that this impression significantly coloured their subsequent dealings with those individuals. Operators who regularly passed on what the police regarded as 'rubbish jobs'—such as minor drug or traffic offences—were soon singled out by officers as 'unhelpful', in large part because they were held responsible for placing already stretched resources under additional strain. Once operators had acquired this reputation with a particular town centre shift, word soon spread to other officers within the area. In schemes in which the majority of operators had this reputation—such as Scheme C2—officers appeared to have drawn the additional conclusion that this was an inevitable consequence of the scheme being run by the local authority and staffed with civilian operators. As one officer at Station C2 put it, civilian CCTV operators could never develop the 'sixth sense' that enabled an experienced police officer to know how to spot a potential offender, or to predict where and when a serious offence was likely to take place: 'At the end of the day, however hard civilians try—and I'm not decrying them as some of them are very switched on—they still don't have the gut feeling and never will have the gut feeling that a police officer is so often trained to have', Police Constable C, Scheme C2.

The belief among operational police officers that they and they alone are possessed of some unique ability that sets them apart from the general public and other criminal justice professionals is not, of course, something that is confined to their attitudes towards CCTV operators at Type C schemes. The importance of acting on 'hunches' and the role played by working rules and instincts in police culture has been discussed at length in the literature of policing.[20] As McConville, Sanders, and Leng note in *The Case for the Prosecution*, acting on instinct is for many officers an essential part of policing, as is the ability to recognize 'something indefinable' that marks a criminal out from the rest of society:

The officer said that he had been a police officer for 10 years and any experienced copper would back him up. He had to trust his instincts most of the time otherwise his job would not get done. He said that he was worried that a lot of young coppers were being taught to act by the book and having instinctive policing trained out of them ... 'When you get to know an area and see a villain about at two in the morning you will always stop him to see what he is about.'[21]

Although this attitude is perhaps understandable in situations where the police find themselves called upon to justify their decisions to critics and the public at large, it is more difficult to explain when it is applied to civilian colleagues who are, ostensibly at least, on the 'police side'.

Based on their comments in both interviews and informal conversation, it is clear that police officers working in conjunction with Type C schemes were far more inclined to see civilian CCTV operators as inherently incapable of developing an officer's 'sixth sense' or discriminating between 'good' and 'bad' jobs, an impression that did much to undermine the working relationship between operators and the police in these areas. As a result, police officers—who in their view already had to go 'out of their way' to drop in on the control room—became even less willing to seek help from operators with ongoing jobs or to exchange information and intelligence. In

---

[20] See e.g. S. Choongh (1997) *Policing as Social Discipline* (Oxford: Clarendon); Holdaway (1983); and R. Reiner (1997) 'Policing and the police' in M. Maguire, R. Morgan, and R. Reiner (eds.) *The Oxford Handbook of Criminology*, 2nd edn. (Oxford: Clarendon), 997.

[21] M. McConville, A. Sanders, and R. Leng (1991) *The Case for the Prosecution* (London: Routledge), 24, as cited in A. Sanders and R. Young (2000) *Criminal Justice*, 2nd edn. (London: Butterworths), 44. Note that the quote cited by Sanders and Young differs from the original as included in *The Case for the Prosecution*, presumably because the later citation is based on an original field note from Sanders' research for the earlier work.

Station C2, for example, few officers knew any of the operators by name, and none of those interviewed was particularly interested in attempting to improve relations between themselves and the scheme. In Town C1—where the scheme was entirely under local authority control and manned on a part-time basis only—the police were even less interested in the development of good relationships with CCTV operators. According to one officer, there was so little crime in the town that the operators were reduced to watching parking lots or following 'suspected' cannabis users, so that they rarely passed on jobs that the police would be interested in. Apparently, it simply was not 'worth the time' to drop in on the scheme on a regular basis, nor was it in the police interest to encourage operators to be more communicative or proactive.

Despite the fact that the police did not appear to place much importance on the development of good relations with operators in Schemes C1 and C2, in Scheme C3 the situation was somewhat different. Unlike their counterparts in the other local authority-led schemes, CCTV operators in Scheme C3 were described by local PCs and town centre officers as 'excellent', 'efficient', and 'switched on'. Officers spoke of enjoying good working relations with supervisors and operators, and all of those interviewed claimed to visit the control room on a regular if not a daily basis—a claim confirmed by the CCTV control room visitor logbook.[22] Although officers still tended to discriminate between different operators according to the types of jobs they passed on or their knowledge of police procedure, on the whole the CCTV operators were seen as both highly competent and reliable. As one officer put it, as far as the local police were concerned, the operators had become an important part of the overall 'policing team' for the town centre.

There are a number of possible reasons why the operators at Scheme C3 enjoyed better relations with the police than their counterparts in the other Type C schemes included in the study. Perhaps most importantly, unlike operators at either Scheme C1 or Scheme C2, all the control room staff at Scheme C3 had previous experience in the private security industry before becoming CCTV operators. Most had worked either as security guards or shop detectives prior

[22] An examination of the logbook showed that most town centre officers called in on the control room at least once per day while on active duty (usually at the beginning of a given shift).

to coming to the scheme—in many cases for companies or local retailers based in Town C3—and nearly all of them were already familiar with the town and with police radio and investigative procedures prior to their arrival at the scheme. Of the eight control room staff interviewed, three also claimed to have developed good working relations with the town centre police before they became operators and said that their familiarity with local policing practices had proved to be extremely helpful in their new role as CCTV operators. This was a point confirmed by the police in interview, when a number of officers commented on the fact that, although the operators were technically civilians, they were far better trained and more experienced than the 'average CCTV operator'. In addition, the fact that the operators were contracted to the scheme by a private security company, and not direct employees of the local council, appeared to carry considerable weight with local PCs. As one officer noted, although disputes often arose between the council and the police regarding the scheme and the extent to which it should be used for policing purposes, the 'loyalty' of the operators to the police was rarely questioned. As far as the town centre officers were concerned, it was clear that the operators were sympathetic to the concerns of the police and shared similar views about how the system should be used.

It is apparent from the interviews conducted with officers working in conjunction with both Type P and Type C schemes that, although the physical location of the CCTV control room does influence the development of police–operator relationships, as far as the police are concerned the crucial issue is operator competency. Irrespective of whether they were working in a police station or a local authority building, or whether they were police or council employees, operators who were viewed as incapable of distinguishing between what the police regarded as 'good' and 'bad' jobs were generally looked down upon by local officers. This said, it appeared that the police working in conjunction with Type P schemes were more likely to make allowances for operator errors on the basis that these operators were seen as part of a working team within the station, and to explain these errors in terms of lack of experience or sufficient training. While this perception did not always mean that relations between the police and these operators were entirely smooth, there was less likelihood that the operators would be 'frozen out' by either local PCs or town centre officers. As the case of Scheme C3 shows, the police also seemed to respond particularly well to operators who not only understood police procedures, but who appeared to share similar working values. As with the operators themselves, where the police were able to distinguish meaningfully between the operators and the managers or owners of the system, there was less chance of operators being blamed for systemic failures or for problems relating to resources.

5.5   Getting along: drawing conclusions

Looking back at the comments of CCTV operators and police officers at each of the six towns, it is clear that operators and local officers at police-led schemes were far more likely to develop good working relations with one another than their counterparts at local authority-led schemes. In addition, despite the fact that operators at both types of scheme shared similar backgrounds and received similar levels of training, there was also considerable evidence to suggest that police officers working in conjunction with Type P schemes regarded CCTV operators with greater levels of personal and professional respect than officers working with Type C schemes.

Crucially, these findings seem to imply that factors such as operator selection and training have less of an impact on police–operator relations than organizational or managerial differences between police- and local authority-led schemes. Although many CCTV operators at Type C schemes believed that they would have enjoyed better relations with the police had they been better trained or prepared, the reality was that local officers tended to be critical of operators not because they were badly trained—although this was a source of criticism—but rather because they were perceived as 'outsiders' and not part of the local 'police team'. Put simply, the fact that Type P operators worked in the local police station and were typically police employees meant that local officers were more likely to accept them and, perhaps most important of all, make allowances for their mistakes.

Of course, the key question that arises from these findings is whether differences in the working relationships between operators and police officers across schemes reflected or translated into differences in working cultures or surveillance practices. Did the fact that operators were more likely to be accepted by the police at police-led schemes make them more sympathetic to police concerns or more likely to adopt 'police values'? Did closer integration between CCTV operators and local officers lead to more police-oriented targeting? These are difficult questions to answer. Certainly, during the course of the research it was clear that Type P operators were far more likely to adopt police terminology than Type C operators; they frequently referred to suspects and offenders, using language that mirrored that of local police officers. Terms such as 'scroat', 'scumbag', and 'tealeaf' were commonly used by operators at police-led schemes to describe well-known local offenders, and most of the operators also appeared comfortable using police shorthand when describing other surveillance targets (the use of police 'IC' categories was especially prevalent amongst Type P operators).[23] Language alone, however, can only tell us so much, and the fact that Type P operators made greater use of police terminology does not necessarily mean that they were also more inclined than operators at Type C schemes to share the same values as their local police colleagues. Similarly, just because Type P operators appeared to be more comfortable in their daily dealings with police officers—a point that was noted many times during the course of the observation period—it does not follow that they did their job any differently from their counterparts at local authority-led schemes.

In order to establish whether there were any actual differences between the working cultures of the police- and local authority-led schemes included in this study, it is instead necessary to compare the targeting practices of Type P and Type C operators and ask questions about how they decided who should be the subjects of CCTV surveillance. Did operators working at police-led schemes, for example, use working rules and categories of suspicion similar to those employed by the police themselves and, if they did, to what extent were these rules learned from the police? Were Type C operators more inclined to use CCTV to pursue goals more in keeping with the needs of their local authority employers than those of the police? These are all questions that are considered in the next chapter, as we begin to look at who was actually watched by the operators and, more crucially, why.

---

[23] The following IC categories are typically used by the police to classify individuals according to their apparent ethnic background: IC1—White European; IC2—Dark European; IC3—Afro-Caribbean; IC4—Asian; IC5—Oriental; IC6—Arab.

6

Choosing Targets

In the early days of CCTV in Britain, most public area surveillance systems were fairly rudimentary affairs. Stationary black and white cameras, returning grainy, often blurred images, were connected to standard video recorders and television monitors, and were watched by operators who were unable to move the cameras or, in some cases, even ensure that they were in focus. As CCTV technology advanced during the late 1980s, however, things began to change. Cameras capable of producing high-quality colour images became standard, as did multiplex recording and 'photo-print' technology. Perhaps the most significant development, however, was the widespread introduction of cameras that could be moved and controlled from afar. Equipped with full pan, tilt, and zoom facilities, this new generation of cameras suddenly enabled operators to *follow* surveillance targets, and transformed the role of the CCTV operator from that of a passive onlooker into an active observer. Suddenly, CCTV operators were required to make decisions about whom and what to watch.

As stated in Chapter 1, one of the major concerns of the research is to determine whether the ways in which CCTV schemes are organized and managed have an impact on the surveillance practices of operators or the extent to which public area CCTV is used by the police. Having established in the previous chapter that police officers and CCTV operators have a tendency to develop better working relationships if a CCTV system is managed by the police and located on police premises, this chapter examines whether these working differences affect the way in which operators exercise their discretion when making targeting decisions. Do operators in police-led schemes and local authority-led schemes watch different types of people, and if so why?

6.1   Why were people targeted?

In the course of the research, a total of 376 targeted surveillances were recorded, 133 at police-led schemes, and 243 at local authority-led schemes. For the purposes of the study, a *targeted surveillance* was deemed to have taken place if an operator intentionally trained a camera on an individual or group for more than 30 seconds.[1] Detailed notes were kept on all of the targeted surveillances observed, with the field notes recording—among other things—the length of the target, where it took place, and basic demographic details for each individual observed.[2] In the case of each targeted surveillance, a note was also made of the operator's initial reason for suspicion, as well as his subsequent motivation for continuing with the surveillance. Thus, in each case, as soon as the researcher saw a camera being trained on an individual or group, a note was made of the operator's apparent reason for interest or suspicion; and after the target had ended, a further note was made of the apparent overall purpose of the surveillance. In an effort to improve the accuracy of these notes and assessments, once the target had been discontinued the operator responsible was immediately asked to explain what he thought the surveillance was about, and to set out the reasons behind his decision to target the individual or group in the first place. During the final data analysis phase, where there was a disparity between the researcher's impression of

[1] Note that the decision to define a target as being any surveillance longer than 30 seconds was made on the basis of both the pilot research and a later examination of Norris and Armstrong's seminal study of operator targeting practices. While it was important to ensure that the minimum length was reasonably long—so that short and relatively trivial targets were not included—it was also essential to ensure that all significant targets were included in the sample. Although Norris and Armstrong only kept data on targets lasting more than one minute, on the basis of the pilot study, a shorter period was chosen on the grounds that targets of 30 seconds or more were of sufficient length to require operators to make active choices about whom they were targeting and why. See Norris and Armstrong (1999*b*), 96.

[2] For each target a note was made of the operator responsible for the target; the length of the target; the location of the target; the reason for the initial target (as per the operator and the researcher); the reason for continuing the target; the apparent age, gender, race, appearance, and demeanour of the primary individual targeted; the reaction (if any) of the primary individual targeted; whether a call to the police or some other authority outside the system was made as a result of the surveillance; whether police officers were deployed as a result of the surveillance; and whether any arrests resulted from the surveillance.

the surveillance and the operator's own account of the incident, in each case a decision was made to record the more plausible or consistent of the two conflicting accounts. In practice, however, this sort of disagreement was extremely rare, with operators confirming the researcher's account of the reasons behind the initial surveillance in over 98 per cent of cases.

Following research on operator targeting practices undertaken by Norris and Armstrong, on completion of the fieldwork eight categories of suspicion were used to classify the reasons behind the initial decision to target certain individuals and groups:

- *Behavioural*: Suspicion based on the behaviour or demeanour of the individual, such as acting aggressively towards others, appearing to be drunk in public, or running down a busy high street.
- *Categorical*: Suspicion based on personal characteristics such as age, dress, gender, or race.
- *Locational*: Suspicion based on an individual's location. Examples might include an individual walking through a car park at night or standing close to a bank cash-point.
- *Personalized*: Suspicion based on the prior knowledge of the individual, such as knowledge of previous criminal behaviour or association with other known or suspected offenders.
- *Protectional*: Monitoring for the purpose of ensuring the safety of the individual targeted. Examples might include following an unaccompanied child or a woman walking alone through a deserted town centre at night.
- *Routine*: Monitoring carried out as part of a set surveillance routine, such as watching security personnel pick up money from a high street bank on a weekly basis.
- *Transmitted*: Suspicion based on information from a source outside the CCTV scheme, or where the initial surveillance was commenced because of an outside request.
- *Voyeuristic*: Surveillance for the purpose of personal interest or gratification, sexual or otherwise.[3]

As these categories are not mutually exclusive, where there were multiple reasons behind the operator's decision to commence

---

[3] With the exception of 'Routine', each of these categories was defined in accordance with the classifications employed by Norris and Armstrong. See Norris and Armstrong (1999*b*), 112. A separate category for routine surveillances was added

surveillance, the incident was classified according to the dominant reason or type of suspicion. Table 6.1 summarizes the results for each type of scheme, as well as the six schemes as a whole.

Looking first at the reasons for initial targeting across all schemes, it is clear from Table 6.1 that the majority of targeting carried out by both Type P (police-led) and Type C (local authority-led) schemes involved operators actively watching out for particular types of people or behaviour. Taken together, 'Behavioural', 'Categorical', and 'Personalized' targeting accounted for 73 per cent of all initial targeting decisions. In contrast, passive surveillance—based on factors such as location—was considerably less important to operators, irrespective of whether they worked at police- or local authority-led schemes.

Within individual categories of suspicion, Table 6.1 also reveals more specific similarities between the initial targeting decisions of Type P and Type C operators.[4] In each case, 'Personalized' suspicion was the single most likely reason for individuals or groups to be targeted by operators, with operators at local authority-led schemes

TABLE 6.1. Reason for initial target/suspicion

Type of suspicion	All schemes		Type P schemes		Type C schemes	
	No.	%	No.	%	No.	%
Behavioural	58	15	30	22	28	11
Categorical	73	20	20	15	53	22
Locational	20	5	12	9	8	3
Personalized	140	37	34	26	106	44
Protectional	13	4	8	6	5	2
Routine	10	3	3	2	7	3
Transmitted	58	15	25	20	33	14
Voyeuristic	4	1	1	1	3	1
Total	376	100	133	101	243	100

Note: Percentages may not add up to 100 due to rounding.

following completion of the pilot study given that the majority of schemes studied carried out some form of regular surveillance either for the police or the local authority, such as monitoring public works or traffic flows.

[4] The individual cells in Table 6.1 are too small to warrant applying tests of statistical significance. As a consequence, the text confines itself to commenting on substantial numerical differences only.

being particularly keen to watch people already known to them. In part, the high rate of 'Personalized' targeting at Type C schemes— 44 per cent as compared with 26 per cent at Type P schemes—can be attributed to the fact that many operators at Scheme C3 had previously worked in other security jobs in and around Town C3 before taking up their current roles as CCTV operators, and they therefore possessed far greater levels of 'local knowledge' than any of the other Type C operators or most Type P operators. Despite the fact that one of the Type C towns (Town C1) did not have an established 'Shop-Safe' radio scheme while all Type P towns did, Table 6.1 shows that rates of targeting based on 'Transmitted' suspicion from outside the system were also reasonably similar across both police- and local authority-led schemes.[5]

Larger differences are, however, apparent in the levels of 'Behavioural', 'Locational', and 'Categorical'-based targeting for operators at police- and local authority-led schemes. Strikingly, CCTV operators working at police-led schemes—where 'Behavioural' targeting made up 22 per cent of all surveillances—were twice as likely to begin targeting an individual on the basis of a judgement about the criminal significance of their behaviour than operators at Type C schemes. What this suggests is that Type P operators were more inclined to treat certain types of behaviour as indicative of potential or actual criminality than Type C operators, and tended to look for 'signs' in the body language or demeanour of the public when making decisions about whom to target. Certainly, this is a point that is illustrated by comments made by the operators themselves during the course of the fieldwork:

FIELD-NOTE EXTRACT: SCHEME P2 (1/74/10.43 a.m.). Operator D spots a black man—casually dressed, probably in his mid to late thirties— walking slowly through the town centre. Although there is nothing about his appearance that makes him stand out from the crowd, his movements are particularly deliberate. When asked why he has decided to target him, the operator responds: 'Well, I spotted him because he wasn't moving right.

[5] All of the CCTV schemes included in the main study except Scheme C1 operated in towns where there were established radio links between all of the major retailers and shopping centres. These networks were typically used by shops to exchange information about the movements of known or suspected shoplifters around the town centre, and to warn private security officers about potential 'problem customers'. Typically, calls put out over the radio scheme were also relayed to CCTV operators so that they could provide camera surveillance as and when necessary.

Almost as though he doesn't know where he's going...' After about a minute of tracking the man as he continues to walk, the operator discontinues the surveillance, noting that 'he seems okay, doesn't look like he's going to cause any trouble'.

FIELD-NOTE EXTRACT: SCHEME P1 (1/82/11.14 a.m.). In a quiet moment, Operator T decides to explain an earlier comment about the importance of body language. Training one of the high street cameras on a pair of young white men walking through the town centre, he observes: 'See these two here? Both of them are walking calmly, all nice and relaxed. No sudden movements, everything flowing. See the one on the left? Hands in his pockets, no indication that he's after a fight...' The two men then pass a couple of young women walking in the opposite direction, who do not appear to notice or react to them. 'See that? They didn't respond to them either.' Satisfied with his explanation, the operator returns to routine scanning.

In addition to comments such as these, many operators at the police-led schemes were quick to stress the importance of body language when responding to interview questions about how they made initial targeting decisions. As the following two quotations taken from formal interviews demonstrate, operators at Type P schemes soon developed their own theories about how to 'read the signs' and predict criminal or other unwarranted behaviour from the body language of members of the public, as well as theories about what constituted normal behaviour or a normal scene:

Quite often it's body language. If you see two people start to gesticulate at one another you can tell by the way they're moving their arms whether it's friendly or not, especially in the evenings when they've been drinking. Again, people who are drunk, you notice them staggering—just different movements from normal. But body language, you get to be quite good at body language 'cause it's something you look out for. So you can tell the hostility in people just by looking at the way they move. (Operator G, Scheme P2)

Firstly you look for what I would say is body language, and the person's demeanour... Whereas with a crowd of people all walking the same way, with the same attitude, there's no aggression shown, everybody's quite happy amongst each other, then clearly everything's going okay. As soon as somebody seems to go against that stream or there's a sudden stop of movement, or heads are turned round looking in one way, that's an indication that there's something happening... (Operator T, Scheme P1)

Significantly, most Type P operators suggested that they had learned to 'read the signs' from local police officers, either by observing their reactions to certain behaviour while in the CCTV control room, or by asking them directly. As one operator at Scheme P2 observed, the fact that the CCTV control room was located across the hall from the Criminal Investigations Department (CID) meant that officers from this division regularly dropped in for coffee with the operators, giving them the chance to ask questions about 'how to spot' certain types of offenders. Such opportunities were valued by operators, and most took full advantage of them to ask numerous and detailed questions about the alleged behaviour of drug dealers, shoplifters, and other groups of offenders. This said, nearly all of the operators interviewed had also clearly formed their own opinions on how to recognize criminal behaviour in the course of their daily observation. Returning to Scheme P2, two of the five operators were regarded by their colleagues in the CCTV control room and by some police officers as having become specialists at recognizing pickpockets and shoplifters according to their supposed body language. As this study did not set out to test such claims, it is difficult to know whether these operators were in fact able to identify accurately certain prospective or actual offenders according to their demeanour or body language. What is clear, however, is that operators *believed* they could read body language and made targeting decisions on this basis, and that they frequently looked to the police in their efforts to improve these alleged skills. In contrast, operators at Type C schemes rarely talked about questions of body language, and did not appear to have developed any theories among themselves about how to recognize different types of potential offender according to their demeanour.

Differences between the targeting decisions of Type P and Type C operators are also apparent in relation to the relative importance of location as a basis for suspicion. As Table 6.1 shows, 'Locational' targeting accounted for 9 per cent of initial targeting decisions in police-led schemes, as opposed to little over 3 per cent in local authority-led schemes. Although these figures show that 'Locational' targeting was relatively infrequent for both types of scheme, the general behaviour of operators at Type P schemes did suggest that these operators were more inclined than their counterparts at Type C schemes to focus regularly on certain key areas in and around the town centre. In many ways, the following two field-note extracts typify the contrast between the attitudes of Type P and Type C operators to the importance of carrying out camera patrols of local 'hot-spots':

FIELD-NOTE EXTRACT: SCHEME P2 (1/21/9.05 a.m.). Operator M comes back into the control room after a short cigarette break. Over the course of the next half hour, he uses a variety of cameras to check out what is going on in a number of key areas around the town, including a local churchyard regarded by the operators as a haven for drunks and drug dealers. During this time he fails to see anything of particular interest, and once he has finished his rounds, he sighs and goes back to the task of more general scanning... When asked why he goes through this routine, he replies: 'Well, you have to have some sort of system. After all, if you don't look you don't find.'

FIELD-NOTE EXTRACT: SCHEME C2 (2/3/11.02 a.m.). After finishing up some paperwork from the previous day, Operator J returns to the monitors and takes control of the cameras one by one. There is no clear or obvious pattern to his surveillance as he moves from one camera to the next, with the time spent controlling each ranging from a few seconds to a couple of minutes. On two occasions he pans the camera without even bothering to look at the screen. After about ten minutes of this, the operator becomes bored and switches to a single camera overlooking the high street, before finally turning away from the monitor and going back to some more paperwork...

One explanation for this difference in practice is that, during their training, operators at Schemes P1, P2, and P3 were encouraged by police managers to carry out regular patrols of areas that the police regarded as crime or pubic order 'hot-spots'. During the course of informal conversations with operators at Scheme P2, for example, it became apparent that they had come to see certain areas within the town as more dangerous or prone to criminal activity than others—on the basis of stories told to them by local police officers. One park in particular, located on the boundary between the town centre and a housing estate, had acquired a reputation with the police for being 'trouble', and operators were frequently urged by police constables visiting the CCTV control room to 'keep an eye on things down there' and to include the park in their routine camera sweeps. As a consequence, operators would almost always target anyone walking through the park, even if only for a couple of seconds. Similarly, an operator at Scheme P1 was clear about the importance of being sensitive to location when using the cameras to patrol the streets in search of potential problems:

FIELD-NOTE EXTRACT: SCHEME P1 (1/70/1.35 p.m.). Operator T trains one of the town centre cameras on a group of three young white men—all in their late teens or early twenties—standing outside a café that is next door to a clothing store. After watching them for about 40 seconds he discontinues the surveillance and explains: 'Three weeks ago that shop had a couple of leather coats nicked by two young blokes. Apparently they just walked in, grabbed them, and ran off. Now I keep an eye on the place. I guess I just find myself aware of it when I'm looking around with the cameras...'

In contrast, Type C operators did not appear to have received similar instructions or guidance, either from senior officers or local PCs. As one operator at Scheme C2 noted ruefully, the only time officers came into the CCTV control room was to pick up tapes or to provide operators with photos of individuals for whom arrest warrants had been issued. Rarely did officers stop to talk to the operators, and as such they were left to their own devices when deciding how to plan their surveillance routines.

Finally, differences can also be seen in the levels of 'Categorical' targeting undertaken at the two types of scheme. While operators at police-led schemes tended to engage in considerable amounts of 'Behavioural' and 'Locational' targeting, operators at local author- ity-led schemes appeared to be less concerned with questions of body language or location when making initial targeting decisions, and more responsive to how people dressed, their age, and other characteristics related to their physical appearance. Returning again to Table 6.1, we can see that 'Categorical' targeting accounted for almost 22 per cent of all surveillances undertaken by Type C operators, as compared with 15 per cent of targeting at police-led schemes. What this suggests is that operators at local authority- led schemes made rather more use of stereotypes about the criminal propensity of certain groups in the community than Type P oper- ators, and were more inclined to notice these groups when looking for potential targets. This raises the question of whether Type C operators were more likely to engage in socially or racially differen- tiated targeting than operators at Type P schemes, a question that is taken up in more detail later in this chapter. At this point, however, it is sufficient to note that, although operators at police- and local authority-led schemes tended to make similar initial targeting deci- sions—focusing primarily on individuals who were already known to them—there were some significant differences between the two types of scheme.

Moving beyond the *initial* decision to target, Table 6.2 classifies each observed incident into one of seven categories according to the

TABLE 6.2. Reasons for continuing surveillance

Category	All schemes		Type P schemes		Type C schemes	
	No.	%	No.	%	No.	%
Association	4	1	0	0	4	2
Crime	209	56	72	54	137	56
Information	7	2	4	3	3	1
Order	73	19	36	27	37	15
Safety/Service	22	6	14	11	8	4
No Obvious	56	15	4	3	52	21
Other	5	1	3	2	2	1
Total	376	100	133	100	243	100

operator's reason for choosing to *continue* surveillance once camera contact had been established. Where, for example, an operator had decided to monitor an individual he believed (for whatever reason) to be a car thief or shoplifter, the continuing surveillance would be classified as crime-related. Similarly, incidents involving public drunkenness, vandalism, and aggressive begging were classified as order-related, and in those cases where an individual was watched because the operator was concerned for their safety, the 'Safety/ Service' category was used. In situations where the reason for the target was not obvious, operators were asked to explain what they were hoping to achieve by continuing to target the individual or group in question. Where there was no apparent reason for the surveillance or when the operator was at a loss to explain the target, the incident was coded as 'Not Obvious'. Again, because these categories had the potential to overlap—particularly the 'Crime' and 'Order' categories—each surveillance was coded according to the dominant reason for the surveillance.

As we can see from Table 6.2, operators in both types of schemes spent over half their time monitoring individuals whom they believed to be involved in some form of criminal activity. This is not particularly surprising given that all of the schemes included in the study had been set up with the specific aim of reducing crime in their local areas.[6] In addition, these figures are also in keeping with similar surveys of operator targeting in Britain. In their study of

[6] See Ch. 3.

three CCTV schemes in the north of England, for example, Norris and Armstrong found that crime-related suspicion was the most likely reason for targeting, accounting for 30 per cent of all surveillances.[7] Both groups of operators also devoted roughly the same amount of time to non-crime-related surveillance, such as searching for missing children and monitoring traffic (categorized as 'Safety/Service'-related targeting). Differences are evident, however, when we move beyond these categories. Operators working in police-led schemes were more inclined to continue targeting individuals whom they regarded as a threat to public order, with the result being that this category accounted for just over 27 per cent of all targets for Type P schemes (as opposed to 15 per cent for Type C). Conversely, operators in council-run schemes were more likely to engage in otherwise unexplained targeting, with surveillances falling into the 'No Obvious' category accounting for one in five (22 per cent) of all targets, a proportion seven times higher than that recorded for the police-led schemes.

This difference in the level of non-specific surveillance between police-led and local authority-led schemes is a significant one. What it suggests is that once operators working at Type C schemes acquired a target—for whatever reason—they were then far more likely to continue to watch that individual or group for reasons unrelated to concerns about crime, public order, or their personal safety. The picture becomes even more interesting when Tables 6.1 and 6.2 are combined and direct connections are drawn between operators' initial targeting decisions and their reasons for continuing surveillance as in Table 6.3.

On the whole, Table 6.3 suggests that once an initial targeting decision had been made, both Type P and Type C operators had very

[7] Note that Norris and Armstrong divided all targeted surveillances recorded in their survey into one of four categories—Crime, Order, No Obvious Reason, and Other—based on the researcher's perception of each incident. This approach was rejected in the current case for two reasons. First, based on the findings of the pilot study, it was felt that additional categories—Association, Information, and Safety/Service—were needed in order to build a more textured picture of those targets that were not directly related to crime or public order. This approach, however, necessitated going beyond categorizing targets according to what they seemed to be about, and actually asking operators to explain targets that were in any way ambiguous. Because of these methodological differences, only qualified comparisons can be drawn between the findings of Norris and Armstrong and those of the current study. See Norris and Armstrong (1999b), 111.

TABLE 6.3. Operators' initial suspicion and reasons for continuing surveillance

Type P schemes		Type C schemes	
Reason for initial targeting	Reason for continuing surveillance	Reason for initial targeting	Reason for continuing surveillance
(1) Personalized 26%	(1) Crime 71% (2) Order 23% (3) Safety/Service 6%	(1) Personalized 44%	(1) Crime 73% (2) Order 17% (3) Safety/Service 6% (4) Association 4%
(2) Behavioural 22%	(1) Crime 43% (2) Order 43% (3) Safety/Service 10% (4) Information 3%	(2) Behavioural 11%	(1) Crime 46% (2) Order 36% (3) No obvious 11% (4) Information 4% (5) Safety/Service 4%
(3) Transmitted 20%	(1) Crime 76% (2) Order 12% (3) Other 8% (4) Safety/Service 4%	(3) Transmitted 14%	(1) Crime 97% (2) Order 3%
(4) Categorical 18%	(1) Crime 50% (2) Order 35% (3) No obvious 10% (4) Information 5%	(4) Categorical 22%	(1) No obvious 68% (2) Crime 21% (3) Order 12%

Note: Percentages may not add up to 100 due to rounding.

similar reasons for continuing surveillance. Regardless of whether they worked at police- or local authority-led schemes, operators tended to continue surveillance of 'Personalized' and 'Behavioural' targets for similar reasons, namely concerns about the possibility of criminal conduct or public disorder. Equally, where a target had been acquired in response to a call to the CCTV control room—'Transmitted' suspicion—operators at both types of scheme tended to continue with the surveillance for crime-related reasons. The one major difference between the two, however, can be found in the level of 'Categorical' targeting. As has already been noted, the fact that operators at local authority schemes were inclined to target individuals and groups on the basis of personal characteristics is a cause for concern. Looking at Table 6.3, we can see that over two-thirds (68 per cent) of all 'Categorical' targets acquired by Type C operators were continued for no obvious reason. In other words, operators at local authority-led schemes were frequently targeting and monitoring members of the public for reasons other than apparent concerns about crime, public order, or personal safety. Although the operators themselves claimed that they were not carrying out the surveillance in question for any particular reason, it is important to consider the possibility that targeting was taking place on the basis of operators' undisclosed assumptions about the inherent criminality of certain individuals or groups, or for other reasons that they were unwilling to discuss. It is therefore necessary to look more closely at who the targets of surveillance were, and ask whether there was any evidence of social, gender, or racial bias in the surveillance decisions of operators at either police- or local authority-led schemes.

6.2 Who was targeted?

During the course of the fieldwork, basic demographic data was recorded for each of the primary individuals targeted for surveillance, including a note of their sex, race, and appearance, as well as an estimate of their age.[8] The data is summarized in Table 6.4. Looking at the findings for all schemes, on the face of it the demographic characteristics of the vast majority of people targeted by

[8] Categorization of individuals according to physical characteristics is of course problematic, and in each case a best estimate of the racial background, age, etc. of the target was made by the author.

TABLE 6.4. Characteristics of surveillance subjects

	All schemes		Type P schemes		Type C schemes	
	No.	%	No.	%	No.	%
Age						
0–19	55	15	33	27	22	9
20–29	231	61	64	48	167	69
30+	90	24	36	25	54	22
Total	376	100	133	100	243	100
Sex						
Female	63	17	16	12	47	19
Male	313	83	117	88	196	81
Total	376	100	133	100	243	100
Race						
Asian	20	5	9	7	11	4
Black	35	9	23	17	12	5
White	321	85	101	76	220	90
Total	376	99	133	100	243	99
Appearance						
Casual	329	87	112	84	217	89
Smart	8	2	4	3	4	2
Scruffy	34	9	13	10	21	9
Uniform	5	1	4	3	1	1
Total	376	99	133	100	243	101

Note: Percentages may not add up to 100 due to rounding.

operators were much the same: over 80 per cent of all surveillance subjects were white, male, and casually dressed. In addition, three-quarters of this group (76 per cent) were young, with the majority being in their late teens or early twenties.

Despite these broad similarities, however, Table 6.4 also reveals that there were substantial differences in the numbers of women, Asians, and black people targeted across police- and local authority-led schemes. Looking first at the sex of those targeted, we can see that although women were far less likely to be subjected to surveillance than men overall, women made up 19 per cent of the total number of targets at local authority-led schemes, as opposed to only 12 per cent at police-led schemes.[9] Further differences also emerge

[9] Norris and Armstrong's study also returned similar rates of targeting by gender. Out of a total of 1,679 individuals targeted by operators in the course of their study, 192 (12 per cent) were women. See Norris and Armstrong (1999b), 109.

when we look at the reasons *why* women were initially targeted by operators. Table 6.5 shows that operators at Type P schemes tended to target women on the basis of their behaviour or out of a concern for their safety, while operators at Type C schemes were more inclined to take an interest in a woman within view of their cameras because she was already known to them. In fact, 'Personalized' targeting of this sort made up almost half (45 per cent) of all targeting of women at local authority-led schemes. It is not surprising, then, when we look at Table 6.6—which links operators'

TABLE 6.5. Reason for initial targeting by sex

Type of suspicion	Type P schemes				Type C schemes			
	Female		Male		Female		Male	
	No.	%	No.	%	No.	%	No.	%
Behavioural	4	25	26	22	6	13	22	11
Categorical	0	0	20	17	7	15	46	24
Locational	1	6	11	9	1	2	7	4
Personalized	3	19	31	27	21	45	85	43
Protectional	6	38	2	2	2	4	3	2
Routine	0	0	3	3	1	2	6	3
Transmitted	1	6	24	21	6	13	27	14
Voyeuristic	1	6	0	0	3	6	0	0
Total	16	100	117	101	47	100	196	101

Note: Percentages may not add up to 100 due to rounding.

TABLE 6.6. Reason for continuing surveillance by sex

Category	Type P schemes				Type C schemes			
	Female		Male		Female		Male	
	No.	%	No.	%	No.	%	No.	%
Association	0	0	0	0	4	9	0	0
Crime	4	25	68	58	24	51	113	58
Information	1	6	3	3	0	0	3	2
Order	1	6	35	30	3	6	34	17
Safety/Service	8	50	6	5	4	9	4	2
No obvious	1	6	3	3	12	26	40	20
Other	1	6	2	2	0	0	2	1
Total	16	99	117	101	47	101	196	100

Note: Percentages may not add up to 100 due to rounding.

reasons for continuing an established target with the subject's gender—that operators at local authority schemes were inclined to continue watching women because they believed that they had either just committed a crime or were about to do so.

In many ways, these findings are supported by various comments made by operators working at local authority-led schemes, particularly those working at Schemes C2 and C3. These operators frequently expressed the view that young women with large carrier bags or pushing prams were more often than not shoplifters, and therefore they routinely targeted these women if they were seen in the town centre or going into local shops. In addition, women seen associating with men believed by these operators to be involved with drugs were also targeted, either on the basis that they were somehow involved in drug dealing themselves or because they were potential customers. On one occasion, an operator at Scheme C3 explained that he was following a young woman because she had previously been seen talking to 'the girlfriend of a known villain and drug dealer', despite the fact that she had not committed any offence nor was she otherwise known to the operator. By way of contrast, comments from Type P operators suggested that they tended to view women as potential *victims* of crime rather than as potential offenders. As one operator at Scheme P3 put it, part of the purpose of the scheme was to protect the particularly vulnerable and to encourage women to use the town centre at night. While a number of Type P operators also expressed the opinion that women were more likely to engage in shoplifting than men, this view did not appear to translate into their targeting practices.

Moving on to the question of race, Table 6.4 shows that Type P operators were more inclined to target Asians and black people than their counterparts at local authority-led schemes. In Towns P1, P2, and P3, Asians made up less than 4 per cent of the total population, but constituted 7 per cent of the total of individuals targeted by operators at police-led schemes.[10] This means that Asians were

---

[10] Racial distributions for each of the towns included in the study were as follows: P1: Whites 96 per cent, Blacks 1 per cent, Asians 1.5 per cent; P2: Whites 96 per cent, Blacks 1 per cent, Asians 3 per cent; P3: Whites 90 per cent, Blacks 4 per cent, Asians 4 per cent; C1: Whites 97 per cent, Blacks 0.8 per cent, Asians 1.3 per cent; C2: Whites 82 per cent, Blacks 6 per cent, Asians 10 per cent; C3: Whites 93 per cent, Blacks 2 per cent, Asians 4 per cent. These figures were drawn from the 1991 National Census and, where possible, more recent local authority surveys.

almost twice as likely to be the targets of CCTV surveillance as their presence in the population would appear to justify. In addition, black people were also over-represented in the targeting figures of Type P operators, but to an even greater extent. Despite making up less than 1 per cent of the population in Towns P1 and P2, and only 4 per cent in Town P3, black people accounted for 17 per cent of all surveillance undertaken by operators at Type P schemes—a figure over four times what might be expected. Although it is important to be cautious about drawing broad conclusions from these relatively simple statistics—particularly given that no data were available for the racial composition of those using the streets covered by each system—the fact remains that these numbers give cause for concern.[11] What they suggest is that operators at police-led schemes were conscious of race when making targeting decisions, and that they were particularly interested in targeting and following black and Asian people.

Looking at the same data for the Type C schemes, black people again appeared to be over-represented, but only marginally so and certainly not to the same extent as in the police-led schemes. In Town C2, blacks made up 6 per cent of the total population, and just under 2 per cent in Towns C1 and C3, but they made up a total of 5 per cent of all those targeted by operators at Type C schemes as a whole. Taking into account the contrasting sizes of Towns C1, C2, and C3, we find that on average black people made up approximately 3.5 per cent of the total population for those areas covered by Type C schemes, which means that the targeting figure of 5 per cent is only slightly above that which might be expected. As regards Asians, they were in fact generally under-represented in the list of individuals targeted by Type C operators. Despite making up 2, 10, and 4 per cent of the population in Towns C1, C2, and C3 respectively, Asian people only accounted for 4 per cent of all those targeted by Type C operators.

Overall, these figures suggest that operators working in police-led schemes were more conscious of race when making targeting and surveillance decisions than their local authority counterparts. Interestingly, however, Tables 6.7 and 6.8 below show that all racial

---

[11] See J. Miller (2000) *Profiling Populations Available for Stops and Searches*, Police Research Series Paper 131 (London: HMSO). Based on the findings contained in his report, Miller argues that levels of racial disparity in police stop-and-search decisions fall dramatically once the representation of different racial groups in the 'available population' is taken into account.

TABLE 6.7. Reason for initial targeting by race

Type of suspicion	Type P schemes						Type C schemes					
	Asian		Black		White		Asian		Black		White	
	No.	%	No.	%	No.	%	No.	%	No.	%	No.	%
Behavioural	1	11	5	22	24	24	2	18	1	8	25	11
Categorical	2	22	3	13	15	15	2	18	1	8	50	23
Locational	1	11	2	9	9	9	0	0	3	25	5	2
Personalized	1	11	5	22	28	28	6	55	5	42	95	43
Protectional	0	0	1	4	7	7	0	0	0	0	5	2
Routine	2	22	1	4	0	0	0	0	0	0	7	3
Transmitted	2	22	6	26	17	17	1	9	2	17	30	14
Voyeuristic	0	0	0	0	1	1	0	0	0	0	3	1
Total	9	99	23	100	101	101	11	100	12	100	220	99

Note: Percentages may not add up to 100 due to rounding.

TABLE 6.8. Reason for continuing surveillance by race

Category	Type P schemes						Type C schemes					
	Asian		Black		White		Asian		Black		White	
	No.	%	No.	%	No.	%	No.	%	No.	%	No.	%
Association	0	0	0	0	0	0	2	18	0	0	2	1
Crime	5	56	14	61	53	53	5	46	7	58	125	57
Information	0	0	1	4	3	3	1	9	1	8	1	1
Order	3	33	4	17	29	29	2	18	3	25	32	15
Safety/Service	0	0	4	17	10	10	0	0	0	0	8	4
No obvious	1	11	0	0	3	3	1	9	1	8	50	23
Other	0	0	0	0	3	3	0	0	0	0	2	1
Total	9	100	23	99	101	101	11	100	12	99	220	102

Note: Percentages may not add up to 100 due to rounding.

groups—white, black, and Asian—were *initially* targeted by Type P operators for much the same reasons. Blacks and whites were subjected to similar rates of 'Personalized', 'Behavioural', and 'Categorical' targeting by these operators, and although Asians were more likely to be the subject of 'Routine' surveillance, on the whole they were initially targeted for much the same reasons as other racial groups. All of this points to the fact that while operators at police-led schemes were more conscious of blacks and Asians when operating their cameras, when they did actually decide to target people from these groups it was generally because the individual was already known to them or on the basis of something to do with their behaviour.

Although it is important not to read too much into these initial targeting figures for blacks and Asians given the small numbers involved, they do suggest that racial stereotyping may have entered into the decision-making of operators at Type P schemes at the *pre-targeting* stage. If, for example, operators are more inclined to notice blacks and Asians when engaged in general surveillance, it follows that even if they choose to target them for the same reasons as they target whites, the outcome will still be an over-representation of ethnic minorities in the number of people surveilled. Yet, irrespective of the stage at which racial considerations entered the targeting decisions of Type P operators, it appears that CCTV surveillance at these schemes did suffer from a degree of (probably unconscious) racial bias. Certainly, these results suggest that further, more specific research into the question of racially biased targeting among CCTV operators is needed.

Finally, turning to the question of age and its impact on targeting, we can see from Table 6.4 that the vast majority of people targeted by operators at both Type P and Type C schemes—over 80 per cent in each case—were below the age of 30. Similarly, as Tables 6.9 and 6.10 show, operators at both types of scheme tended to target and monitor these individuals for what were essentially the same reasons. Irrespective of whether they were being watched by operators working at Type P or Type C schemes, the majority of young people were initially selected for surveillance either because they were already known to operators or because their behaviour or appearance was felt to be in some way suspicious. Once targeted, they were likely to be kept under surveillance by operators for reasons relating to crime or public order. In short, it made little

TABLE 6.9. Reason for initial targeting by age

Type of suspicion	Type P schemes						Type C schemes					
	0–19		20–29		30+		0–19		20–29		30+	
	No.	%	No.	%	No.	%	No.	%	No.	%	No.	%
Behavioural	6	18	16	25	8	22	2	9	20	12	6	11
Categorical	8	24	11	17	1	3	8	36	32	19	13	24
Locational	3	9	5	8	4	11	1	5	5	3	2	4
Personalized	6	18	17	27	11	31	7	32	79	47	20	37
Protectional	1	3	3	5	4	11	3	14	2	1	0	0
Routine	2	6	0	0	1	3	0	0	4	2	3	6
Transmitted	7	21	11	17	7	19	1	5	22	13	10	19
Voyeuristic	0	0	1	2	0	0	0	0	3	2	0	0
Total	33	99	64	101	36	100	22	101	167	99	54	101

Note: Percentages may not add up to 100 due to rounding.

TABLE 6.10. Reason for continuing surveillance by age

Category	Type P schemes						Type C schemes					
	0–19		20–29		30+		0–19		20–29		30+	
	No.	%	No.	%	No.	%	No.	%	No.	%	No.	%
Association	0	0	0	0	0	0	0	0	4	2	0	0
Crime	23	70	32	50	17	47	10	45	105	63	22	41
Information	0	0	2	3	2	6	0	0	3	2	0	0
Order	7	21	20	31	9	25	2	9	15	9	20	37
Safety/Service	2	6	5	8	7	19	3	14	3	2	2	4
No obvious	1	3	3	5	0	0	7	32	35	21	10	19
Other	0	0	2	3	1	3	0	0	2	1	0	0
Total	33	100	64	100	36	100	22	100	167	100	54	101

Note: Percentages may not add up to 100 due to rounding.

difference who was watching them; regardless of the type of scheme in operation, young people were regarded by those behind the cameras as potential troublemakers or criminals and were targeted as such.

In summary, it is clear that there were considerable similarities between the surveillance practices of Type P and Type C operators, with both groups spending the majority of their time targeting young, white men either because they were already known to operators or because their behaviour or appearance was perceived as being somehow out of the ordinary. Broadly speaking, this overall result is consistent with the findings of Norris and Armstrong, who also uncovered similar patterns of age-related targeting among CCTV operators working in local authority schemes.[12] Significant differences do emerge between the two types of scheme, however, in the targeting of certain racial minorities and women. Operators at police-led schemes showed a particularly strong bias towards the targeting of blacks, with the result that blacks were over-represented in the surveillance statistics for these schemes. In contrast, operators at local authority-led schemes tended to follow a higher proportion of women, mostly for crime-related reasons.

The question that now arises is whether the similarities and differences in the targeting practices of Type P and Type C operators actually matter. Does the fact that operators at police-led schemes target a disproportionate number of black people translate into higher numbers of blacks being stopped by the police in these areas? To what extent do operator targeting practices and patterns of CCTV surveillance affect the actions of the police and the likelihood of certain groups being singled out for police attention?

6.3   Does it matter? Operator practices and police responses

During the course of the field research, various forms of referral and deployment data were recorded for each of the 346 surveillances observed, including whether a call was made from the CCTV operator to the police in connection with the surveillance, and the nature of the police response in each case. As Table 6.11 shows, only ten out of a total of 133 surveillances undertaken by Type P operators

[12] See Norris and Armstrong (1999b), 98–116.

TABLE 6.11. Call-ins and police deployment by scheme

	Type P schemes		Type C schemes	
	No.	%	No.	%
Calls from CCTV operators to officers or police control room	10	7.5	3	1.2
Police deployments resulting from operator calls	6	4.5	1	0.4

Note: Percentage of all surveillances observed.

resulted in a call either to the police control room or to officers on the street, with the police being subsequently deployed on only six occasions. Looking at the same figures for Type C schemes, the numbers were even lower, with only three calls and one police deployment arising out of a total of 243 surveillances.[13]

In light of some of the claims made by operators and police officers during the course of the study about the impact of CCTV on levels of police deployment, these results are surprising. On the one hand, the extremely low rate of call-ins for Type C operators suggests that far from constantly calling in 'bad jobs' or creating additional work for the police—a complaint often made by officers working in areas covered by local authority-led schemes—the reality was that Type C operators seldom contacted the police, and on the few occasions that they did so, the police rarely responded by deploying officers. Similarly, the suggestion that Type P operators were taken more seriously as a result of their close working relations with the police also seems somewhat questionable in light of the fact that only half of their calls resulted in a police response. Despite the inclination of Type P operators to target for crime and public order-related reasons, less than 5 per cent of all surveillances by these operators resulted in some form of police deployment.[14] In short, while it appears operators at police-led schemes were marginally

---

[13] Note that these results are in line with those reported by Norris and Armstrong, who noted that 'nearly 600 hours of observation resulted in only forty-five deployments'. Given that Norris and Armstrong recorded 857 surveillances in the course of their fieldwork, this means that the police were only called out in response to 5 per cent of targets observed. Norris and Armstrong (1999b), 166.

[14] Four of the six deployments were to incidents that were classified as crime-related, with the remaining two being in response to public order disturbances.

more inclined to call the police than their local authority counterparts, there is no evidence that their calls were taken any more seriously.

Returning to the theme of the previous section, these findings also cast doubt on the actual impact of differences in operator targeting practices on young men, women, and racial minorities within the community. Although it may be true, for example, that Type A operators were more inclined to target black and Asian people rather than whites, this unwarranted surveillance rarely, if ever, resulted in any form of immediate police intervention. This does not, of course, mean that such surveillance is acceptable. Even if individuals do not have a recognizable right to privacy in public spaces, it is widely accepted that they should be free from unwarranted and unnecessary scrutiny.[15] Therefore, while CCTV targeting of blacks and Asians may not lead to more police interventions, arrests, convictions, and so on, black and Asian people are none the less more likely to be subjected to gratuitous surveillance.

Furthermore, notwithstanding the disproportionate targeting of minorities, the fact that public area surveillance is being carried out at all is in and of itself significant. As Garland and other social theorists have argued, the spread of surveillance technologies like CCTV is indicative of a larger 'neo-liberal' strategy that has shifted responsibility for the management of risk and public insecurity away from the state to local agencies such as regional police forces and town councils.[16] In this sense, the question of whether CCTV targeting translates directly into police responses is beside the point. The mere fact that the police and local authorities have become involved in such surveillance activities speaks to an important change in the way in which governments and the public have come to think about crime and the problem of crime control.

Given that the police rarely respond to the calls of camera operators, however, what then is the impact of CCTV on policing? If

---

[15] For a discussion of privacy rights in public spaces, see von Hirsch (2000); Feldman (1997); and Goold (2002b).

[16] See D. Garland (1996) 'The limits of the sovereign state: strategies of crime control in contemporary society' British Journal of Criminology 36: 4; and A. Barry, T. Osbourne, and N. Rose (1996) Foucault and Political Reason: Liberalism, Neo-liberalism and Rationalities of Government (London: UCL Press).

levels of deployment are not significantly affected by the presence of cameras—irrespective of who is behind them—are police officers and policing practices affected in other ways? To answer these questions, we must now turn our attention from the CCTV operators to the police themselves.

7

The Effect of CCTV on Policing

One of the most important questions raised by the advent of CCTV is whether the spread of public area surveillance in Britain has brought about any significant changes in the way in which towns and city centres are policed. As both supporters and opponents of CCTV have argued, closed circuit cameras have the potential to transform not only how the police patrol the streets and gather evidence, but also how the police see themselves and, perhaps more importantly, how they see the public.[1] If it is true that the emergence of public area CCTV is indicative of a move towards new forms of policing, to what extent has this shift been reflected in current police practices? This chapter examines the impact of CCTV on a variety of police activities and aspects of police organization, and considers whether the introduction of CCTV technology has led the police to re-evaluate their role and their relationship with the public.[2]

7.1 CCTV and beat policing

Central to the policing of most towns and cities in Britain is the police beat. All uniformed officers spend at least the first two years of service 'on the beat', and in the minds of the vast majority of police officers it remains one of the most important activities undertaken by the police.[3] Not only does beat policing provide a steady

---

[1] See e.g. K. S. Williams and C. Johnstone (2000) 'The politics of the selective gaze: closed circuit television and the policing of public space' *Crime, Law and Social Change* 34(2): 183.

[2] Sections of this chapter are taken from B. J. Goold (2003) 'Public area surveillance and policing: the impact of CCTV on police behaviour and autonomy' *Journal of Surveillance and Society* 2(1): 191. The author is grateful to the editors for their permission to reproduce this material.

[3] For a discussion of the importance to the police of the 'beat', see C. Emsley (1996) *The English Police* (Harrow: Longman), 225–337. See also more generally

source of information about crime within a town or city, many within the police also believe that putting officers on the streets can help to deter potential offenders, build public confidence, and reduce overall levels of crime and public disorder. As a consequence, and in spite of falling police numbers and mounting resource pressures, police forces in Britain remain committed to this style of policing.

According to a number of the senior officers interviewed in the course of this study, one of the major reasons why the Southern Region Police decided to support the use of CCTV was because it was felt that the introduction of cameras would help to improve the efficiency of existing police beats. Although there was no suggestion that cameras would eventually lead to the removal of officers from the streets, there was nevertheless a hope that CCTV would enable the police to devote more resources to the patrolling of housing estates and problem areas outside towns such as P2, P3, C2, and C3. As one senior officer noted, the idea was that cameras would free up resources by making local patrols less tied to the town centre proper and therefore more flexible:

In theory, I would like to think that if you're going to put a dozen cameras in a town centre, then you can take . . . not take away the police officers, but you can restructure your policing of that town centre so that the officers no longer need to be concentrated in the town centre, but on the outskirts of the town centre or housing estates or industrial estates or whatever else is around. Because for the majority of the time, while the officer is patrolling the town centre he or she is doing no more than observing. If you can have a camera doing those aspects of your policing and your patrol work, then you could be doing something else. (Chief Inspector A, Police Headquarters)

The same officer was forced to admit, however, that after almost five years of CCTV in the Southern Region there was little to suggest that any change had occurred in either the organization of town centre beats or the daily practices of town centre officers. In towns such as P1, P2, and P3, where police-led CCTV schemes were in operation and there was regular, informal contact between police officers and CCTV operators, there was no evidence that shift sergeants or local inspectors had attempted to integrate the scheme

Holdaway (1983); and M. Brogden, T. Jefferson, and S. Walklate (1988) *Introducing Policework* (London: Unwin).

into the town's overall policing strategy. Where records of local and town centre beats had been kept by the police, they showed that there had been no change in patrol patterns since the introduction of CCTV. Officers continued to walk the same beats as before, despite the fact that they were in constant radio contact with CCTV operators, who were frequently watching the very same streets on their monitors back in the station. Although a number of police constables claimed that the presence of the cameras meant that they could now leave the town centre and be confident that 'someone was watching over things', in practice this did not translate into any formal or even informal policy of extending existing beats to outlying areas as had been originally envisioned.

There are a number of possible reasons why the introduction of CCTV appears to have had little impact on the practice of beat policing. To begin with, the failure of management to provide local inspectors or shift sergeants with any form of guidance regarding the use of CCTV appears to have been a decisive factor. As one senior officer acknowledged, the reason why the organization of local beats had remained unchanged was because PCs and town centre officers had little idea of how to make best use of the cameras, or how to integrate them into existing policing strategies: 'What we're not doing is telling them to use the cameras to their advantage... And if your next question is why aren't we doing it, then the answer is that although we're putting some effort into training managers, we're not putting effort into educating the police officers' (Chief Inspector A, Police Headquarters).

In part, this lack of education appeared to be a result of pressures on training resources within the force. As other senior officers later admitted, legislation like the Crime and Disorder Act 1998 had led to a shift in police training priorities, away from traditional concerns such as patrol practices and town centre policing, and instead towards issues relating to restorative justice and the development of local partnerships. There is a certain irony to this. While officers were given training on how best to work with local authorities under the requirements of the new Act, very few, if any, received instruction on how to integrate the use of closed circuit television into local policing strategies. This was despite the fact that in four of the towns included in the study—towns P1, P2, P3, and C2—the town centre CCTV scheme represented the largest joint project between the police and the local authority. As a local intelligence officer in Town P2 observed wryly, the police were so concerned with forming new partnership arrangements that they appeared to 'have forgotten about their old ones', including CCTV.

Looking beyond issues relating to training and the education of individual officers, concerns about the impact of changes in patrol practices on public opinion may also help to explain why local beats have remained relatively unaffected by the introduction of CCTV. One of the primary reasons why the police have continued with the practice of beat policing is because many officers—at both the management and the operational level—feel that putting officers on the streets is essential to the maintenance of good relations with the public.[4] As a consequence, although reorganizing existing police beats to include industrial estates and shopping centres not covered by CCTV may help to reduce the overall level of crime in a given area, the question remains as to whether the majority of the public would support such a change. As one shift sergeant in station P2 observed, the police were not only committed to reducing crime but also to making the general public feel safe, and while the presence of cameras might make beat policing less relevant to the maintenance of order, it was not clear that the public viewed cameras as a substitute for having officers out on the street.[5] According to this officer, until such time as the public (and, for that matter, the police themselves), come to accept cameras as a partial alternative to foot patrols, it is unlikely that organization of beats in towns like P2 will be changed.

Finally, as a number of senior officers pointed out throughout the course of the research, there was also 'cultural resistance' within the lower police ranks to changing existing police patrol strategies in order to accommodate and take advantage of CCTV. According to one chief inspector, regardless of whether there are CCTV cameras or not, officers will still want to be in the town centre, playing an active part in keeping the peace and making arrests:

In my view, the policing strategies of town and city centres that have had CCTV installed should change, but the point is that they haven't. In other

---

[4] S. Holdaway (ed.) (1979) *The British Police* (London: Arnold); and Brogden *et al.* (1988).

[5] On the question of public attitudes to CCTV see Ditton (1998); and J. Ditton and E. Short (1999) 'Yes, it works, no, it doesn't: comparing the effects of open-street CCTV in two adjacent Scottish town centres' in Painter and Tilley (1999*b*), 201.

words, [Towns P1, P2, and P3] and anywhere else that's got closed circuit television are, I suspect, being policed in very much the same way now as they were five or ten years ago. Particularly on Friday and Saturday nights, because then you have major cultural barriers to break down within the force...The young officers will still want to be in that town centre on a Friday and a Saturday, wanting to make arrests and thinking that they're being judged on the number of prisoners they've brought in. (Chief Inspector A, Police Headquarters)

It should come as no surprise that existing patrol practices and widely held beliefs amongst officers can have a significant effect on how individuals and the force as a whole respond to and use technologies like CCTV. Indeed, Manning has argued that it is essential to take factors such as cultural resistance into account when attempting to predict how police officers will adapt to technology: '[T]he vague notion that available, even conventionally acceptable technology will be used and employed without constraint of police practices and local political traditions is untenable'.[6]

Although commentators like Reiner are right to acknowledge that police culture is not 'monolithic, universal or unchanging', traditionally the police have been extremely conservative, both in their approach to the task of street policing and in their willingness to embrace new technology.[7] It is therefore no surprise that the police have been hesitant to change existing beat practices to accommodate CCTV, particularly given the perception that such change might result in fewer officers on the streets. While some politicians and advocates of CCTV may see town centre cameras as an alternative to increasing police numbers, it was clear from the current study that few serving officers regarded cameras as the equivalent of 'having a police officer on every corner'.

---

[6] P. Manning (2000) 'Information technologies and the police' in P. Gill (ed.) *Rounding up the Usual Suspects? Developments in Contemporary Law Enforcement Intelligence* (Aldershot: Ashgate), 391.

[7] R. Reiner (1992c) *The Politics of the Police*, 2nd edn. (Hemel Hempstead: Harvester Wheatsheaf), 109. On the subject of police conservatism, see: J. Skolnick (1966) *Justice without Trial* (New York: Wiley); J. Skolnick and D. H. Bayley (1986) *The New Blue Line* (New York: Free Press); R. Reiner (1978) *The Blue Coated Worker* (Cambridge: Cambridge University Press); and R. Reiner (1991) *Chief Constables* (Oxford: Oxford University Press).

7.2 CCTV and resource management

Although the introduction of CCTV appears to have had little or no effect on the way in which local beats are organized, it would be wrong to assume that police resource management has not been affected by the presence of closed circuit cameras. Of the 55 police officers interviewed in the course of the field research, more than two-thirds felt that CCTV had affected the way in which they responded to incidents within their town centres. Officers working in conjunction with police-led schemes were particularly adamant that CCTV cameras had improved response times and had made police resourcing more efficient, in part because PCs and police control room staff were able to determine how serious an incident was before making a decision about the number of officers or cars to send. As one shift sergeant noted,

If we get a shout that there is a fight in the High Street, we will radio through to the [CCTV] operator—'How many people are involved? Are there any weapons involved?'—and that will give us an initial understanding of what we're going to deal with. If there are fifteen, twenty people involved in a fight and there's weapons, then we're not going to send a single crew car... (Police Sergeant B, Scheme P2)

Indeed, as the same sergeant later went on to observe, knowing that the cameras are watching and collecting evidence while a public disturbance is in progress may, from the point of view of the police at least, eliminate the need to send officers into a potentially dangerous or life-threatening situation:

If there are weapons involved and the fight looks like it is too big for the amount of police horses we've got at the moment, we will not go to it. The CCTV camera can do its job, it can record the offenders, it can record the incident, for a future sweeping-up, if you like, of all the people who have been involved and have committed crime. (Police Sergeant B, Scheme P2)

Certainly, a number of incidents observed in the course of the fieldwork suggested that the police control rooms have indeed begun to use CCTV to help reduce the danger to officers on the street. As the following two extracts show, one of the key ways in which this is accomplished is by providing officers with detailed information about the nature of the disturbance and—where there is a possibility of violence—prior knowledge of which individuals are particularly dangerous:

FIELD-NOTE EXTRACT: SCHEME P1 (N1/5/11.34 p.m.). Operator M re-ceives a call from the police control room asking for camera coverage of the door of a local nightclub. According to the message from control, a fight has broken out inside the club and the police have been called by security to help them remove those involved. By the time the operator manages to find the nightclub with the cameras, however, the disturbance has already spilled out onto the street and a number of separate fights have broken out. Zooming out to get a better picture of what is going on, the operator manages to take in the entire scene and then radios the police control room to ask whether they have a good enough picture of the situation on their monitor. Police control respond, asking the operator to hold the current view, and then they begin to relay information to PCs on the ground via the police radio. Three main protagonists—all of whom are still fighting—are identified by the police control room and their descriptions sent out over the radio. Approximately one minute later a police car arrives carrying two PCs, who stay in the car until they are joined by two more officers on foot thirty seconds later. One of the officers then confirms the description of the offenders and then the four officers step into the fight, immediately locate the three identified 'troublemakers', and restrain them before escorting them back to the patrol car. The other participants in the fight are largely ignored, and within a minute the fight has petered out. In all, the interven-tion has taken less than a minute and is accomplished with little difficulty. The operator continues to cover the officers while they put the offenders into the police car and then drive away.

FIELD-NOTE EXTRACT: SCHEME P3 (N1/31/2.13 a.m.). Operator A spots two young white men running through the town centre. After about ten seconds they stop and begin fighting, before being joined by three more men who immediately start a separate fight alongside. The operator informs the police control room of the fight via the police radio, passing on a detailed description of the individuals and their location. Units are deployed and within about two minutes a police car arrives on the scene. From the car, one of the PCs asks for permission from the police control room to speak directly with the CCTV operator, which is granted. The officer then asks the operator 'who started it' and whether she has seen any weapons such as knives or bottles. The operator replies, giving descriptions of the first two men before explaining that she hadn't seen any weapons since the fight started. The two PCs then get out of the car, approach the five men and restrain the original pair. With this, the other three men stop fighting and turn towards the officers to watch what is going on. The first two men are put in the car, and then one of the officers begins speaking to the men still on the street. By this point things have calmed and another car has arrived. The operator continues watching, until a call over the radio from one of the officers on the ground comes in, thanking her for 'making life a lot easier.'

Less dramatically, officers also suggested during interviews that cameras had helped improve resource management by substantially reducing the amount of time wasted attending hoax calls. In many cases, reports of fights or disturbances in the town centre could now be confirmed by CCTV operators before officers were sent to investigate, and when prank calls were made repeatedly from telephone boxes in the town centre, CCTV surveillance could be used to help identify and apprehend the culprits. As a number of PCs observed, CCTV had improved resource use by making them less reliant on the public for information about what was going on in the town centre, and better placed to decide whether a report or complaint required an immediate response. This was a point that was echoed by nearly all of the police control room staff interviewed, irrespective of whether they were working in conjunction with a police-led or local authority-led CCTV scheme. According to one control room sergeant, one of the major advantages of CCTV was that it enabled police control—via their own slave CCTV monitors—to assess a given problem in the town centre before deciding how best to deal with it and what sorts of resources were required:

I think it's eased our job in the control room a lot, because if something is happening in the town we can visualize it properly, as opposed to relying on information coming to us from another source. We've sidestepped that, and I suppose it eases the stress because instead of hearing things happening in the background, and trying to get resources to deal with incidents etc., we can now actually see it for ourselves and control it ourselves. So I suppose the bottom line is that we can take control of incidents in the town centre instead of relying on other people to give us information. (Control Room Sergeant A, Scheme P3)

Although most of the police officers interviewed in the course of the study felt that the CCTV had improved resource management within their local town centre, it is difficult to test whether response times had in fact fallen as a result of the introduction of closed circuit cameras or, even more problematically, whether resource allocations had become more efficient. The police do not keep accurate or extensive records on response times or the number of officers dispatched to a given incident, and while many senior officers made claims about the beneficial impact of CCTV on police resource management, all of them acknowledged that the evidence they were forced to rely upon was largely anecdotal. What is clear, however, is that regardless of the type of CCTV scheme in operation, most police officers *believed* that the introduction of CCTV had made them more efficient. Where differences in opinion between officers did arise, they tended to focus not on whether gains had been made, but rather on their extent. Officers working in conjunction with Type C schemes were, for example, less enthusiastic when talking about response times than their Type P counterparts, despite the fact that both groups agreed that these times had improved since the introduction of the cameras. This difference may in part be explained by the fact that none of the operators at Type C schemes had a direct radio link to their local police control room, and instead they had to rely on 'phoning in' incidents picked up by the cameras. In addition, poor communication and strained relations between individual operators and the police—a common problem in Type C schemes—may also have blunted the impact of the cameras on police response times, both by making operators less confident about calling in incidents and by making the police less receptive to information coming from the CCTV control room.

Aside from making claims about the beneficial impact of CCTV on police response times, many officers also maintained that police resource management had also been affected by the introduction of CCTV cameras in other ways. Nearly all of the PCs and middle-ranking officers interviewed in the course of the study were convinced that public area CCTV had placed additional pressure on police resources, primarily because it helped to bring more 'jobs' to their attention:

The problem is that as a result of CCTV we are now responding to things that we wouldn't have responded to before. You know, if there was a punch-up up in the town and there was no complaint, and it wasn't seen by a policeman, then it wouldn't be any great thing. But if the CCTV operator sees it and quite rightly calls it up as a fight in progress, then the police will attend. And that has implications for our resources. But I think its value as a deterrent far outweighs its problems as far as giving us too many things we can't commit ourselves to. (Police Inspector F, Scheme P2)

Obviously CCTV hasn't decreased our workload. In some respects, you could say it's actually increased the amount of work because the cameras are spotting things, spotting offences that wouldn't normally be picked up by the police. Obviously that's a good thing though, because anything that increases our workload like that means crime is being detected, which is our primary role. (PC 5, Scheme P3)

As discussed in the previous chapter, there was in fact no evidence to suggest that the number of police deployments had increased as a result of the introduction of CCTV, regardless of whether the scheme in place was police- or local authority-led. CCTV operators rarely called the police control room or officers on the street, and, when they did, police deployment was not an automatic result.[8] This being the case, it is difficult to say why many police officers felt that the introduction of CCTV had led to increased resource pressures and 'more jobs'. One possible answer is that many officers had exaggerated the impact of CCTV in interviews and informal conversations, choosing to explain problems arising from a general shortage of resources by reference to the introduction of cameras. Alternatively, it is possible that the additional work pressures complained of by PCs were not a consequence of the introduction of CCTV, but rather a result of other local changes that had resulted in increased demands being placed upon the police. According to one senior officer, for example, overall levels of police activity in towns such as P2, P3, and C2 had been rising steadily for some years, mostly as a result of a growth in the number of licences being granted to new pubs and nightclubs in these areas:

The increased workload may or may not be attributable to CCTV. Yes, officers are drawn into the town centre to respond to incidents, but is it because of CCTV or is it because of the fact that so many more nightclubs have opened up? Although it might be true that the cameras are drawing more things to your attention, equally you can be made aware of incidents in the town by the nightclubs themselves phoning you, or people walking by seeing a fight and calling you in. So although there is more pressure on police resources in the town centre, while some of it might be due to CCTV picking more things up, I suspect that quite a lot of it is actually due to the change of the environment and the growing number of nightclubs ... There is a push for a 24-hour economy—shopping in the day and entertainment in the evening—and as the nightclub scene expands in places like Town P3, it takes up more and more of our time. (Police Inspector G, Scheme P3)

Irrespective of whether the level of police activity in those towns studied had increased as a result of the introduction of CCTV cameras or other factors, what is clear is that the majority of officers interviewed believed that the presence of CCTV had created extra work for them and their colleagues. Accordingly, while officers

[8] See Ch. 6, Sect. 6.3.

were keen to point out that CCTV had become an 'essential tool', most had come to regard the cameras as a mixed blessing. As one PC working in Town P1 noted ruefully, although CCTV may have improved response times and some aspects of police resource management, neither he nor any of the other officers on his shift had noticed any change in their workloads; in fact, if anything CCTV had simply made them more aware of what they were 'missing' and how much more needed to be done.

7.3   Police safety

In addition to improving certain aspects of police resource management, the introduction of cameras also appears to have had a positive impact on perceptions of police safety in all of the towns included in the study. Without exception, all of the officers interviewed—regardless of rank or whether they were working in association with a Type P or Type C CCTV scheme—were convinced that the presence of CCTV cameras had dramatically improved levels of police safety and had reduced the incidence of assaults on police officers. Although some officers believed that this change could be attributed to some kind of deterrent effect—for example, suspects were less likely to attack officers or resist arrest if they knew they were being watched by CCTV—the vast majority sought to explain the alleged change in terms of improvements in communication and response planning. As one officer at Scheme P1 noted, having CCTV cameras in and around the town centre means that the police control room is able to monitor disturbances and assess whether backup is required without the need for constant 'radio updates', leaving the officers involved free to concentrate entirely on the actual incidents themselves. This is a point that was also made by a control room sergeant at Scheme P3:

If the patrol officers are in the town centre by themselves and respond to a violent incident, they have the assurance of knowing that we can actually see them. Before the cameras came in, we would have to rely on being given an update on their welfare via third parties, because very often units going to a job like that have to concentrate on what's happening in front of them and can't keep updating the control room in terms of what's happened to them. Now we can actually see them, and it has happened that on a couple of occasions at least, probably seven or eight, that we've actually put up an assistance shout for officers based on what we've seen from the camera.

Sometimes when officers are in danger, we may only hear a partial transmission or we may not catch the call sign or the location, and suddenly we've got to look all over the place to see what's happening. At least now as regards the town centre, which always has the potential for being the worst area in that respect, we can see what is happening to the officers and almost anticipate problems. (Control Room Sergeant A, P3)

Although this study did not examine whether the introduction of CCTV had in fact reduced the number of assaults on police officers or the number of injuries sustained by police officers in the line of duty, it was clear that the presence of CCTV had made officers *feel* safer.[9] Even those officers who had previously expressed doubts about the competency of their local CCTV operators or the effectiveness of the technology appeared to be absolutely convinced that having CCTV made them less vulnerable on the streets and had improved overall levels of officer safety.

7.4   Policing the police

Traditionally, one of the key features of street-level policing has been the degree of autonomy enjoyed by individual officers. Although in principle the powers employed by the police—such as stop-and-search and the power of arrest—are regulated by law and subject to various forms of review, in practice decisions made at street level are rarely, if ever, directly supervised or exposed to external criticism.[10] Unlike in many other forms of organization, in the police service personal discretion increases as one moves down the hierarchy, with the effect that officers on the street exercise considerable power over the public. Van Maanen has noted that

because police tasks at the lower level are ill-defined, episodic, non-routine, accomplished in the regions of low visibility, and are dispatched in ways that most often bypass the formal chain of command in the organisation, control over the work resides largely in the hands of those who perform the work. In this sense, police agencies resemble symbolic or mock bureauc-

---

[9] Accurate data on assaults against police officers was not available for each of the towns included in the study, and as a result it was impossible to determine whether the number of attacks or attempted assaults on officers in those areas covered by cameras had fallen as a result of the introduction of CCTV.

[10] J. Q. Wilson (1968) *Varieties of Police Behavior* (Cambridge, Mass.: Harvard University Press), 17.

racies where only the appearance of control, not the reality, is of central concern.[11]

As Holdaway and others have argued, historically the police have been keen to maintain this autonomy, either by ensuring that decision-making continues to be low visibility, or by resisting the efforts of government and others to impose restrictions on the exercise of officer discretion.[12] As researchers discovered in the years following the introduction of the Police and Criminal Evidence Act (PACE), the police are extremely adept at circumventing rules that attempt to limit their powers or constrain their discretion.[13] With the introduction of public area CCTV, however, many police officers now find themselves faced with the prospect of being watched and possibly recorded as they go about their daily routine on the streets.[14] How this change affects the exercise of police discretion and the way the police respond to incidents in view of the cameras was one of the key concerns of this project.[15]

[11] J. van Maanen (1983) 'The boss: first-line supervision in an American police agency' in M. Punch (ed.) *Control in the Police Organization* (Cambridge, Mass.: MIT Press), 277. See also J. Goldstein (1960) 'Police discretion not to invoke the criminal process: low visibility decisions in the administration of justice' *Yale Law Journal* 63: 543; P. Manning (1977) *Police Work: The Social Organization of Policing* (Cambridge, Mass.: MIT Press), and McConville *et al.* (1991), 18. According to Shapland and Vagg, most beat officers only see a supervising officer once a day, and not because they are necessarily required to do so but typically because they are in need of advice: J. Shapland and J. Vagg (1980) *Policing by the Public* (London: Routledge).

[12] Holdaway (1979). See also Holdaway (1983) and Choongh (1997).

[13] According to McConville *et al.*, 'As a general rule, conformity with the detailed substantive and procedural rules is not an important consideration for police officers in respect of most of their powers. Thus, powers of stop-and-search do not standardly inform police decision-making but rather rationalise behaviour undertaken for other reasons.' See McConville *et al.* (1991), 183. See also Sanders and Young (2000), 90.

[14] On the question of how the introduction of CCTV cameras inside police stations may affect police behaviour, see Newburn and Hayman (2002).

[15] The idea that police are subject to surveillance from their own devices is, of course, nothing new. As Ericson and Haggerty point out, 'the very communication formats and technologies police officers use to conduct surveillance of others are also used for surveillance of their own work' Ericson and Haggerty (1997), 35. Indeed, Manning goes further to suggest that far from being autonomous agents, the police are in fact dominated by the very machines that serve them: 'They are servants of the public in name only, for although the public pays them, they work for the machines that lurk behind them, glow in front of them, click and buzz in their ears and fill the

During the course of the research, police officers at each of the six schemes were asked whether they believed that the introduction of cameras had affected how they or their colleagues behaved on patrol or responded to incidents within the town centre. Typically, officers *initially* responded by stating that the presence of CCTV had not had any impact on the way in which they carried out their duties or exercised their powers. Comments such as 'I don't really notice the cameras' and 'You don't really think about being recorded until afterwards' were common, as were statements such as the following:

Being watched by the cameras doesn't bother me in the slightest. And it shouldn't—it shouldn't bother anyone because your job shouldn't change because the cameras are there. You should be doing it by the book wherever you go, whether the cameras are watching you or not. So to that end, no, it doesn't affect me at all... Sometimes you might go away thinking, 'Was that excessive?' And then you look at the cameras, and nine times out of ten, no, it's not. I did everything fine then. (PC 2, Scheme P1)

At the end of the day, we've just got to make sure what we do is by the letter of the law and according to our own guidelines and procedures. And as long as police officers aren't doing anything wrong, it's the same for them as for the public: they have nothing to worry about. (PC 3, Scheme P1)

The cameras certainly don't affect the way that I deal with things. I'm not thinking as I'm going to an incident, 'Oh, I've got to be careful because CCTV is there'. I mean, you deal with an incident as you find it. (PC 1, Scheme C2)

When pressed further on the issue of how CCTV had affected their behaviour on the streets, however, over two-thirds of the officers interviewed conceded that the introduction of cameras had forced them to be 'more careful' when out on patrol. Some, for example, had heard stories of officers being prosecuted for unlawful arrest or assault on the basis of CCTV evidence—stories that had left them anxious about being watched and the possibility of their own activities being scrutinized. Others, particularly younger officers, found that being under constant surveillance made them nervous and uncomfortable. Irrespective of the reason

air with dull electronic sounds' P. Manning (1988) *Symbolic Communication: Signifying Calls and the Police Response* (Cambridge, Mass.: MIT Press), 155.

for their concern, many of these officers had come to the conclusion that the introduction of CCTV made it essential for them to 'go by the book', or at least to create the appearance of doing so. One officer at Scheme P1 confessed:

It affects our thinking of things a lot because obviously the cameras are there to identify possible crime about to happen, or even people who are actually committing crimes at the time. But having said that, it also records police actions. Therefore when you arrive at an incident, you've got to be aware of the fact that the cameras are watching you. We are being recorded, the same as anybody else. Therefore what we do has to be right, it has to *look* right. Therefore it makes it quite a priority for most officers entering the town centre—they're thinking, 'I'm on camera'. (PC 3, Scheme P1)

In a similar vein, after some reflection, another officer at Scheme P1 also admitted that the introduction of cameras had affected the thinking of officers at the station, particularly those who in his opinion needed to improve their attitude and approach to policing the town centre:

I think CCTV is good for everybody. It can't *not* be. I mean, the only negative thing I can think of is if perhaps officers were not doing what they should be doing when they're arresting people and speaking to people, but then those people shouldn't be doing the job, in my opinion. So, if the cameras are forcing them to perhaps think about the way they're policing and think about doing it properly, then I think it's a good thing. (PC 4, Scheme P1)

In the course of informal conversations with police officers at Schemes P1 and P2, it also became clear that many officers working at these stations had been 'warned' by their shift sergeants and local inspectors to remember that they were being watched by the cameras, and to be particularly aware of CCTV whenever they attended an incident in the town centre. In a small number of cases, officers had received more specific advice, namely about making sure that when they effected an arrest they did so in view of the cameras, in part for the purposes of evidence but more importantly to protect themselves against complaints of unlawful arrest. According to one shift sergeant at Scheme P2, it was essential for officers to make use of the cameras and to incorporate them in their day-to-day thinking when working the town centre 'for their own sake as well as for the sake of the community'. As a consequence, during shift briefings he made a point of reminding officers of CCTV and suggesting ways in which they could turn it to their advantage, such as making sure that the camera operators were actually watching and recording an incident *before* the police arrived, so that if trouble developed the tape would help to put the actions of the police in their 'proper' context.

The opinion that care needed to be taken with CCTV to ensure that police actions were not 'misinterpreted' was one that was frequently expressed by officers of all ranks during the course of the study. Although the majority of officers interviewed initially claimed to be unconcerned or unaffected by the presence of CCTV cameras, over time it became apparent that many harboured private concerns about the possibility of their actions being exposed to external scrutiny. According to a number of PCs at Scheme P2, for example, officers around the station had become increasingly worried about the prospect of CCTV evidence being used 'against police officers', particularly in relation to the investigations of complaints by the Police Complaints Authority. In part, these apprehensions may have been sparked by concern over a complaint made about a local officer that eventually led to his suspension for unlawful arrest. Central to the complaint was CCTV footage taken by local cameras, which showed the officer effecting an arrest with his baton. According to the officer concerned—who had returned to the station but had been taken off town centre patrol duty—part of the 'problem' in his case was that the tape only told part of the story:

An incident started up in one of the local nightclubs and spilled out violently onto the street. At some point, I had to use my baton on someone. I felt at the time that I had used it just as we had practised, but that incident went to court, and the magistrates viewed the videotape from the CCTV cameras. I believe that because they didn't understand the techniques they saw, they misunderstood the amount of force that had been used . . . (PC 3, Scheme P2)

Circumspect about his suspension and its effect on his career, the officer claimed that the incident had forced him to reconsider his previous opinion of CCTV and its use by the police. In particular, he argued that his own experience had made him acutely aware of how misleading camera footage could be, and of the need for police officers, lawyers, and the courts to become wary of relying solely on CCTV evidence:

The essential problem with the CCTV is that it cannot capture the perception of the people or of the officers who are actually experiencing the situation. If you see two people fighting and it gets caught on the video, it doesn't tell you the background to it, it doesn't necessarily tell you what happened immediately before, and sometimes it doesn't tell what happened during or immediately after. I think that is one of the main downfalls of CCTV. This idea that many people see it as a panacea, of evidence, when really and truly it has got some quite severe difficulties. (PC 3, Scheme P2)

Going further, he also stressed that part of the problem arose from the fact that unless magistrates and prosecutors understood police techniques, it was likely that the number of successful but unfounded complaints based on CCTV evidence of arrests would eventually begin to rise:

People that are involved in the criminal justice system who get to see CCTV evidence have to be given some advice on the police techniques that they may see on CCTV. Because there are no two ways about it. Some police techniques, some of the restraints we use, do look violent. But that's only because they haven't seen the technique being trained or seen the officers being trained in it. (PC 3, Scheme P2)

During the weeks spent at Scheme P2, it became clear that the experiences of this officer had become well known around the local police station, and had led other PCs and more senior officers to reconsider their own opinions about CCTV. Although in conversation the majority of PCs played down the incident and described it as either 'unfortunate' or a 'one-off', according to one officer the affair had affected thinking on his shift and the way officers approached potentially difficult situations:

I think they are a lot more cautious about being hands-on, and certainly a lot more cautious with the use of force. And that tends, in my personal view, to go against the training we are told to use, and has the potential to make officers more vulnerable. My personal feeling is that there will come an occasion, it might not happen now and it might not happen tomorrow, but sometime an officer will get a severe beating or even worse as a result of possibly being over-cautious. (PC 4, Scheme P2)

This suggestion that the introduction of cameras had made some police officers less willing to use force on the streets was echoed by several operators during the course of the study. At Schemes P1, P2, and C3, for example, operators complained on numerous occasions about what they saw as the reluctance of officers to step in and end fights that had been detected by the cameras. One operator at Scheme C3 became particularly incensed when describing an incident where, after being called to a fight outside a nightclub, two patrol officers remained in their car observing the fight for almost ten minutes before finally deciding to attempt to arrest the main protagonists. It is difficult to know, however, whether this reluctance on the part of the officers stemmed from a fear of being 'caught on camera' and possible exposure to complaints about the use of force, or whether it simply represented a healthy concern for their own safety.

In any event, during the course of the research it became increasingly clear that officers at all of the towns were worried about the possibility of camera footage being used in support of complaints against them or their colleagues. Notwithstanding the suspension of the officer at Town P2, however, the introduction of CCTV into the Southern Region had not actually led to an increase in the number of complaints against the police.[16] An examination of the tape logs at each of the six schemes revealed only two instances of tapes being removed in connection with complaints against the police. In addition, statements made by a handful of senior officers suggested that when CCTV footage was examined in response to a complaint against a police officer, the result was most likely the dropping of the complaint altogether. According to one inspector at Town P2, for example, the presence of CCTV had led to a *reduction* in the number of formal complaints being made against his officers:

I deal with complaints as an inspector, and quite often you have people come in and complain. Then you'll go and look at the video, and quite often they actually back up the officer's side of things because lots of these things are night-time type confrontations, and people's memories of them are clouded by alcohol . . . (Police Inspector C, Scheme P1)

Given that it was rare for complaints to be made or upheld on the basis of CCTV evidence, why were officers in the Southern Region concerned about the possibility of video footage being used against them? In part, their concern may have stemmed from an awareness of the fact that—at a national level at least—CCTV footage is being

---

[16] Although the overall number of complaints had risen marginally during the period immediately following the introduction of cameras, nearly all of this rise could be attributed to a change in Force policy regarding the distinction drawn between formal and informal complaints.

used increasingly by the Police Complaints Authority (PCA) in England to investigate complaints against police officers.[17] In an article published by *The Sunday Times*, for example, it was reported that during 1999 alone CCTV footage was used in nearly 300 successful complaints against police officers, and that more recent figures suggest that this number is rising.[18] As Richard Offer, spokesperson for the PCA, observed when being interviewed for the article, CCTV can not only be used to protect the public from crime and criminals, but also from the police: 'It has been used to tackle crime, but one side-effect has been that it makes it much easier to deal with police complaints... It is giving citizens protection against errant officers, and officers protection on malicious complaints. It's certainly a valuable tool.'[19]

The concern expressed by officers during the course of the study may, therefore, have had less to do with how CCTV was actually being used to investigate complaints in the Region, and more to do with a fear about how CCTV might be used against them in the future. Whatever the reason, however, officers reported that this concern had translated into more circumspect behaviour on the part of many PCs, particularly when it came to using force or making arrests within view of the cameras. In this regard, it is interesting to note how closely public area surveillance has come to resemble Jeremy Bentham's original idea of the Panopticon. Although in the wake of Foucault's *Discipline and Punish* there has been a tendency for criminologists and sociologists to examine surveillance technologies such as CCTV in terms of social control, it is important to remember that, for Bentham, one of the great virtues of his

---

[17] The PCA is an independent body set up by the government to oversee public complaints against police officers in the 43 police services in England and Wales, as well as officers exercising a police function with British Transport, the Ministry of Defence, the Port of Liverpool, the Port of Tilbury, the Royal Parks, and UKAEA (United Kingdom Atomic Energy Authority) police. The PCA can investigate complaints made by members of the public or complaints referred directly by police services. Note that in 1998–9, the PCA considered the detailed evidence in 4,134 fully investigated cases, with the result that police officers were charged with a total of 333 disciplinary offences. This compared with 237 charges in 1997–8.

[18] *The Sunday Times*, 'Street cameras turn tables on police behaving badly' (13 Aug. 2000), 5.

[19] ibid. See also The *Independent*, 'Thousands of new cameras filming streets' (18 Jan. 2000).

panoptic prison was that it exposed prison guards as well as prisoners to outside scrutiny. As Janet Semple observes:

The final application of the inspection principle was of the whole of the prison by the whole of the outside world. The central tower would enable judges and magistrates to inspect the prison quickly and safely...The design of the building would also enable any member of the public to enter the prison and to view every prisoner in it.[20]

In helping to bring about the 'panopticonization' of streets and town centres, public area CCTV has the potential to transform the way in which the police, as well as the general population, see and use public spaces. Indeed, as Richard Ericson and Kevin Haggerty have observed, 'coincident with the surveillance of suspect citizens is the surveillance of the police as a suspect population...surveillance that arises out of distrust that is endemic in risk society'.[21] This being the case, it is important to ask whether the presence of CCTV led officers to alter their behaviour in other, less positive ways than those already discussed.

7.5   Staying out of sight

Having already noted that the police have traditionally been extremely keen to protect their autonomy on the streets, it is important to examine whether the introduction of cameras produced any form of 'protective response' from officers in the towns included in this research study. Certainly, previous studies of the police have shown that officers will attempt to circumvent external supervision or surveillance wherever possible, either to disguise specific incidents or to maintain an environment of low visibility in which the unfettered exercise of police discretion can take place. As a case in point, Ericson and Haggerty found that Canadian police officers go to considerable lengths to avoid being the subjects of video surveillance:

Like other police technologies, video cameras are potentially able to trace police officer activity. However, we found that there were a number of ways in which this capacity was circumvented. For example, officers might

---

[20] J. Semple (1993) *Bentham's Prison: A Study of the Panoptic Penitentiary* (Oxford: Clarendon Press), 142.
[21] Ericson and Haggerty (1997), 56.

position the camera in a way which would produce a recording fashioned to induce the viewer to empathize with the officers rather than the suspect. As one officer declared, 'I'm not a great lover of Rodney King or anything, but it will be nice to show our side of things for a change.'[22]

Turning to the more specific case of public area CCTV, Norris and Armstrong reported that, at one of the CCTV schemes included in their study, operators were occasionally given a signal by police officers—typically by raising their arm and waving their hand—to move the cameras away from a potentially sensitive or embarrassing incident. In one case, for example, four town centre officers were 'caught' by the cameras standing in a group talking when they should have been on patrol, the result being a signal to the CCTV operator to move the cameras away quickly before they were spotted by their superiors:

When this [signal to the operator to move away] was also spotted by the Controller the message both silently from those surveilled and verbally from behind him was move the camera—which the operator did. The Controller went on to explain that the Divisional Commander had his monitor on and if he saw four patrol officers standing in a group he would 'go mad'.[23]

In addition, Norris and Armstrong also found evidence to suggest that the police, on occasion, deliberately ignore or suppress CCTV footage that may give support to a formal complaint or force the police to take disciplinary action against a serving officer:

One Thursday night a large-scale public order situation was a product of a local officer leaving a night-club and picking a fight with three black youths. The latter sitting in a car outside a snooker club were approached by him and were not impressed by his suggestion that drug dealers like them should 'fuck off to where they came from'; in the ensuing fight the CCTV system located the PC, shirt off brawling as more black youths spilled out of the snooker club. The end product was the deployment of

---

[22] ibid., 139. On the same page, Ericson and Haggerty also describe a similar incident which involved tampering with video cameras: 'During our fieldwork a supervisor expressed a concern that the video system he was about to have installed would display the speed of the police vehicle as well as the speed of the vehicle being pursued. He worried that police vehicles would regularly be shown to be travelling at excessive speeds, even during routine patrols... The installer agreed to remove the speed display for the police vehicle, so that only the speed of the oncoming vehicle would be registered.'

[23] Norris and Armstrong (1999b), 89–190.

20 uniformed officers to the scene and the spiriting away in the rear of the police car of the offending officer. Two black youths were arrested. According to the CCTV operator the tape was never released to either the police or any other agency and the officer was never disciplined for his actions.[24]

Although in the current study there was no evidence to suggest that officers had actually directed operators to deflect attention from them, there was reason to believe that police officers at some of the schemes had attempted to remove tapes that they feared might contain footage of police misconduct. At the police-led schemes, operators claimed that on a number of occasions officers had come up to the CCTV control room following incidents in which they had been required to use force and had asked to 'check the tape'. One operator at Scheme P2, for example, complained of having to ask officers to leave the control room after they had attempted to remove a tape from the previous day—a tape that showed one of them restraining a young woman who had allegedly resisted arrest. According to the operator, many of the officers at the station did not appear to regard themselves as being bound by the Code of Practice directions about tape handling and access to evidence, and he went so far as to joke that the padlock on the tape storage cupboard was not there to protect the tapes from the possibility of theft from intruders, but rather from theft by the police. Although when interviewed the operator downplayed the incident and claimed that the officers were easily dissuaded from trying to take the tapes, it was clear that some tension had arisen as a result of the incident and that the operators had subsequently begun to take issues of system and tape security far more seriously.

As might be expected, episodes of this kind appeared more likely to take place at Type P schemes, in part because the police had greater access to the CCTV control room and in part because Type P operators and police officers tended to enjoy closer working relations. As was noted in Chapter 5, it was clear from interviews with both the police and CCTV operators that officers working in conjunction with Type P schemes were more inclined to view the system as existing primarily for their benefit, and often displayed signs of regarding themselves as the 'rightful' owners of all evidence produced by the cameras. This general attitude may explain why cer-

[24]   Norris and Armstrong (1999b), 190.

tain officers at Type P schemes felt comfortable asking operators for access to tapes and, on rare occasions, bold enough to attempt to remove tapes without authorization. In contrast, none of the operators interviewed at local authority-led schemes claimed that local police officers had attempted either to direct cameras away from them or to gain unauthorized access to tapes. In light of the fact that relations between operators and officers at these schemes were rarely as friendly as at the police-led schemes, this lack of interference on the part of the police is perhaps to be expected. Operators working at Type C schemes were rarely visited by local police officers, and therefore any efforts by those officers to interfere with the system would have been both obvious and unwelcome.

Given some of the fears that have been expressed by civil libertarians regarding the possibility of CCTV being misused by the police, these findings suggest that there is indeed reason to be concerned about the independence and integrity of police-led CCTV systems. It can be argued, for example, that as Type P schemes are more susceptible to police interference than local authority-led schemes, the police should be prevented from running public area CCTV systems altogether. As we have already seen, however, none of the systems considered in the course of this study was subject to comprehensive or effective regulation.[25] None of the codes of practice or procedural guidelines at *any* of the schemes was sufficiently well-drafted or consistently enforced as to ensure that the systems were safe from outside interference, regardless of whether they were police- or local authority-led. As a consequence, a degree of caution needs to be exercised before coming to the conclusion that police-led CCTV schemes are *necessarily* more vulnerable than local authority-led schemes. What is clear is that effective regulation is especially important in the case of Type P schemes, if only because the possibility of police interference with such systems is inevitably higher.

7.6   CCTV and police interviews

Police interrogation is central to nearly all criminal investigations.[26] According to section 30(1) of the Police and Criminal Evidence Act

---

[25] See Ch. 4.
[26] According to Code C, para. 11.1A of the Police and Criminal Evidence Act (PACE) 1984, an interview is defined as 'the questioning of a person regarding his

(PACE) 1984, once a person has been arrested, the police are obliged to conduct a formal interview at the police station, during which they may ask the suspect questions relating to the alleged offence or other crimes in which they believe him or her to have been involved.[27] In practice, however, police interviews rarely take the form of a simple question-and-answer session. As many commentators have noted, the police have come to rely on the pre-charge interview as a means by which to secure confessions and convictions, as well as an opportunity to obtain information and intelligence about past or planned crimes.[28] Similarly, for many suspects the interview represents an opportunity to deny involvement in the offence, to secure their release from detention, or to attempt to bargain with the police:

> Police interviews with suspects are not usually simple chats. In an accusatorial system they are often adversarial. Some suspects are happy to tell the police everything they know. They may be confident of their ability to establish their innocence or be anxious to clear their conscience by confessing. For many suspects, however, telling the police what they know gains them nothing and can lose them a lot. In the main, then, the interview is about negotiating release of information (in exchange for something worth gaining) and/or attempting to persuade suspects to provide information which they do not want to provide.[29]

The use of interrogation tactics by the police is well known, and at present there are few restrictions on the use of these tactics during the pre-charge interview. As Sanders and Young note, PACE is silent

involvement or suspected involvement in a criminal offence or offences which, by virtue of para. 10.1 of Code C, is required to be carried out under caution'. For a discussion of the distinction between 'interviews' and 'mere conversations' (which are not governed by Code C), see Sanders and Young (2000), 271–3.

[27] It is important to distinguish between interviews conducted before and after the suspect is charged. Once a person has been charged with an offence, according to Code C of PACE he or she cannot be interviewed regarding the offence unless it is necessary either to prevent or minimize harm or loss to some other person or the public, or to clear up an ambiguity in a previous answer or statement. The police may also conduct an interview after a charge has been made where it is in the interests of justice that the defendant be given the opportunity to comment on information concerning the offence that has come to light since he or she was charged. Where the interview takes place prior to charge, none of these restrictions apply.

[28] Sanders and Young (2000), 149. See also D. Hobbes (1988) *Doing the Business* (Oxford: Oxford University Press); McConville *et al.* (1991).

[29] Sanders and Young (2000), 280.

as to the legality of most interrogation tactics, as are the PACE Codes of Practice.[30] Although evidence obtained 'unfairly' is liable to be excluded under section 78 of PACE, for example, the courts have so far been unwilling to treat many police interrogation tactics as unfair.[31] Similarly, prohibitions on the use of inducements or oppression by the police contained in section 76 appear to have had little impact on police interrogation practices except in certain extreme cases.[32]

As Choongh and others have observed, the police have learned to make the most of the freedom afforded to them by the law, and are quick to turn any attempts to redress the balance of power in the interview room to their advantage.[33] Many police interrogation manuals highlight the importance of maintaining control over information in the pre-charge interview, advising officers to release as little evidence as possible to the suspect or their solicitor.[34] These

[30] ibid., 282. As Sanders and Young also observe, while torture is a crime under section 134 of the Criminal Justice Act 1988, the courts have yet to apply the definition of torture to include practices which do not include some form of physical abuse or direct physical threat.

[31] Practices that have been held by the courts to be 'unfair' according to PACE include: the telling of lies by officers in the course of an interrogation (*R v Mason* [1988] 1 WLR 139); the questioning of a juvenile in the absence of an appropriate adult (*R v Fogah* [1989] Crim LR 141); and the failure to keep a contemporaneous note of a suspect's statements in interview (*R v Canale* [1990] 2 All ER 187).

[32] As Sanders and Young note, since the decision of the Court of Appeal in *R v Fulling* [1987] QB 426 the courts have 'yet to clarify what is meant in the law by oppression': Sanders and Young (2000), 284. According to Lord Lane in *Fulling*, oppression could be defined as the exercise of 'authority or power in a burdensome, harsh or wrongful manner, unjust or cruel treatment of subjects, inferiors etc; the imposition of unreasonable or unjust burden', with the added qualification being that the police must also have acted improperly.

[33] Choongh (1997), ch. 5. See also M. McConville and J. Hodgson (1993) *Custodial Legal Advice and the Right to Silence*, RCCJ Study No. 16 (London: HMSO); and J. Baldwin (1993a) 'Police interview techniques: establishing truth or proof?' *British Journal of Criminology* 33: 325.

[34] Although the PACE does address the issue of coercive or oppressive interrogation tactics, the restrictions laid down in Code C, para. 11.3 offer suspects little real protection in interview. According to para. 11.3: 'No police officer may try to obtain answers to questions or to elicit a statement by the use of oppression ... [or] ... shall indicate, except in answer to a direct question, what action will be taken on the part of the police if the person being interviewed answers questions, makes a statement or refuses to do either'. For a discussion of the effectiveness of the PACE provisions, see Sanders and Young (2000), 280.

manuals frequently remind officers of the need to think tactically when interviewing suspects, and of the importance of using information in ways that are likely to increase their chances of inducing a confession or giving suspects the opportunity to incriminate themselves.[35] As Sanders and Young note, asserting and retaining control of the interview is of central concern to the police:

> The police control where, when and how interrogations take place, what is asked, what information is given to suspects, and what is said to suspects or solicitors outside the interrogation. This keeps suspects on the defensive, nervous, less able to exercise their normal powers of judgement, and unsure of the applicability of any rights of which they may have knowledge.[36]

One of the key ways in which the police maintain control in the interview room is by using the rules of disclosure to their advantage. Although the rules are clear after a person is charged, at present the law does not specifically require the police to disclose evidence to a suspect or their solicitor prior to or during the interview stage of an investigation.[37] Under the provisions set out in PACE, interviewing officers are only obliged to disclose the custody record and, in identification cases, any initial description given by witnesses.[38] The police are free, therefore, to withhold all other evidence—including CCTV footage—until a charge is laid in the hope that a suspect may lie or implicate themselves, either by denying their involvement in the offence or by refusing to answer questions.[39]

---

[35] According to some sources, as many as three-quarters of all defendants who appear for trial in the Crown Court have made some kind of incriminating statement to the police, either in the form of a full confession or some other disclosure that has weakened their defence. See Choongh (1997), 132.

[36] Sanders and Young (2000), 280–1.

[37] The rules relating to the disclosure of evidence in criminal cases are contained in the Criminal Procedure and Investigations Act 1996. According to the provisions of the Act, once the defendant has been charged, almost all of the material in the possession of the police and the prosecution must be disclosed. Failure by the prosecution to comply with the rules of disclosure set down in the Act can result in the court staying the proceedings on the grounds that there has been an abuse of process under section 5(1)(b) and section 10. In addition, failure to disclose may give rise to an action for damages or some other form of relief under the terms of the Human Rights Act 1998.

[38] According to Code D of PACE, the first description provided of a suspect must be recorded (para. 2.0) and disclosed to the defence in the pre-trial procedure, particularly before any formal identification procedures are commenced.

[39] On the basis of the rules of disclosure contained in part II of the Criminal Justice and Public Order Act 1994, for example, there is nothing to suggest that the police

Given what is known about interrogation practices, there is good reason to suspect that the police have already begun to take tactical advantage of the presence of CCTV. The idea that the 'camera never lies' is a powerful one, and the belief that CCTV evidence is somehow incontrovertible is one that is widely shared by both the police and the general public. CCTV evidence linking a suspect to the offence is therefore likely to be regarded by many officers as sufficient to gain a conviction, and as a powerful tool for inducing the suspect to plead guilty.

Although it was not within the scope of the study to examine police interrogation and charging practices in any systematic way, anecdotal evidence provided by many of the officers interviewed suggests that the introduction of CCTV has changed the way in which many police interviews are conducted and the behaviour of suspects under interrogation. Officers frequently spoke of suspects admitting to an offence as soon as they heard that the police were in possession of CCTV evidence, and many argued that the introduction of CCTV had therefore made the task of interviewing and charging suspects 'quicker and easier'. As one police sergeant at Station P1 noted, few suspects questioned either the reliability or admissibility of CCTV evidence, and once they realized that they had been 'captured on camera', they simply admitted guilt and accepted their fate:

Once a person is confronted with their actions on tape, it's normally going to be a guilty plea with a view to getting a lesser sentence. Because some of the horror stories that I have seen on CCTV, I would guarantee you any judge or jury on viewing that incident on the cameras would recommend

are under any obligation to disclose information to the defence before an inference from silence can be made. This interpretation of the Act has recently been confirmed in the case of *R v Imran* [1997] Crim LR 754. Here the court held that it was wrong to suggest that the police are required to disclose the whole of the evidence against the defendant prior to interview, even if this may have prevented the suspect from making false statements in interview. Further support for this position can be found in the decision of the Court of Criminal Appeal in *R v Argent* [1997] 2 Cr App R 27 in which the court held that an inference could be drawn under section 34 of the Criminal Justice and Public Order Act 1994 despite the fact that there had not been full disclosure at interview (although the court did recognize that lack of disclosure could be a factor to take into account, and held that the jury was entitled to decide for itself whether the failure to answer questions in the face of less than full disclosure was reasonable). See G. Hutton and D. Johnston (2001) *Blackstone's Police Manual: Evidence and Procedure* (London: Blackstone), 295.

that that person goes to prison. And a lot of people have got off going to prison or have got some sort of reduction by their own admission, after seeing themselves on CCTV. There's no point fighting it. If you're there in black and white, hold your hands up, get a reduced sentence. That's how the criminal justice system works. (Police Sergeant H, Scheme P1)

Although it is unclear whether the introduction of CCTV has led to a rise in the number of guilty pleas, many police officers *believe* that the availability of CCTV evidence has made obtaining confessions considerably easier.[40] Many of the officers interviewed were also convinced that sentencing practices have changed as a result of the introduction of CCTV, with judges being more likely to hand down custodial sentences for violent offences that are recorded by the cameras. As the same police sergeant from Scheme P1 noted, in many cases the availability of CCTV evidence enables the police to pressure the Crown Prosecution Service (CPS) into accepting a more serious charge or the court into handing down what the police believed to be an appropriate sentence:

Where a serious incident such as grievous bodily harm with intent has been captured by CCTV, and there is a possibility that the Crown Prosecution Service might go for a lesser standard of charge, we will always attempt to ensure that the judge or anybody doing any sentencing has access to the film. If we do that, then there is always a chance that the court will consider a more serious charge and a longer sentence. (Police Sergeant H, Scheme P1)

It is interesting that although the police appear to have begun to rely on CCTV evidence as a means of extracting confessions and ensuring convictions, there is no conclusive evidence to suggest that they make tactical use of CCTV footage at the interrogation stage. At Station P3, a memo had been distributed by the officer in charge of the CCTV scheme advising officers to wait until suspects had made a statement before revealing the existence of CCTV evidence. Few officers in the station, however, appeared to have paid any

---

[40] As records of whether CCTV evidence was referred to in pre-charge interviews were not kept at any of the stations under study, it was extremely difficult to identify connections between the introduction of CCTV and changes in the number of guilty pleas across towns and cities in the Southern Region. According to Williams and Johnstone, however, there is evidence to suggest that in many cases involving CCTV evidence, suspects frequently admit guilt once they become aware that their actions have been recorded by the cameras. See Williams and Johnstone (2000), 196.

attention to this advice. In fact, all of the officers interviewed strenuously denied having ever withheld disclosure of CCTV footage, at either the pre-charge or post-charge stage of an investigation. The reason for this appears to have less to do with the police taking a particularly ethical stance to the use of CCTV, and more to do with a mistaken belief in the need to disclose such evidence in interview:

There is no point holding it back. The reason is that defence solicitors are obviously looking for a method and a means to try and get their client off. They're doing the best for their client. If we were to breach the disclosure rules by not disclosing that we've got the CCTV evidence, then we're going to make ourselves look bad. Let's tell them up front. We tend now to be very up front. 'This is what we've got. We've got a statement from A, B, and C. We also have CCTV evidence and that evidence shows your client doing this.' ... There's no way we could arrest someone, interview them about an incident, get an admission from them, where they admit they were there, and then all of a sudden the defending solicitor finds out that there is a closed circuit TV film of it. (Police Sergeant J, Scheme P2)

It is possible that this mistaken belief stems from a misunderstanding of the rules laid down by the amended Data Protection Act 1998. Many of the officers interviewed claimed that the new data protection provisions placed them under a positive obligation to disclose CCTV evidence to the suspect or their solicitor as soon as is practicable, and asserted that a failure to do so would place them in breach of the Act and render any CCTV evidence inadmissible. Others believed instead that they were specifically required to disclose CCTV evidence under PACE, although none of them could point to a specific section in the Act or provisions in the Codes of Practice to support this belief.[41]

Police officers' belief in the need to disclose CCTV evidence may also stem from a desire to avoid giving the suspect's defence solicitor some form of tactical advantage at the prosecution stage. As a number of charge sergeants observed, the fact that the law does not oblige the police to disclose CCTV evidence in the pre-trial stage does not mean that it is always in their best interests to withhold it. According to Hutton and Johnston, the failure of the police to

---

[41] Note that the procedures for video identification set out in Annex B to Code D of the Police and Criminal Evidence Act 1984 do not apply to footage taken by closed circuit television cameras. See *R v Jones (Mark Anthony)* (1994) 158 JP 293.

disclose material such as CCTV footage may be a factor that the defendant later relies upon in court to show that a failure to mention possible defences when interviewed was reasonable in the circumstances.[42] Although police officers may not be making tactical use of CCTV evidence at this stage, it is also possible that pragmatic reasons—as well as mistaken beliefs—are behind the decision to withhold or disclose CCTV evidence before or during the police interview, with the police having to balance any desire to 'trip up' the suspect against the possibility of giving the defence grounds on which to challenge the evidence against them.

7.7   Police information and intelligence

Central to the effective policing of any town or city is the gathering and processing of information. Traditionally, the police have relied extensively on street patrols, undercover officers, informants, and members of the general public to provide them with information about their local environment and the activities of suspect populations within the community. In addition to providing the basis for the majority of police investigations, this information is crucial in shaping the development of policing strategies at both the local and the force level, helping senior management to direct resources and respond to changing crime patterns and trends. With the introduction of CCTV, the police now have at their disposal a tool capable of gathering large and diverse amounts of information about everything from traffic flows and illegal parking to the movements of suspected shoplifters and drug dealers.

Given its potential, it seems reasonable to expect that the police would have embraced CCTV and taken steps to integrate it into

---

[42] Hutton and Johnston (2001), 295. It is important to note that, although there are no specific rules either in the 1994 Act or the subsequent case-law that consider the question of whether CCTV evidence should be disclosed at the pre-trial stage, it is clear from the case of *DPP v Chipping* (11 Jan. 1999, unreported) that a failure to disclose such evidence after charges have been laid may result in a case being dismissed as an abuse of process under section 5(1)(b) and section 10. In *DPP v Chipping*, the prosecution failed to disclose the existence of CCTV evidence containing footage of the site at which the offence was alleged to have occurred (footage which the police had examined and later erased believing it to be of no use in the case). In this instance, the failure to disclose was held to be an abuse of process and the case dismissed.

their existing information-gathering networks. Certainly, one of the main concerns of critics of CCTV has been that the police will quickly absorb this new technology and use it to enhance their existing surveillance capacity. According to Norris and Armstrong, the introduction of public area CCTV has already begun to transform the way in which the police deal with public disturbances and demonstrations:

In public order policing, the priority has traditionally been the preservation of public tranquillity rather than the detection and prosecution of offenders. However, the potential of the new technologies is increasingly being exploited with the use of surveillance and intelligence gathering squads and footage being retrospectively examined and analysed to provide evidence for prosecution. Not only, therefore, is the net widened, but the potential for deviancy amplification in public order situations is increased. And as previously marginal demonstrators are caught up in the mêlée and subsequently identified, arrested and prosecuted, their fledgling deviant identities may well become entrenched.[43]

Although Norris and Armstrong offer no specific evidence in support of these broad claims, it is true that the police in Britain have used public area CCTV for information-gathering and intelligence purposes in the past and continue to do so in certain circumstances. London's so-called 'Ring of Steel', for example, was established with a view to improving the ability of the police to gather information about potential terrorist activities in the capital and, as Armstrong and Giulianotti have noted, CCTV has also been used by Scotland Yard's Football Intelligence Unit to collect information on football hooligans.[44]

In the regions covered by this study, however, there was no evidence of any significant or systematic attempt by the police to incorporate CCTV into their existing information or surveillance networks. None of the stations had made any effort to establish a system whereby information collected by CCTV could be made available to other police divisions or departments such as the Local Information Unit or Criminal Investigations Division (CID). Nor had any provision been made for keeping CCTV operators informed of ongoing police surveillance operations being carried out in their local area. What little information exchange there was

[43] Norris et al. (1998a) 268–9.
[44] Armstrong and Giulianotti (1998).

between CCTV and police information units was informal, haphazard, and extremely rare. As a consequence, videotapes that may
have contained useful information on the whereabouts of suspects
or about changing patterns of crime, were not systematically examined. Indeed, detailed study of the tape logs at each of the schemes
revealed that CCTV tapes were rarely examined by the police at all,
and that the vast majority were routinely erased without anyone
other than the camera operators having ever viewed them. Furthermore, despite the fact that all of the CCTV schemes maintained
detailed logbooks and 'rogues' galleries' (containing pictures of
known or suspected offenders and their associates), these were
rarely if ever consulted by officers aside from the occasional town
centre PC. Finally, as a number of officers noted, so far the police
had made little effort to put operators 'in the picture' or to take
advantage of their knowledge or experience of information
gathering:

It's a tool which is not utilized to its full potential, purely and simply
because the operators are not given as much information, intelligence
information-wise, as they should be. They don't go along to police briefings, and when they do get information from us a lot of it is very much
on an ad hoc basis. They should be made an integral part of the shift,
spearheading our strategy within the town, and we should be working according to the information they produce...(Police Sergeant B,
Scheme P2)

This was a point that was echoed by a number of operators at
Type P schemes, who noted with a certain dismay that they were
rarely if ever kept informed about changes in general police strategy
for their respective towns or of various police operations that were
being carried out in the town centre. Responding to a question
about an ongoing surveillance operation based just outside the
central shopping area of Town P2, an operator claimed to have
heard about it some months after it had commenced—despite the
fact that the area under surveillance was also covered by the town
centre cameras—and only then when he was asked to review some
police tapes to see if he recognized any of the surveillance targets:
'Don't know how much of this goes on. We only get told about
[police surveillance] operations that are relevant to us. Everything is
on a need to know basis only' (Operator G, Scheme P2).

Certainly, during the course of the field observation operators
were never invited to attend town centre shift briefings or asked to

attend meetings of local intelligence officers. This failure on the part of the police to integrate CCTV into their existing information networks was a source of great frustration for many of the middle-ranking and senior officers interviewed in the course of the study. As a number of officers observed:

Information from the CCTV cameras should be mixed with information coming in from informants and from other sources, and there should be some person drawing it all in and turning it into intelligence. I think it can be utilized far more as an information-gathering tool, feeding information into the system. Why we aren't making better use of it I just don't know. (Police Sergeant B, Scheme P2)

You give somebody a side-handled baton and they will go on a training course to learn how to use it and to learn what to do and not do with it. If you give them CS spray, the same thing applies, and with the radio the same thing applies, and so and so on. You don't let somebody drive a car until they are qualified to drive it, and yet we're putting millions of pounds' worth of cameras up there and we aren't telling our officers what they can do with it. A CCTV system does absolutely nothing but gather information. That's all it does. And we aren't telling them what to do with that information or how to make best use of it. If we did, then it would become second nature... (Chief Inspector A, Police Headquarters)

There are a number of possible explanations as to why this integration has not occurred. On the one hand, the physical location of many of the CCTV control rooms may prevent the easy exchange of information between those responsible for the system and local intelligence officers or detectives within the CID. All of the local authority-led CCTV control rooms were located on council premises and were not easily accessible to officers because of security restrictions, a fact that may have dissuaded officers from attempting to set up lines of communication between themselves and the schemes. This does not explain, however, why there was also no systematic information exchange at Schemes P1 and P3, where the CCTV control room was located at the heart of the local police station. The location of CCTV control rooms notwithstanding, the failure of the police to provide resources for the routine interrogation of CCTV tapes makes it extremely difficult for local intelligence units to develop any system of regular information exchange between themselves and local CCTV schemes, regardless of whether they are working alongside a police- or local authority-led CCTV system. Sifting through CCTV tapes and extracting information from them is an extremely time-consuming and labour-intensive process, and one which detectives and intelligence officers were only inclined to engage in when they already knew what they were looking for. Combined with the fact that CCTV operators were not asked to provide intelligence reports or briefings, this additional failure routinely to examine CCTV footage meant that there was no mechanism by which information could pass from any of the schemes into the police intelligence network other than by personal contact between operators and police officers.

Finally, from the broader picture it can be argued that the main reason why the police have failed to integrate CCTV in to their existing information networks is because those networks are fundamentally inflexible and resistant to change. There is a considerable body of research to suggest that the traditional structure of policing has made it extremely difficult for the police to respond to developments in information technology.[45] Just as the police in Britain were slow to move to computerized records and databases during the late 1960s and early 1970s because of organizational inertia, the current reluctance to take advantage of the intelligence potential of CCTV may stem from a similar set of cultural and institutional circumstances.

Moreover, these findings cast doubt over claims that police involvement in the establishment of new surveillance networks like public area CCTV is evidence of a shift towards a greater emphasis on 'risk-based policing'.[46] Given that the police make little use of the information generated by these systems—and, more crucially, do not share this information with other organizations or agencies also interested in controlling risk—the spread of CCTV has had virtually no effect on how the police respond to risk or formulate overall strategy. While the desire to better manage risk and reduce public insecurity may have been behind the initial decision to become involved in public area surveillance, most of the information generated by CCTV is routinely ignored by the police and its

[45] See Ackroyd et al. (1992), 121–41; and H. Goldstein (1990) Problem Oriented Policing (New York: McGraw-Hill).

[46] See Ericson and Haggerty (1997); and U. Beck (1992) Risk Society: Towards a New Modernity (London: Sage). For a discussion of Ericson and Haggerty's work in the context of CCTV and surveillance theory more generally, see McCahill (2002), 16–17; and D. Lyon (2001) Surveillance Society: Monitoring Everyday Life (Buckingham: Open University Press), 120–2.

potential as a risk assessment and intelligence tool largely over-looked.

7.8 Conclusion

At the end of this examination of the impact of CCTV on policing, where do we find ourselves? Having considered a variety of different police activities—ranging from police patrols and resource management to police interrogation and information gathering—a contradictory picture emerges. In certain key respects, CCTV does appear to have had a limited impact on the way in which the police respond to incidents and on various aspects of police safety. Thanks to the introduction of town centre cameras, police control staff are better able to assess incidents in progress, and officers on the streets are generally made to feel safer in the execution of their duty. Similarly, police interrogation practices seem to have been affected by the introduction of cameras and the availability of CCTV footage at the interview stage. In many other key respects, however, CCTV appears to have had at best a marginal effect on current police practices, particularly when it comes to how towns and cities are actually policed. Regardless of whether CCTV was run by the police or the relevant local authority, shift patterns and policing strategies in the six towns included in the study were not affected by the introduction of CCTV, nor were local intelligence networks or the activities of departments such as the CID. In short, the arrival of CCTV did not *fundamentally* affect the way in which policing was carried out in the Southern Region.

In light of many of the issues raised at the beginning of this book, this is a striking conclusion. Far from revolutionizing the way in which towns and cities are policed, the introduction of CCTV has in fact had little effect on the police either as individuals or as an organization. What now remains then is to return to the questions raised in Chapter 1, and consider what these findings tell us about how the police respond to technological change. Does the emergence of technologies like public area CCTV necessarily lead to more intrusive and authoritarian forms of policing? Does the 'techno-policing' thesis provide an accurate description of how the police make use of new technologies? How will the continued use of public area CCTV affect the future of policing in Britain?

8

Conclusions

One creates a machine for a particular and limited purpose. But once the machine is built, we discover, always to our surprise, that it has ideas of its own; that it is quite capable not only of changing our habits but . . . of changing our habits of mind.

Neil Postman[1]

A major problem with many contemporary accounts of new technologies is their implied determinism. Technological innovation is all too frequently seen as the prime mover, producing information societies and even cyber societies . . . Such idolatries follow the ancient pattern of mystification and dependency-creation, not to mention a signal failure to produce the promised goods.

David Lyon[2]

In Chapter 1, two questions were identified as the primary concerns of this book. The first—how has the introduction of CCTV affected policing practices in Britain?—has largely been answered. Contrary to the expectations of many politicians, academics, and civil libertarians, this study finds that the spread of CCTV has had little significant impact on the practices and organization of the police in the Southern Region. Although some elements of police resource management and discipline have improved as a result of the introduction of CCTV, there have been no major changes in the way in which the towns included in this study are policed or patrolled. Regardless of whether CCTV schemes are run by the police or local authorities, officers on the street and in the station have not rushed to embrace this new technology or integrate it into the daily work

---

[1] N. Postman (1983) *The Disappearance of Childhood* (London: W. H. Allen), 24.
[2] Lyon (2001), 23–4.

routines. Instead, most have simply acknowledged the presence of the cameras and continued to go about the task of policing as they have always done.

The second critical question—what does the police response to CCTV tell us about the future of policing?—is the subject of this final chapter. Since the publication of Foucault's *Discipline and Punish*, criminologists and social theorists have speculated about how continuing advancements in surveillance technology will affect policing. For many, the introduction of CCTV in the early 1990s marked the beginning of the end for traditional forms of policing and social control, and a major step towards the establishment of a 'maximum surveillance society'. However, having now seen how little policing has in fact changed as a result of the introduction of CCTV, there is a need to re-examine this view, and with it much of our thinking about the relationship between the police and the technology of surveillance.

8.1   Techno-police or 'business as usual'?

Underlying much of the concern about recent developments in the area of public surveillance is a particularly deterministic account of how the police make use of new technologies. Although the alarmist works of social theorists like Neil Postman, Jacques Ellul, and Marshall McLuhan are now rarely if ever referred to directly by writers interested in questions of policing and surveillance technology, their influence none the less remains apparent.[3] Gary T. Marx, for example, has argued that policing has been transformed by the emergence of new surveillance technologies that have made covert observation both cheap and easy. While Marx is hardly a simple determinist, his description of a world in which total social control

---

[3] Lyon (2001), 111. According to Lyon, many sociological studies of policing, such as Gary T. Marx's *Undercover Policing* and Richard Ericson and Kevin Haggerty's *Policing the Risk Society*, begin with a 'deferential nod towards Ellul'. For representative works, see: N. Postman (1993) *Technopoly: The Surrender of Culture to Technology* (New York: Vintage); J. Ellul (1964) *The Technological Society* (New York: Vintage); M. McLuhan and Q. Fiore (1967) *The Medium is the Message* (New York: Bantam); and M. McLuhan and B. Powers (1989) *The Global Village: Transformations in World Life and Media in the 21st Century* (Oxford: Oxford University Press). McLuhan is perhaps most famous for coining the term 'global village' to describe what he saw as a newly emergent global society both linked and divided by the electronic mass media.

has become a reality—the so-called 'surveillance society'—relies heavily on a deterministic view of the spread of computer and information technology.[4] According to McCahill and Norris, this deterministic tendency can also be found in the writings of criminologists concerned with the use of CCTV for crime prevention, as well as in many recent sociological works on the Panopticon and the spread of disciplinary power.[5] Both of these strands of criminology and social theory are, it is argued, implicitly deterministic because of their willingness to assume that CCTV systems can only be used in certain, pre-defined ways—ways that inevitably bring about specific outcomes and institutional effects:

One thing that unites these two very different approaches is their tendency to take as given the way CCTV systems are applied in practice. It is assumed that either visual surveillance systems have been introduced to detect and prevent crime or to extend the disciplinary potential of panoptic systems. What is often missing in this literature is a detailed micro-sociological account of the construction and operation of visual surveillance systems in different institutional settings.[6]

While it is clear that deterministic theories continue to underpin many academic accounts of the spread of surveillance technology, their influence is even more explicit in the arguments of civil libertarians and privacy advocates. As has already been discussed in Chapter 1, civil liberties groups have been quick to portray the police as an organization extremely adept at incorporating new technologies such as CCTV into their existing surveillance and information networks. Similarly, privacy advocates have consistently maintained that strict laws and regulations are needed to prevent the police from using new data processing and information technologies to undermine individual privacy rights and due process protections in countries such as Britain and the United States.

Within the literature of policing, this view of the relationship between the police and new technology is often referred to as the

---

[4] According to Marx, 'with computer technology, one of the final barriers to total social control is crumbling'. See G. T. Marx (1985) 'The surveillance society: the threat of 1984-style techniques' *The Futurist* (June), 21.

[5] McCahill and Norris (2002a), 4. Specifically, McCahill and Norris point to work by Skinns and Tilley (on questions of crime prevention) and by Reeve (on the subject of the Panopticon and power). See Skinns (1998); N. Tilley (1998) 'Evaluating the effectiveness of CCTV schemes' in Norris *et al.* (1998b), 139; and Reeve (1998a).

[6] McCahill and Norris (2002a), 4.

'techno-policing' thesis. According to proponents of this thesis such as Sarah Manwaring-White, recent changes in the technology of policing are indicative of a qualitative shift in the whole nature of policing in our society, a sinister development that has taken place without any commensurate changes in constitutional and legal controls.[7] Deterministic in character, the techno-policing thesis maintains that as new technologies are developed, they exert a powerful influence over the thinking of the police, driving them towards more authoritarian styles of policing and oppressive methods of social control. New surveillance technologies such as CCTV are seen as being particularly attractive to the police, as they promise to free the police of their dependence on the public for information, and give them greater power over their environment.

All of this assumes, of course, that the police are able to make effective use of technologies like closed circuit television. As Clive Walker has pointed out, the techno-policing thesis is based in part on a questionable assumption—that technical change is introduced and assimilated into the police service in a 'calculated, controlled and ruthlessly efficient manner, and that the full implications of such change are understood'.[8] However, as detailed in the previous chapters, the Southern Region Police were at least initially hesitant to adopt new CCTV technology. Furthermore, since becoming involved in the running of various CCTV schemes, local officers have made little effort to incorporate CCTV into their existing policing strategies and information networks. When they have done so, their attempts have been haphazard and superficial. Far from aggressively assimilating this new technology and being shaped by it, as the techno-policing thesis would predict, the Southern Region Police remain relatively unchanged by the introduction of public area CCTV.

Why has this been the case? Why are the police unable or unwilling to make greater use of CCTV, despite the apparent conviction of many individual officers that the technology has much to offer? In part, the answer to these questions lies with the particular circumstances that surrounded the introduction of CCTV to the Southern Region. The fact that the initial impetus behind the spread of CCTV came from local and central government meant that the police were never fully committed to the idea of public area surveillance. Equally, it seems that concerns about being perceived as an insidious

---

[7] Manwaring-White (1983).   [8] Walker (1983), 694.

'Big Brother' blunted the impact of this technology on the force as a whole, with senior officers being hesitant to embrace the technology wholeheartedly and adjust overall policing strategies to accommodate the schemes.

The major reason for the failure to make extensive use of CCTV, however, appears to be far more fundamental than either of these factors. Put simply, the Southern Region Police made little use of CCTV because they were unwilling and unable to change existing practices to take advantage of the new technology. Although much of the literature of surveillance presents a picture of the police as a rational bureaucracy capable of easily assimilating new technologies and techniques, the reality is substantially different. Throughout the course of the research, the overwhelming impression of the police was one of inflexibility and conservatism, and of a failure on the part of senior management to engage with the opportunities and challenges presented by CCTV.

This organizational inflexibility should come as no surprise to anyone familiar with the organization or working culture of the police. The police are notorious for being deeply suspicious of change, particularly when it comes to the management and execution of their core tasks such as street policing and order maintenance.[9] According to Manning, 'police organisations differ markedly from other organisations in ways that tend to amplify their conservative tendencies', and, as Herman Goldstein rightly observes, it is this inherent conservatism that makes the police particularly ill-suited to absorbing new technologies.[10] Although CCTV may offer the prospect of reduced police response times, better resource management, and improved police intelligence and surveillance networks, no actual change is likely to occur unless the police have a clear idea and a clear will to transform their existing practices in order to accommodate and exploit this new technology. As this book has demonstrated, the Southern Region Police have consistently failed to engage with this issue and as such remain largely unaffected by the introduction of public area CCTV to their region.

As with any study of this size, there is a question of how far its findings can be extended to the general case. Is there any reason to

[9] See e.g. D. Bailey and E. Bittner (1985) 'The tactical choices of police patrol officers' *Journal of Criminal Justice* 14: 329; and Manning (1977).
[10] Manning (1992) 354; Goldstein (1990).

believe that the response of the Southern Region Police has been somehow atypical when compared with that of other police forces across Britain? As was noted at the beginning of this book, one of the reasons why the Southern Region Police Force was chosen as the site for this research was because it is a large force, encompassing a wide area and a range of different CCTV schemes. In addition, the Southern Region has a reputation for being an innovative force, keen to test new policing techniques and to embrace multi-agency partnerships. If anything, then, there are good reasons to think that the Southern Region Force would be *more* receptive to the introduction of CCTV than many other forces in Britain. Accordingly, there is no reason to believe that CCTV is likely to have had a major impact on policing strategies and practices across the rest of the country.

If all this is true, why does the techno-policing thesis continue to exert such influence over many academics and civil libertarians concerned with the spread of public area surveillance? If, in reality, CCTV does not significantly affect the way in which the police operate or organize themselves, why do pro-privacy organizations persist in maintaining that the police state is just around the corner? There are, of course, many possible answers to this question. On the one hand, unease over the use of CCTV by police is inexorably bound up with deeper concerns about the growing use and sophistication of surveillance technologies in society more generally. Taking this view, the spread of CCTV represents just one aspect of the move towards a Foucaultian future, a future in which public streets and shopping centres become modern Panopticons, and personal privacy is rendered virtually non-existent. Alternatively, it can be argued that much of the opposition to CCTV is motivated by a desire on the part of civil libertarians to prevent *any* expansion in existing police powers, and not by any larger concern about the growing pervasiveness of surveillance in society. While both of these arguments are persuasive, there is another, less obvious explanation for the popularity of the techno-policing thesis—namely that we fear CCTV because it provokes very specific and disturbing 'Orwellian nightmares'.

8.2   Visions of dystopia

Looking at the discourse of surveillance and technology over the past fifty years, it is difficult to overestimate the impact that

Orwell's novel *Nineteen Eighty-Four* has had on popular and academic imaginations. Stanley Cohen has noted that 'key literary works of twentieth-century dystopianism have passed into popular consciousness', bringing with them the spectre of a future in which state-sponsored surveillance has all but extinguished privacy and other forms of personal freedom.[11] From *Brazil* to GATTACA, contemporary pop culture is awash with images and ideas drawn directly from Orwell, Huxley, and others. Equally, academic writers have made extensive use of *Nineteen Eighty-Four* in their attempts to understand and explain the relationship between surveillance and social control. David Flaherty, for example, openly acknowledges using Orwell's world as a benchmark against which actual efforts to establish a 'surveillance society' can be measured, with each new technological advance being judged according to whether it brings us closer to the sort of nightmare envisaged in *Nineteen Eighty-Four*.[12]

Despite the fact that this image of the future provides a ready set of metaphors to frame our thinking about technology, surveillance, and social control, however, Orwell's vision has also induced a degree of collective myopia when it comes to debating the pros and cons of new technologies like CCTV. As Garland has noted, not only do 'surveillance dystopias continue to exert their appeal', they also inspire an underlying and often unconscious mistrust of any attempt by the government to learn more about us or aspects of our lives that we consider to be private.[13] This is a point that has also been raised by the social theorist David Lyon:

[D]ystopian visions... have the virtue of directing our attention to the negative, constraining, and unjust aspects of surveillance, and of helping us to identify which kinds of trends are especially dangerous from this

---

[11] S. Cohen (1985) *Visions of Social Control* (Cambridge: Polity Press), 202. For a survey of the 'literature of dystopia', see M. R. Hillegas (1967) *The Future as Nightmare: H. G. Wells and the Anti-utopians* (New York: Oxford University Press); F. Polak (1973) *The Image of the Future* (Amsterdam: Elsevier); C. Walsh (1962) *From Utopia to Nightmare* (New York: Harper and Row); and in particular F. G. Manuel and F. P. Manuel (1979) *Utopian Thought in the Western World* (Oxford: Blackwell). All four of these works are referred to by Cohen in his discussion of the dystopia literature and its impact on social theory.

[12] D. H. Flaherty (1989) *Protecting Privacy in Surveillance Societies* (Chapel Hill, NC: University of North Carolina Press), 6.

[13] Garland (1995).

point of view. But their disadvantage is that they thus exaggerate the negative by seeing only one side of surveillance, promote pessimism about whether such negative traits can be countered, and fail to offer any indication as to what the content of the alternative might be.[14]

It is this very mistrust that privacy groups have consistently relied upon in their campaign to ban technology like public area CCTV. Rather than produce evidence to show that the introduction of cameras has led to more authoritarian forms of policing, the prevailing tactic has instead been to draw parallels—however tendentious—between current developments and the nightmare of *Nineteen Eighty-Four*.

Unless we move away from this pessimistic and overly deterministic view of the relationship between surveillance and technology, developments like public area CCTV will continue to be greeted with suspicion and hostility. As Garland rightly points out, surveillance technologies like CCTV are inherently neutral, and not *necessarily* bound up with the exercise of authoritarian power by organizations such as the police.[15] Instead, surveillance and social control can, in the right circumstances, be benign:

[I]t might be worth reminding ourselves of the positive senses of the word [surveillance]—'inspection', 'superintendence', 'supervision', 'oversight'— and the indispensable need for such activity in spheres such as child-rearing, education, health or business, not to mention science and the acquisition of systematic knowledge.[16]

As this book has demonstrated, there is a pressing need for us to re-examine the ways in which we think about surveillance and to resist the pull of dystopic visions when looking at the impact of technology like CCTV. Cameras are not in and of themselves intrusive—they only become so when used in particular settings and in particular ways. Accordingly, it is important to determine whether those particular settings and particular ways coincide at all with

---

[14]   Lyon (1994), 204.

[15]   See also J. Young (1999) *The Exclusive Society: Social Exclusion, Crime and Difference in Late Modernity* (London: Sage), 196–9. Walker also questions the implicit assumption made by proponents of the techno-policing thesis that technology is inherently malevolent. As he observes, how technology affects organizations like the police 'all depends on how it is used, by whom, and under what conditions'. Walker (1983), 695.

[16]   Garland (1995), 5.

reality before looking for parallels in the fictionalized worlds of writers such as Orwell and Huxley. The introduction of new technology into an organization as complex and conservative as the police is rarely a simple affair, and as a result predicting how such technology will ultimately affect working practices is extremely difficult.

While surveillance technologies like CCTV have the potential to transform human institutions such as the police, these technologies are also shaped by the values and practices of those who use them. Norris writes, 'CCTV in its operation and effects is contingent on a host of social processes which shape how the technology is actually used. We simply cannot know in advance what CCTV is, means and does, and how effective it is since it is dependent upon its organisational implementation.'[17] Rather than assume that organizations like the police are inevitably becoming more repressive as a result of the introduction of CCTV—or that the spread of public area surveillance technology is yet more evidence of the arrival of the 'risk society'—this book has tried to provide insight into how cameras are *actually* being used by the police. Given how much has been written in recent years by about Panopticonism, insecurity, and the relationship between surveillance and social control, there is a danger that such issues have been largely removed from their real-life contexts and have become over-theorized.

Ironically, the need for more empirical explorations of surveillance was made some 30 years ago by one of the pioneers of surveillance theory. Writing in 1973, the sociologist James Rule sounded a clear warning to future researchers interested in the growth of mass surveillance, cautioning against the temptation to speculate on the outcome of some new technological development before first undertaking the 'close documentation of existing practices and painstaking analysis of their relations to their social contexts'.[18] For Rule, the central aim was to discover how changes in the technology of surveillance bring about social change and to challenge those who—in their efforts to draw attention to the possibility of an Orwellian future—move too quickly from facts to inference and speculation:

[O]ne feels that the authors have stopped thinking critically, and instead are contenting themselves with playing to the grandstand of alarmed public

[17] Norris (1997).   [18] Rule (1973), 34.

opinion...Such statements [about the possibility of a totalitarian future] are not factually incorrect; their speculative nature makes it impossible to submit them to proof or disproof. But they are unhelpful in that they carry speculation to such an extreme as to blur the distinction between the concrete, verifiable trends, and fancy.[19]

As the experience of the Southern Region Police demonstrates, speculative and deterministic predictions about how the police are likely to be affected by technologies like CCTV may be wide of the mark. Contrary to the expectations of both supporters and opponents of CCTV in the region and elsewhere, policing practices in the six towns included in this study did not change significantly as a result of the introduction of CCTV. Cameras alone do not make the police more repressive or authoritarian, any more than they make the police more effective or efficient.

8.3   Conclusions

Aside from raising important questions about the way in which the police adapt to technological change, the findings of this study point to the need for a re-examination of some of our central assumptions about the relationship between surveillance and social control. Writers such as Orwell and Foucault have been instrumental in shaping the way many criminologists and social theorists now think about questions of surveillance and its role in contemporary society. There is a danger, however, that unless we make more of an effort to understand how changes in the technology of surveillance actually affect institutions like the police, the theoretical literature of social control will become increasingly divorced from reality.

This book has attempted to provide, in McCahill and Norris's words, an account of 'the construction and operation of visual surveillance systems' in one particular institutional setting—the police.[20] The findings presented here suggest that, while the spread of CCTV may one day result in a fundamental change in British policing, that change has not yet occurred. Furthermore, it is clear

---

[19] Rule (1973), 32–3. Although Rule himself concedes that his interest in the topic of surveillance was initially sparked by reading Orwell's *Nineteen Eighty-Four*, he stresses that as the underlying questions concerning the growth of mass surveillance are inherently sociological, they must be investigated using sociological methods.

[20] McCahill and Norris (2002*a*), 4.

that so long as the police remain committed to their existing methods of town centre policing and information gathering, there is little chance that current police practices in relation to the use of CCTV will change in the near future. Unless the organization and working culture of the police in Britain change, the technology of public area surveillance will continue to be little more than an adjunct to more traditional modes of policing.

Bibliography

Ackroyd, C., K. Margolis, J. Rosenhead, and T. Shallice (1980) *The Technology of Political Control* (London: Pluto).

Ackroyd, S., and J. A. Hughes (1991) *Data Collection in Context*, 2nd edn. (London: Longman).

——R. Harper, J. A. Hughes, D. Shapiro, and K. Soothill (1992) *New Technology and Practical Police Work: The Social Context of Technical Innovation* (Buckingham: Open University Press).

Agre, P., and M. Rotenburg (eds.) (1997) *Technology and Privacy: The New Landscape* (Cambridge, Mass.: MIT Press).

Alderson, J. C., and P. J. Stead (1973) *The Police We Deserve* (London: Wolfe Publishing).

Aldhouse, F. (1998) 'CCTV systems and the Data Protection Act', Memorandum to the House of Lords Select Committee on Science and Technology Sub-Committee 11: Digital images as evidence. Published in House of Lords Select Committee on Science and Technology 'Digital images as evidence', Evidence HL Paper 64–1 (London: HMSO).

Aldridge, J. (1994) 'Effective CCTV security and safety systems' *CCTV Today* 1: 12.

——and G. Knupfer (1994) 'Public safety: improving the effectiveness of CCTV security systems' *Journal of the Forensic Science Society* 34: 257.

Ansell, J. (1998) 'Closed circuit television: the human element', unpublished M.Sc. dissertation (Scarman Centre for the Study of Public Order, Leicester University).

Appleyard, B. (2001) 'Nowhere to hide' *The Sunday Times Magazine* (15 Apr.).

Arlidge, J. (1994) 'Welcome Big Brother' *Independent* (2 Nov.), 22.

Armitage, R. (2002) 'To CCTV or not to CCTV? A review of current research into the effectiveness of CCTV systems in reducing crime' *NACRO Community Safety Practice Briefing* (London: NACRO).

——G. Smyth, and K. Pease (1999) 'Burnley CCTV evaluation' in Painter and Tilley (1999*b*), 225.

Armstrong, G. and R. Giulianotti (1998) 'From another angle: police surveillance and football supporters' in Norris *et al.* (eds.) (1998*b*), 113.

Aubrey, C. (1981) *Who's Watching You?* (Harmondsworth: Penguin).

Bailey, D., and E. Bittner (1985) 'The tactical choices of police patrol officers' *Journal of Criminal Justice* 14: 329.

Baldwin, J. (1993a) 'Police interview techniques: establishing truth or proof?' *British Journal of Criminology* 33: 325.

—— (1993b) 'Power and police interviews' *New Law Journal* 143: 1194.

Bannister, J., N. Fyfe, and A. Kearnes (1998) 'Closed circuit television and the city' in Norris *et al.* (eds.) (1998b), 21.

Barry, A., T. Osbourne, and N. Rose (1996) *Foucault and Political Reason: Liberalism, Neo-liberalism and Rationalities of Government* (London: UCL Press).

Baxter, J. D. (1990) *Protecting Privacy: State Security, Privacy and Information* (Brighton: Harvester Wheatsheaf).

Bayley, D. (1977) *The Police and Society* (London: Sage).

—— (1994) *Police for the Future* (New York: Oxford University Press).

—— and C. Shearing (1996) 'The future of policing' *Law and Society Review* 30(3): 585.

Bean, P. (1999) 'Technology and criminal justice' *Law, Computers & Technology* 13(3): 365.

Beck, A., and A. Willis (1995) *Crime and Security: Managing the Risk to Safe Shopping* (Leicester: Perpetuity Press).

—————— (1999) 'Context-specific measures of CCTV effectiveness in the retail sector' in Painter and Tilley (1999b), 251.

Beck, U. (1992) *Risk Society: Towards a New Modernity* (London: Sage).

Becker, H., and B. Geer (1989) 'Participant observation: The analysis of qualitative field data' in Burgess (1989e), 239.

Beninger, J. R. (1989) *The Control Revolution: Technological and Economic Origins of the Information Society* (Cambridge, Mass.: Harvard University Press).

Benn, S. I. and G. F. Gaus (eds.) (1983) *Public and Private in Social Life* (New York: St Martin's Press).

Bennett, T. (1989) 'The neighbourhood watch experience' in Morgan and Smith (1989), 138.

—— (1990) *Evaluating Neighbourhood Watch* (Aldershot: Gower).

—— (ed.) (1996) *Preventing Crime and Disorder: Targeting Strategies and Responsibilities* (Cambridge: Institute of Criminology).

—— and L. Gelsthorpe (1996) 'Public attitudes towards CCTV in public places' *Studies on Crime and Crime Prevention* 5(1): 72.

Benson, D., and J. A. Hughes (1991) 'Evidence and inference' in G. Button (ed.) *Ethnomethodology and the Human Sciences* (Cambridge: Cambridge University Press).

Bentham, J. (1970) *An Introduction to the Principles of Morals and Legislation* (London: Athlone Press).

Berg, B. L. (1998) *Qualitative Research Methods for the Social Sciences* (Boston: Allyn and Bacon).

Bird, J. (ed.) (1993) *Mapping the Futures* (London: Routledge).

Birks, P. (ed.) (1997) *Privacy and Loyalty* (Oxford: Clarendon Press).

Bittner, E. (1970) *The Functions of the Police in a Modern Society* (Washington: US Government Printing Office).

Black, T. R. (1993) *Evaluating Social Science Research* (London: Sage).

Blumenthal, H. J. (1988) 'CCTV: The big picture' *Security Management* 32(11): 7.

Bogard, W. (1996) *The Simulation of Surveillance in Telematic Society: Social Control in the 1990s* (Cambridge: Cambridge University Press).

Bottoms, A. (1990) 'Crime prevention facing the 1990s' *Policing and Society* 1: 3.

——(2000) 'Theory and research in criminology' in King and Wincup (2000).

——and P. Wiles (1996) 'Understanding crime prevention in late modern societies' in Bennett (1996).

Bouley, J. (1994) 'Night vision technology cuts through darkness' *Security* 31(2): 23.

Bradburn, N., S. Sudman, and E. Blair (1979) *Improving Interview Method and Questionnaire Design* (San Francisco: Jossey-Bass).

Brake, M., and C. Hale (1992) *Public Order and Private Lives: The Politics of Law and Order* (London: Routledge).

Brantingham, P., and P. Brantingham (1981) *Environmental Criminology* (Beverly Hills, Calif.: Sage).

Brenner, M., J. Brown, and D. Canter (eds.) (1985) *The Research Interview: Uses and Approaches* (London: Academic Press).

Bright, J. (1991) 'Crime prevention: the British experience' in Stenson and Cowell (1991), 62.

——(1997) *Turning the Tide: Crime, Community and Prevention* (London: Demos).

Brin, D. (1999) *The Transparent Society: Will Technology Force us to Choose between Privacy and Freedom?* (Cambridge: Perseus).

British Society for Social Responsibility in Science (BSSRS) Technology of Political Control Group (1985) *TechnoCop: New Police Technologies* (London: Free Association Books).

British Sociological Association (1992) 'Statement of ethical practice' *Sociology* 26: 703.

British Standard 7858:1996 (1996) *Code of Practice for Security Screening of Personnel Employed in a Security Environment* (London: British Standards Institute).

Brogden, M., T. Jefferson, and S. Walklate (1988) *Introducing Policework* (London: Unwin).

Brown, A. (1998) *Police Governance in England and Wales* (London: Cavendish).

Brown, B. (1995) 'CCTV in town centres: three case studies' Crime Detection and Prevention Series, Paper No. 68 (London: Police Research Group, Home Office Police Department).

Bulmer, M. (1980) 'Comment on "The ethics of covert methods" by R Holman' *British Journal of Sociology* 31(1): 59.

—— (1982) *Social Research Ethics* (London: Macmillan).

Bulos, M., W. Chaker, M. Farish, V. Mahalingham, and C. Sarno (1995) *Towards a Safer Sutton? Impact of Closed Circuit TV on Sutton Town Centre* (London: London Borough of Sutton).

—— and D. Grant (eds.) (1996) *Towards a Safer Sutton? CCTV One Year On* (London: London Borough of Sutton).

—— and C. Sarno (1994) *Closed Circuit Television and Local Authority Initiatives: The First National Survey* (London: School of Land Management and Urban Policy, South Bank University London).

—— —— (1996) *Codes of Practice and Public Closed Circuit Television Systems* (London: Local Government Information Unit).

Bunyan, M. (1997) 'Judge angry as boy thugs go free' *Daily Telegraph* (7 June).

Bunyan, T. (1977) *The Political Police in Britain* (Harmondsworth: Penguin).

Burgess, R. (1989a) 'Keeping field notes' in Burgess (1989e), 191.

—— (1989b) 'Some role problems in field research' in Burgess (1989e), 46.

—— (1989c) 'Styles of data analysis: approaches and implications' in Burgess (1989e), 235.

—— (1989d) 'The unstructured interview as conversation' in Burgess (1989e), 107.

—— (ed.) (1989e) *Field Research: A Sourcebook and Field Manual* (London: Routledge).

Burnham, D. (1983) *The Rise of the Computer State* (New York: Vintage).

Burrows, J. N. (1979) 'The impact of closed circuit television on crime in the London Underground' in Mayhew *et al.* (1979).

Burrows, Q. (1997) 'Scowl because you're on candid camera: privacy and video surveillance' *Valparaiso University Law Review* 31: 1083.

Butler, A. J. P. (1984) *Police Management* (London: Gower).

Bygrave, L. A. (1998) 'Data protection reform in Scandinavia' *Privacy Law & Policy Reporter* 5: 9.

—— and A. H. Aarø (2001) 'Privacy, personality, and publicity: an overview of Norwegian law' in Henry (2001).

Cahill, M. (1994) *The New Social Policy* (Oxford: Blackwell).

Campbell, D. (1995) 'Spy cameras become part of the landscape' *Guardian* (30 Jan.), 6.

Cate, H., and M. H. Armacost (1997) *Privacy in the Information Age* (Washington: The Brookings Institution).

Chan, J. (1997) *Changing Police Culture* (Cambridge: Cambridge University Press).

Chatterton, M. R. and S. J. Frenz (1994) 'CCTV: its role in reducing burglaries and the fear of crime in sheltered accommodation for the elderly' *Security Journal* 3(3): 133.

Choongh, S. (1997) *Policing as Social Discipline* (Oxford: Clarendon).

Clarke, R. V. (1995) 'Situational crime prevention' in M. Tonry and D. P. Farrington (eds.) *Building a Safer Society: Strategic Approaches to Crime Prevention*, Crime and Justice Series, vol. 19 (London: University of Chicago Press), 91.

—— (1997) *Situational Crime Prevention: Successful Case Studies*, 2nd edn. (Albany, NY: Harrow and Heston).

—— and M. Hough (1984) *Crime and Police Effectiveness* (London: Home Office).

Cohen, S. (1980) 'Ethnography without tears' *Urban Life* 9(1): 25.

—— (1985) *Visions of Social Control* (Cambridge: Polity Press).

—— (1989) 'The critical discourse on "social control": note on the concept as a hammer' *International Journal of the Sociology of Law* 17: 347.

—— (1994) 'Social control and the politics of reconstruction' in Nelken (1994).

Coleman, C., and C. Norris (2000) 'CCTV and crime prevention: questions for criminology' in C. Coleman and C. Norris *Introducing Criminology* (Cullompton, Devon: Willan Publishing).

Coleman, R. and J. Sim (1998) 'From the dockyards to the Disney store: surveillance, risk and security in Liverpool city centre' *Law, Computers & Technology* 12(1): 27.

—— —— (2000) 'You'll never walk alone: CCTV surveillance, order and neo-liberal rule in Liverpool city centre' *British Journal of Sociology* 51(4): 623.

Conservative Central Office (1979) *Conservative Manifesto 1979* (London: McCorquodale Printer Ltd.).

—— (1983) *Conservative Manifesto 1983* (London: McCorquodale Printer Ltd.).

Constant, M. (2001) 'Digital transfers' *CCTV Today* (Sept./Oct.).

—— and P. Turnbull (1994) *The Principles and Practice of Closed Circuit Television* (Hertfordshire: Paramount Publishing Ltd.).

Cornish, D., and R. Clarke (1983) *Crime Control in Britain: A Review of Policy Research* (Albany, NY: State University of New York Press).

Crawford, A. (1997) *The Local Governance of Crime* (Oxford: Oxford University Press).

—— (1998) *Crime Prevention and Community Safety: Politics, Policies, and Practices* (Harlow: Addison Wesley Longman Ltd.).

Crawford, A., and M. Jones (1995) 'Inter-agency cooperation and community-based crime prevention: some reflections on the work of Pearson and colleagues' *British Journal of Criminology* 35(1): 17.

Currie, E. (1996) 'Social crime prevention strategies in a market society' in Muncie *et al.* (1996), 343.

Damjanovski, V. (1999) *CCTV* (Burlington: Elsevier Science).

Dandeker, C. (1990) *Surveillance Power and Modernity* (Cambridge: Polity Press).

Davies, M. (1992) *Beyond Blade Runner: Urban Control and the Ecology of Fear* (Westfield, NJ: Open Magazine Pamphlet Series).

——(1998) *City of Quartz: Excavating the Future in Los Angeles* (London: Pillico).

Davies, S. (1994) 'They've got an eye on you' *Independent* (2 Nov.), 22.

——(1995) 'Welcome home Big Brother' *Wired* (May).

——(1996a) *Big Brother: Britain's Web of Surveillance and the New Technological Order* (London: Pan Books).

——(1996b) 'The case against: CCTV should not be introduced' *International Journal of Risk, Security and Crime Prevention* 1(4): 327.

——(1997) '10 reasons why public CCTV schemes are bad' KDIS Online, http://merlin.legend.org.uk/-brs/cctv/tenreasons.html, Apr.

——(1998) 'CCTV: a new battleground for privacy' in Norris *et al.* (1998b), 243.

Dawson, T. (1994) 'Framing the villains' *New Statesman* (23 Jan.), 12.

Delfour, J. J. (1996) 'La vidéosurveillance et le pouvoir du voir (Du panoptisme comme modèle de société)' *Lignes* 27: 151.

Denzin, N. (1970) *The Research Act* (Chicago: Aldine).

Diffley, C., and E. Wallace (1998a) *CCTV: Making it Work: Training Practices for CCTV Operators* (St Albans: Home Office Police Scientific Development Branch).

————(1998b) *CCTV: Making it Work—Recruiting and Selection of CCTV Operators* (St Albans: Home Office Police Scientific Development Branch).

Ditton, J. (1979) *Contrology beyond the New Criminology* (Oxford: Macmillan).

——(1998) 'Public support for town centre CCTV schemes: myth or reality?' in Norris *et al.* (1998b), 221.

——and E. Short (1996) 'Does CCTV affect crime?' Paper presented at the conference CCTV Surveillance and Social Control (University of Hull, 9 July 1996).

————(1998a) 'Evaluating Scotland's first town centre CCTV scheme' in Norris *et al.* (1998b), 155.

————(1998b) 'Seen and now heard: talking to the targets of open street CCTV' *British Journal of Criminology* 38(3): 404.

———— (1999) 'Yes, it works, no, it doesn't: comparing the effects of open-street CCTV in two adjacent Scottish town centres' in Painter and Tilley (1999b), 201.

Dixon, D., K. Bottomley, C. Coleman, M. Gill, and D. Wall (1989) 'Reality and rules in the construction and regulation of police suspicion' *International Journal of the Sociology of Law* 17: 185.

—— C. Coleman, and K. Bottomley (1990) 'Consent and legal regulation of policing' *Journal of Legal Studies* 17: 345.

Douglas, J. D. (1976) *Investigative Social Research* (Beverly Hills, Calif.: Sage).

Downes, D., and R. Morgan (1994) '"Hostages to fortune"? The politics of law and order in post-war Britain' in Maguire *et al.* (1994), 183.

———— (1997) 'Dumping the "hostages to fortune": the politics of law and order in post-war Britain' in Maguire *et al.* (1997), 87.

—— and J. Young (1987) 'Crime and government' *New Society* (21 May), 55.

Drury, I. (2001a) 'Bus lane super highway' *CCTV Today* (Sept./Oct.).

—— (2001b) 'More peaks to scale as UK market reaches plateau' *CCTV Today* (Nov./Dec.).

Dworkin, R. (1977) *Taking Rights Seriously* (London: Duckworth).

Eck, J. E. (1997) 'Preventing crime at places' in Sherman *et al.* (1997).

Ekblom, P., and K. Pease (1995) 'Evaluating crime prevention' in Tonry and Farrington (1995), 582.

Ellul, J. (1964) *The Technological Society* (New York: Vintage).

Emsley, C. (1996) *The English Police* (Harrow: Longman).

Ericson, R., and K. Carriere (1994) 'The fragmentation of criminology' in Nelken (1994), 89.

Ericson, R., and K. Haggerty (1997) *Policing the Risk Society* (Oxford: Clarendon).

Etzioni, A. (2000) *The Limits of Privacy* (New York: Basic Books).

Evans, D., N. R. Fyfe, and D. Herbert (eds.) (1992) *Crime, Policing and Place: Essays in Environmental Criminology* (London: Routledge).

—— and D. Herbert (eds.) (1989) *The Geography of Crime* (London: Routledge).

Farish, M. (1995) 'The response of special interest groups to CCTV' in Bulos *et al.* (eds.).

Fassbender, J. (2001) 'When image is everything' *CCTV Today* (Sept.).

Fawcett, J. E. S. (1987) *The Application of the European Convention on Human Rights*, 2nd edn. (Oxford: Clarendon Press).

Fay, S. J. (1998) 'Tough on crime, tough on civil liberties: some negative aspects of Britain's wholesale adoption of CCTV surveillance during the 1990s' *Law, Computers & Technology* 12(2): 315.

Feeley, M., and J. Simon (1994) 'Actuarial justice: the emerging new criminal law' in Nelken (1994), 173.

Feenberg, A. (1991) *A Critical Theory of Technology* (New York: Oxford University Press).

—— (1999) *Questioning Technology* (London: Routledge).

Feldman, D. (1993) *Civil Liberties and Human Rights in England and Wales* (Oxford: Clarendon Press).

—— (1994) 'Secrecy, dignity or autonomy? Views of privacy as a civil liberty' *Current Legal Problems* 47: 41.

—— (1997) 'Privacy-related rights and their social value' in Birks (1997), 15.

Felson, M., and R. V. Clarke (1997) 'The ethics of situational crime prevention' in Newman, *et al.* (1997), 197.

Fielding, N. (1993) 'Ethnography' in Gilbert (1993), 154.

—— and J. L. Fielding (1986) *Linking data* Sage University Paper Series on Qualitative Research Methods, vol. 4 (Newbury Park, Calif.: Sage).

Flaherty, D. H. (1988) 'The emergence of surveillance societies in the Western world: towards the year 2000' *Government Information Quarterly* 5(4): 377.

—— (1989) *Protecting Privacy in Surveillance Societies* (Chapel Hill, NC: University of North Carolina Press).

Foote Whyte, W. (1989) 'Interviewing in field research' in Burgess (1989*e*), 111.

Foucault, M. (1977) *Discipline and Punish: The Birth of the Prison* (London: Allen Lane).

Francis, P., and J. Braggins (1995) 'Editorial' *Criminal Justice Matters* (summer) (20): 2.

Fyfe, N. R. (1995*a*) 'Controlling the local spaces of democracy and liberty? 1994 criminal justice legislation' *Urban Geography* 16(3): 192.

—— (1995*b*) 'Law and order policy and the spaces of citizenship in contemporary Britain' *Political Geography* 14(2): 177.

—— and J. Bannister (1996) 'City watching: closed circuit television surveillance in public places' *Area* 28(1): 37.

Gadher, D. (1999) 'Smile, you're on 300 candid cameras...' *The Sunday Times* (14 Feb.).

Gamble, A. (1988) *The Free Economy and the Strong State: The Politics of Thatcherism* (London: Macmillan).

Gandy, O. (1993) *The Panoptic Sort: A Political Economy of Personal Information* (Boulder, Col.: Westview Press).

Garfinkel, H. (1967) *Studies in Ethnomethodology* (Englewood Cliffs, NJ: Prentice Hall).

Garfinkel, S. (2001) *Database Nation: The Death of Privacy in the 21st Century* (Cambridge: O'Reilly & Associates).

Garland, C. (1985) *Punishment and Modern Society: A Study in Social Theory* (Oxford: Clarendon).

Garland, D. (1985) *Punishment and Welfare: A History of Penal Strategies* (Aldershot: Gower).

—— (1995) 'Panopticon days: surveillance and society' *Criminal Justice Matters* (20): 4.

—— (1996) 'The limits of the sovereign state: strategies of crime control in contemporary society' *British Journal of Criminology* 36: 4.

—— (2000) 'The culture of high crime societies: some preconditions of recent "law and order" policies' *British Journal of Criminology* 40: 3.

—— (2001) *The Culture of Control: Crime and Social Order in Late Modernity* (Oxford: Oxford University Press).

Geake, E. (1993a) 'The electronic arm of the law' *New Scientist* (8 May), 21.

—— (1993b) 'Tiny Brother is watching you' *New Scientist* (8 May), 21.

Geertz, C. (1988) *Works and Lives: The Anthropologist as Author* (Stanford, Calif.: Stanford University Press).

—— (1993) *The Interpretation of Cultures* (London: Fontana).

Giddens, A. (1981) *A Contemporary Critique of Historical Materialism, Vol. 1: Power, Property, and the State* (Berkeley: University of California Press).

—— (1985) *The Nation-State and Violence* (Cambridge: Polity Press).

Gilbert, N. I. (ed.) (1993) *Researching Social Life* (London: Sage).

Gill, M. and V. Turbin (1997) *An Evaluation of the Effectiveness of CCTV in Two Retail Stores* (Leicester: Scarman Centre for the Study of Public Order).

———— (1999) 'Evaluating "Realistic evaluation": evidence from a study of CCTV' in Painter and Tilley (1999b), 179.

Gill, P. (2000) *Rounding up the Usual Suspects? Developments in Contemporary Law Enforcement Intelligence* (Aldershot: Ashgate), 391.

Gluckman, M. (1961) 'Ethnographic data in British social anthropology' *Sociological Review* 9(1): 5.

Goffman, E. (1972) *Behaviour in Public Places* (Harmondsworth: Pelican).

Goldstein, H. (1990) *Problem Oriented Policing* (New York: McGraw-Hill).

Goldstein, J. (1960) 'Police discretion not to invoke the criminal process: low visibility decisions in the administration of justice' *Yale Law Journal* 63: 543.

Goold, B. J. (2002a) 'CCTV and public area surveillance in Japan: balancing privacy rights and police powers' *Hosei Riron* (*Journal of Law and Politics*) 35(2): 149.

—— (2002b) 'Privacy rights and public spaces: CCTV and the problem of the "unobservable observer"' *Criminal Justice Ethics* 21(1): 21.

Goold, B. J. (2003) 'Public area surveillance and policing: the impact of CCTV on police behaviour and autonomy' *Journal of Surveillance and Society* 2(1): 191.

Gormley, K. (1992) 'One hundred years of privacy' *Wisconsin Law Review* 1345.

Graef, R. (1989) *Talking Blues* (London: Collins).

Graham, S. (1997) 'Urban planning in the information society' *Town and Country Planning* (Nov.), 298.

—— (1998a) 'The end of geography or the explosion of place? Conceptualizing space, place, and information technology' *Progress in Human Geography* 22(2): 165.

—— (1998b) 'Spaces of surveillant simulation: new technologies, digital representations, and material geographies' *Environment and Planning: Society and Space* 16: 494.

—— (1998c) 'Towards a fifth utility? On the extension and normalisation of public CCTV' in Norris *et al.* (1998b), 89.

—— J. Brooks and D. Heery (1996a) 'Towns on television: closed circuit TV in British towns and cities', Paper presented at the conference CCTV Surveillance and Social Control (University of Hull, 9 July).

—— —— —— (1996b) 'Towns on the television: closed circuit TV in British towns and cities' *Local Government Studies* 22(3): 3.

—— and S. Marvin (1996) *Telecommunications and the City: Electronic Spaces, Urban Places* (London: Routledge).

Granholm, J. M. (1987) 'Video surveillance on public streets: the constitutionality of invisible citizen searches' *Detroit Law Review* 64: 694.

Green, C. (2000) 'User options' *CCTV Today* (Nov./Dec.).

Green, P. and A. Rutherford (eds.) (2000) *Criminal Policy in Transition* (Oxford: Hart).

Grimshaw, R., and T. Jefferson (1987) *Interpreting Policework* (London: Unwin).

Grollier Multimedia Encyclopaedia (1995) (Calif.: Grollier Electronic Publishing Incorporated).

Grombridge, N., and K. Murji (1994) 'Obscured by cameras?' *Criminal Justice Matters* 17: 9.

Gropp, W. (1993a) *Besondere Ermittlungsmaanahmen zur Bekämpfung der Organisierten Kriminalität—Ein rechtsvergleichendes Gutachten im Auftrag des Bundesministeriums der Justiz und des Bayerischen Staatsministeriums der Justiz* (Freiburg im Briesgau: Max-Planck-Institut für ausländisches und internationales Strafrecht).

—— (1993b) 'Special methods of investigation for combating organised crime' *European Journal of Crime, Criminal Law and Criminal Justice* 1: 20.

Guardian, 'Someone's watching' (22 Mar. 1995), 2.

—— 'Fears over crime outweigh reality' (4 Oct. 1995), 5.

—— 'Fear of crime "driving out high street shoppers"' (8 Nov. 1995), 10

Hacking, L. (1983) *Representing and Intervening* (Oxford: Oxford University Press).

Hagan, J., and R. Peterson (eds.) (1995) *Crime and Inequality* (Stanford, Calif.: Stanford University Press).

Hall, S. (1979) *Drifting into a Law and Order Society* (London: Cobden Trust).

—— (1985) 'Authoritarian populism' *New Left Review* 115.

Hammersley, M. (1989) *The Dilemma of Qualitative Method: Herbert Blumer and the Chicago Tradition* (London: Routledge).

—— (1992) *What's Wrong with Ethnography?* (London: Routledge).

—— (1998) *Reading Ethnographic Research: A Critical Guide* (Harlow: Addison Wesley Longman Ltd.).

—— and P. Atkinson (1983) *Ethnography: Principles in Practice* (London: Tavistock).

Hancox, P. D., and J. B. Morgan (1975) 'The use of CCTV for police control at football matches' *Police Research Bulletin* 25: 41.

Harvey, D. (1990) *The Condition of Postmodernity: An Enquiry into the Origins of Cultural Change* (Oxford: Blackwell).

—— (1993) 'From space to place and back again: reflections on the condition of postmodernity' in Bird (1993).

Hassemer, W. (1992) 'Brauchen wir den "Großen Lauschangriff"?' *Deutsche Richterzeitung* (Sept.), 355.

Hay, C. (1995) 'Mobilization through interpellation: James Bulger, juvenile crime and the construction of a moral panic' *Social and Legal Studies* 4(2): 197.

Heal, K. (1992) 'Changing perspectives on crime prevention: the role of information and structure' in Evans *et al.* (1992), 257.

—— and J. Burrows (eds.) (1983) *Crime Prevention: A Co-ordinated Approach* (London: HMSO).

—— and G. Laycock (1988) 'The development of crime prevention: issues and limitations' in Hope and Shaw (1988), 236.

Hempel, L., and E. Töpfer (2002) *Working paper No. 1: Inception report*, Urban eye project: On the threshold to urban Panopticon? Analysing the employment of CCTV in European cities and assessing its social and political impacts (Berlin: Centre for technology and society, Technical University Berlin).

Henry, M. (ed.) (2001) *International Privacy, Publicity and Personality Laws* (London: Butterworths).

Hillegas, M. R. (1967) *The Future as Nightmare: H. G. Wells and the Anti-utopians* (New York: Oxford University Press).

Hirsch, A. von (2000) 'The ethics of public television surveillance' in von Hirsch *et al.* (eds.) (2000), 59.

Hobbes, D. (1988) *Doing the Business* (Oxford: Oxford University Press).

Hobbs, D., and T. May (eds.) (1993) *Interpreting the Field: Accounts of Ethnography* (Oxford: Clarendon).

Hogwood, B. (1992) *Trends in British Public Policy* (Buckingham: Open University Press).

Holdaway, S. (ed.) (1979) *The British Police* (London: Arnold).

—— (1983) *Inside the British Police* (Oxford: Blackwell).

—— (1989) 'Discovering structure: studies of the British police occupational culture' in Weatheritt (ed.), 55.

Homan, R. (1980) 'The ethics of covert methods' *British Journal of Sociology* 31(1): 46.

—— (1991) *The Ethics of Social Research* (London: Longman).

Home Office (1979) *The Private Security Industry: A Discussion Paper* (London: HMSO).

—— (1984) 'Crime prevention', Home Office Circular 8/1984 (London: Home Office).

—— (1986) 'Review of Public Order Law' (London: HMSO).

—— (1990*a*) 'Crime prevention: the success of the partnership approach', Home Office Circular 44/1990 (London: Home Office).

—— (1990*b*) *Digest of CCTV schemes* (London: HMSO).

—— (1993) 'Disclosure of criminal records for employment vetting purposes', Home Office Green Paper (London: HMSO).

—— (1994) 'CCTV: looking out for you', Pamphlet (London: HMSO).

—— (1995) *CCTV Challenge Competition 1996/7: Bidding Guidance* (London: HMSO).

—— (1997) *Closed Circuit Television Challenge Competition (Round 4) 1998/99* (London: The Home Office Crime Prevention Agency).

—— (1998*a*) 'Recruitment and selection of CCTV operators', Police Scientific and Development Branch Report (London: Home Office).

—— (1998*b*) 'Training practices for CCTV operators', Police Scientific and Development Branch Report (London: Home Office).

—— (2003) 'National evaluation of CCTV: early findings on scheme implementation and an effective practice guide', Home Office Development and Practice Report (London: HMSO).

Honess, T., and E. Charman (1992) 'Closed circuit television in public places: its acceptability and perceived effectiveness', Crime Prevention Unit Series, Paper 35 (London: Home Office Police Research Group).

Hoogenboom, A. B. (1989) 'The privatisation of social control' in R. Hood (ed.) *Crime and Criminal Policy in Europe: Proceedings of a European Colloquium, 3–6 July 1988* (Oxford: University of Oxford Centre for Criminological Research), 121.

Hook, P. (1994) 'Faces in the crowd' *Police Review* (22 July), 22.

Hope, T. (1999) 'Privatopia on trial? Property guardianship in the suburbs' in Painter and Tilley (1999*b*), 15.

—— and M. Shaw (eds.) (1988) *Communities and Crime Reduction* (London: HMSO).

Horrocks, I., J. Moff, and P. Topps (eds.) (2000) *Democratic Governance and New Technology: Technologically Mediated Innovations in Political Practices in Western Europe* (London: Routledge).

House of Lords Select Committee on Science and Technology (1997) 'Enquiry into digital images as evidence: oral evidence' (London: HMSO).

Hoyle, C. (2000) 'Being "a nosy bloody cow": ethical and methodological issues in researching domestic violence' in King and Wincup (2000), 395.

Hughes, G. (1998) *Understanding Crime Prevention* (Buckingham: Open University Press).

Hutton, G., and D. Johnston (2001) *Blackstone's Police Manual: Evidence and Procedure* (London: Blackstone).

Inness, J. (1992) *Privacy, Intimacy and Isolation* (Oxford: Oxford University Press).

Janßen, K.-H. (ed.) (1984) *Ihr glücklichen Augen . . .* (Frankfurt: Robinson).

Jenkins, J. (1992) 'Eye can see you' *New Statesman and Society* (21 Feb.), 14.

Jenkins, S. (1996) *Accountable to None: The Tory Nationalisation of Britain* (London: Penguin).

Johnston, L. (1992) *The Rebirth of Private Policing* (London: Routledge).

—— (2000) *Policing Britain: Risk, Security and Governance* (Harlow: Longman).

Jones, P., D. Hiller, and D. Turner (1997) 'Exploring the role of CCTV surveillance systems in town centre management' *Management Research News* 20: 35.

Jones, T., and T. Newburn (1994) 'How big is the private security industry?' *Policy Studies Institute* (Aug.), 32.

—— —— (1996) 'The regulation and control of the private security industry' in Saulsbury, Mott, and Newburn (eds.), 105.

—— —— (1998) *Private Security and Public Policing* (Oxford: Clarendon).

—— —— and D. Smith (1994) *Democracy and Policing* (London: Policy Studies Institute).

Jupp, V. (1996) *Methods of Criminological Research* (London: Routledge).

Justice (1997) 'Digital images as evidence: report to the House of Lords Select Committee on Science and Technology' (London: Justice).

KDIS Online (1997) 'CCTV: Big Brother in Bradford', http//merlin.legend.org.uk/~brs/cctv/kdis12.html, Mar.

Kettle, M. (1980) 'The drift to law and order' *Marxism Today* (Oct.), 20.

Kettle, M. (1982) *Uprising!: The Police, the People and the Riots in Britain's Cities* (London: Pan).

King, R. D., and E. Wincup (eds.) (2000) *Doing Research on Crime and Justice* (Oxford: Oxford University Press).

Kitchen, H. (1996) *A Watching Brief: A Code of Practice for CCTV* (London: Local Government Information Unit).

Koch, B. C. M. (1998) *The Politics of Crime Prevention* (Aldershot: Ashgate).

Kramer, B. (1992) 'Videoaufnahmen und andere Eingriffe in das Allgemeine Persönlichkeitrecht auf der Grundlage des § 163 StPO' *Neue Juristische Wochenschrift* 2732.

Kruegle, H. (1996) *CCTV Surveillance: Video Practices and Technology* (Burlington, Vt.: Butterworth-Heinemann).

Kuhns, E., and S. V. Martorane (eds.) (1981) *Qualitative Methods for Institutional Decision-Making* (San Francisco: Jossey-Bass).

Kulter Films Inc. (1995) *Caught in the Act.*

Laycock, G., and K. Heal (1989) 'Crime prevention: the British experience' in Evans and Herbert (1989), 315.

Lea, J., and J. Young (1984) *What is to be Done about Law and Order?* (Harmondsworth: Penguin).

Leishman, F., B. Loveday, and S. P. Savage (eds.) (1996) *Core Issues in Policing* (London: Longman).

Lianos, M., and M. Douglas (2000) 'Dangerisation and the end of deviance: the institutional environment' in Sparks and Garland (eds.).

Liberty (1989) 'Who's watching you? Video surveillance in public places', Liberty Briefing Paper No. 16 (London: Liberty).

—— (1995) *Defending Diversity, Defining Dissent: What's Wrong with the Criminal Justice and Public Order Act 1994* (London: National Council for Civil Liberties).

—— (1998) 'Digital images as evidence', Submission to the House of Lords Select Committee on Science and Technology (London: Liberty, 1997). Also published in House of Lords Select Committee on Science and Technology 'Digital images as evidence', Evidence HL Paper 64-1 (London: HMSO).

Lloyd, I. (1996) 'Review of *Big Brother: Britain's Web of Surveillance and the New Technological Order* by Simon Davies' *Journal of Information, Law and Technology* 3.

Loader, I. (1997) 'Private security and the demand for protection in contemporary Britain' *Policing and Society* 7: 143.

—— (1998) 'Criminology in the public sphere: arguments for utopian realism' in Walton and Young (eds.), 190.

Local Government Association (1998) *Local Government Association (LGA) CCTV Directory 1997/1998* (London: Local Government Association).

Lofland, J. (1971) *Analysing Social Settings* (New York: Wadsworth).

—— (1974) 'Styles of reporting qualitative field reports' *American Sociologist* 9(3): 307.

Lofland, L. H. (1973) *A World of Strangers: Order and Action in Urban Public Space* (New York: Basic Books).

Lowman, J., R. Menzies, and T. Plays (eds.) (1987) *Transcarceration: Essays in the Sociology of Social Control* (Aldershot: Gower).

Lustgarten, L. (1986) *The Government of the Police* (London: Sweet and Maxwell).

Lyon, D. (1994) *The Electronic Eye: The Rise of Surveillance Society* (London: Polity Press).

—— (2001) *Surveillance Society: Monitoring Everyday Life* (Buckingham: Open University Press).

—— and E. Zureik (eds.) (1996) *Computers, Surveillance and Privacy* (Minneapolis: University of Minnesota Press).

McCabe, S., and P. Wallington (1988) *The Police, Public Order and Civil Liberties: The Legacy of the Miners' Strike* (London: Routledge).

McCahill, M. (1998) 'Beyond Foucault: towards a contemporary theory of surveillance' in Norris *et al.* (1998b), 41.

—— (2002) *The Surveillance Web: The Rise of Visual Surveillance in an English City* (Collumpton, Devon. Willan Publishing).

—— and C. Norris (1999) 'Watching the workers: crime, CCTV and the workplace' in P. Davies, V. Jupp, and P. Francis (eds.) *Invisible Crimes: Their Victims and their Regulation* (London: Macmillan), 208.

—— —— (2002a) 'Working paper No. 2: literature review', Urban eye project: On the threshold to urban Panopticon? Analysing the employment of CCTV in European cities and assessing its social and political impacts (Berlin: Centre for technology and society, Technical University Berlin).

—— —— (2002b) 'Working paper No. 3: CCTV in Britain', Urban eye project: On the threshold to urban Panopticon? Analysing the employment of CCTV in European cities and assessing its social and political impacts (Berlin: Centre for technology and society, Technical University Berlin).

—— —— (2002c) 'Working paper No. 6: CCTV in London', Urban eye project: On the threshold to urban Panopticon? Analysing the employment of CCTV in European cities and assessing its social and political impacts (Berlin: Centre for technology and society, Technical University Berlin).

McConville, M., and J. Hodgson (1993) *Custodial Legal Advice and the Right to Silence*, RCCJ Study No. 16 (London: HMSO).

—— and D. Shepherd (1992) *Watching Police, Watching Communities* (London: Routledge).

——A. Sanders and R. Leng (1991) *The Case for the Prosecution* (London: Routledge).

McKenzie, I. K. (ed.) (1998) *Law, Power and Justice in England and Wales* (Westport, Conn.: Praeger Publishers).

McLuhan, M., and Q. Fiore (1967) *The Medium is the Message* (New York: Bantam).

—— and B. Powers (1989) *The Global Village: Transformations in World Life and Media in the 21st Century* (Oxford: Oxford University Press).

Maanen, J. van (1983) 'The boss: first-line supervision in an American police agency' in Punch (ed.), 277.

—— and P. Manning (eds.) (1978) *Policing: A View from the Streets* (New York: Random House).

Maguire, M. (1998) 'Restraining Big Brother? The regulation of surveillance in England and Wales' in Norris *et al.* (1998*b*), 229.

——R. Morgan, and R. Reiner (eds.) (1994) *The Oxford Handbook of Criminology* (Oxford: Clarendon).

——————(eds.) (1997) *The Oxford Handbook of Criminology*, 2nd edn. (Oxford: Clarendon).

Mahalingham, V. (1996) 'Sutton town centre public perception survey' in Bulos and Grant (1996).

Mainprize, S. (1996) 'Elective affinities in the engineering of social control: the evolution of electronic monitoring' *Electronic Journal of Sociology* 2.

Manning, P. (1977) *Police Work: The Social Organisation of Policing* (Cambridge, Mass.: Massachusetts Institute of Technology Press).

——(1979) 'The social control of police work' in Holdaway (1979), 41.

——(1988) *Symbolic Communication: Signifying Calls and the Police Response* (Cambridge, Mass.: MIT Press) 155.

——(1992) 'Information technologies and the police' in Tonry and Morris (1992), 349.

——(2000) 'Information technologies and the police' in Gill (2000), 391.

Manuel, F. G., and F. P. Manuel (1979) *Utopian Thought in the Western World* (Oxford: Blackwell).

Manwaring-White, S. (1983) *The Policing Revolution: Police Technology, Democracy and Liberty in Britain* (Brighton: Harvester).

Marenin, O. (ed.) (1995) *Policing Change: Changing Police* (New York: Garland).

Marshall, G. (1965) *Police and Government* (London: Methuen).

Marx, G. T. (1985) 'The surveillance society: the threat of 1984-style techniques' *The Futurist* (June), 21.

—— (1987) 'The interweaving of public and private police in undercover work' in Shearing and Stenning (1987), 172.

—— (1988) *Undercover: Police Surveillance in America* (Berkeley: University of California Press).

—— (1995a) 'Electric eye in the sky: some reflections of the new surveillance and popular culture' in J. Ferrell and R. Sanders, *Cultural Criminology* (Boston: North Eastern University Press), 106.

—— (1995b) 'The engineering of social control: the search for the silver bullet' in Hagan and Peterson (1995) 225.

Matchett, A. (2002) *CCTV for Security Professionals* (Amsterdam: Elsevier Science).

Mathiesen, T. (1983) 'The future of control systems: the case of Norway' in D. Garland and P. Young (eds.) *The Power to Punish: Contemporary Penality and Social Analysis* (London: Heinemann), 130.

Mayhew, P., R. G. V. Clarke, J. N. Burrows, J. M. Hough, and S. W. C. Wincester (1979) *Crime in Public View*, Home Office Research Study, No. 49 (London: HMSO).

Meyer-Larsen, W. (ed.) (1983) *Der Orwell-Statt 1984* (Reinbek: Rowohlt).

Michael, A. (Minister of State) (30 July 1997) *Hansard House of Commons Debates* (London: HMSO).

Miller, J. (2000) *Profiling Populations Available for Stops and Searches*, Police Research Series Paper 131 (London: HMSO).

Mitchell, J. C. (ed.) (1969) *Social Networks in Urban Situations* (Manchester: University of Manchester Press).

Moran, J. (1998) 'A brief chronology of photographic and video surveillance' in Norris *et al.* (1998b), 277.

Morgan, R. (1989) 'Police accountability: current developments and future prospects' in Weatheritt (1989), 169.

—— and D. J. Smith (eds.) (1989) *Coming to Terms with Policing* (London: Routledge).

Morison, J. (1987) 'New strategies in the politics of law and order' *Howard Journal* 26(3): 203.

Münchhausen, von A. (1984) 'Die stummen Aufpasser: ein dichtes Netz von Videokameras, der unser öffenliches Leben überwacht' in Janßen (1984), 90.

Muncie, J., E. McLaughlin, and M. Langan (eds.) (1996) *Criminological Perspectives: A Reader* (London: Sage).

Murphy, T. (1999) 'The admissibility of CCTV evidence in criminal proceedings' *Law, Computers & Technology* 13(3): 383.

Musheno, M., J. Levine, and D. Palumbo (1978) 'Television surveillance and crime prevention: evaluation of an attempt to create defensible space in public housing' *Social Science Quarterly* 58(4): 647.

Narayan, S. (1996) 'What's happening?' *CCTV Today* (Nov.), 20.

Nash, M., and S. P. Savage (1994) 'A criminal record? Law, order and Conservative policy' in Savage, Atkinson, and Robbins, (eds.), 211.

Naughton, J. (1994) 'Smile you're on TV' *Life: The Observer Magazine* (13 Nov.).

Nelken, D. (ed.) (1994) *The Futures of Criminology* (London: Sage).

New Scientist (1996) 'Crime watch' (Jan.) 6(13): 47.

Newburn, T. and S. Hayman (2002) *Policing, Surveillance, and Social Control: CCTV and the Police Monitoring of Suspects* (Collumpton, Devon: Willan Publishing).

Newman, G., R. V. Clarke, and S. G. Shoham (eds.) (1997) *Rational Choice and Situational Crime Prevention* (Aldershot: Ashgate).

Nieto, M. (1997) *Public Video Surveillance: Is it an Effective Crime Prevention Tool?* (Sacramento, Calif.: California Research Bureau).

Nock, S. (1993) *The Costs of Privacy* (New York: Aldine de Gruyter).

Nogala, D. (1998) 'Social control technologies: Verwendungsgrammatiken, Systematisierung and problemfelder technisierter sozialer Kontrollarrangements', unpublished dissertation (Berlin: Free University).

Norris, C. (1995) 'Algorithmic surveillance' *Criminal Justice Matters* (summer) (20): 7.

—— (1997) 'Surveillance, order and social control: end of award report to the Economic and Social Research Council' (Hull: Department of Social Policy, University of Hull).

—— and G. Armstrong (1998) 'Introduction: power and vision' in Norris *et al.* (1998*b*), 3.

—— —— (1999*a*) 'CCTV and the social structuring of surveillance' in Painter and Tilley (1999*b*), 157.

—— —— (1999*b*) *The Maximum Surveillance Society: The Rise of CCTV* (Oxford: Berg).

—— J. Moran, and G. Armstrong (1996) 'Algorithmic surveillance: the future of automated visual surveillance', Paper presented at the conference: CCTV Surveillance and Social Control (University of Hull, 9 July 1996).

—— —— —— (1998*a*) 'Algorithmic surveillance: the future of automated visual surveillance' in Norris *et al.* (1998*b*), 255.

—— —— —— (eds.) (1998*b*) *Surveillance, Closed Circuit Television and Social Control* (Aldershot: Ashgate).

O'Brien, J. (1992) 'CCTV watches the world go by' *Security Management Journal* 36(6): 27A.

Ocqueteau, F., and M. L. Pottier (1995*a*) 'Videosurveillance et gestion de l'insécurité dans un centre commercial: les leçons de l'observation' *Les Cahiers de la Sécurité Intérieure* (21): 55.

—— —— (1995*b*) *Vigilance et sécurité dans les grandes surfaces* (Paris: L'Harmattan).

O'Malley, P. (1992) 'Risk, power and crime prevention' *Economy and Society* 21(3): 252.

—— (1996) 'Post-Keynesian policing' *Economy and Society* 25(2): 137.

Orlander, J. D., and M. H. Greenberg (eds.) (1977) *Criminal Justice through Science Fiction* (New York: New Viewpoints).

Painter, K., and D. P. Farrington (1999) 'Street lighting and crime: diffusion of benefits in the Stoke-on-Trent project' in Painter and Tilley (1999*b*), 77.

—— and N. Tilley (1999*a*) 'Editor's introduction: seeing and being seen to prevent crime' in Painter and Tilley (1999*b*), 1.

—— —— (eds.) (1999*b*) *Surveillance of Public Space: CCTV, Street Lighting, and Crime Prevention* (Monsey, NY: Criminal Justice Press).

Parker, J. (2001) *Total Surveillance: Investigating the Big Brother World of E-spies, Eavesdroppers and CCTV* (London: Piatkus).

Parratt, L. (1995) 'Mistaken identities? ID cards: a solution looking for a problem' *Criminal Justice Matters* (summer) (20): 10.

Pattison, B. (1995) 'The use of CCTV by local authorities' *Prison Service Journal* 102: 39.

Pawson, R., and N. Tilley (1997) *Realistic Evaluation* (London: Sage).

Pease, K. (1996) 'Opportunities for crime prevention: the need for incentives' in Saulsbury *et al.* (1996), 96.

—— (1997) 'Crime prevention' in Maguire *et al.* (1997), 971.

—— (1999) 'A review of street lighting evaluations: crime reduction effects' in Painter and Tilley (1999*b*), 47.

Perceptics, *License Plate Reader*, Advertising Brochure.

Phillips, C. (1999) 'A review of CCTV evaluations: crime reduction effects and attitudes towards its use' in Painter and Tilley (1999*b*).

Photoscan (1996) *Photoscanner: The Journal of Photoscan*, Issue No. 23.

Plowden, P., M. Stockdale, and D. Elliot (1997) 'New techniques and new devices: video evidence and the criminal courts' *New Law Journal* (4 Apr.), 502.

Polak, F. (1973) *The Image of the Future* (Amsterdam: Elsevier).

Poole, R. (1991) *Safer Shopping: The Identification of Opportunities for Crime and Disorder in Covered Shopping Centres* (London: West Midlands Police and Home Office).

—— and D. Williams (1996) 'Success in the surveillance society' *Security Management* 40: 29.

Postman, N. (1983) *The Disappearance of Childhood* (London: W. H. Allen).

—— (1993) *Technopoly: The Surrender of Culture to Technology* (New York: Vintage).

Potter, K. (1995) 'Lens support' *Police Review* (8 Sept.), 18.

Poyner, B. (1997) 'Situational crime prevention in two parking facilities' in Clarke (1997).

—— (1999) 'Video cameras and bus vandalism' *Journal of Security and Administration* 11: 44.

Pratt, J. (1999) 'Governmentality, neo-liberalism and dangerousness' in Smandych (ed.).

Privacy International (1997*a*) '10 reasons to stop the cameras' (London: Privacy International).

—— (1997*b*) 'Statement on closed circuit television (CCTV) surveillance devices' (London: Privacy International).

—— (1998) *Privacy and Human Rights: An International Survey of Privacy Laws and Practices* (London: Privacy International).

Punch, M. (1979) *Policing the Inner City* (London: Macmillan).

—— (ed.) (1983) *Control in the Police Organization* (Cambridge, Mass: MIT Press).

Rawlings, P. (1995) 'The idea of policing: a history' *Policing and Society* (5): 129.

Reeve, A. (1996) 'The private realm of the managed town centre' *Urban Design International* 1(1): 61.

—— (1998*a*) 'The panopticisation of shopping: CCTV and leisure consumption' in Norris *et al.* (1998*b*), 69.

—— (1998*b*) 'Risk and the new urban space of managed town centres' *International Journal of Risk, Security and Crime Prevention* 3(1): 43.

Regan, P. (1995) *Legislating Privacy Technology, Social Values, and Public Policy* (Chapel Hill, NC: University of North Carolina Press).

Reiner, R. (1978) *The Blue Coated Worker* (Cambridge: Cambridge University Press).

—— (1991) *Chief Constables* (Oxford: Oxford University Press).

—— (1992*a*) 'Police research in the United Kingdom: a critical review' in Tony and Morris (1992), 435.

—— (1992*b*) 'Policing a postmodern society' *Modern Law Review* 55(6): 761.

—— (1992*c*) *The Politics of the Police*, 2nd edn. (Hemel Hempstead: Harvester Wheatsheaf).

—— (1997) 'Policing and the police' in Maguire *et al.* (1997), 997.

—— (2000) 'Police research' in King and Wincup (2000), 205.

Reiss, A. J. (1992) 'Police organisation in the twentieth century' in Tonry and Morris (1992), 51.

Reynolds, P. (1982) *Ethics and Social Science Research* (Englewood Cliffs, NJ: Prentice Hall).

Robb, G. C. (1980) 'Police use of CCTV surveillance: constitutional implications and proposed regulations' *University of Michigan Journal of Law Reform* 13: 582.

Roberts, A., and S. Goulette (1996) 'CCTV surveillance: the local authority's role—A review of current practice' *Proceedings of the Institute of
Civil Engineers-Municipal Engineers* 115(2): 61.

Robertson, G., and I. Craw (1994) 'Testing face recognition systems' *Image
and Vision Computing* 12(9): 609.

Rosen, J. (2001*a*) 'A cautionary tale for a new age of surveillance' *New
York Times* (7 Oct.).

——(2001*b*) *The Unwanted Gaze: The Destruction of Privacy in America*
(New York: Vintage).

Rosenbaum, D. P. (1988) 'A critical eye on neighbourhood watch: does it
reduce crime and fear?' in Hope and Shaw (1988), 126.

Royal Borough of Windsor and Maidenhead (1996) 'CCTV: closed circuit
television making Windsor and Eton safer places', Pamphlet (Windsor:
Royal Borough of Windsor and Maidenhead Windsor).

Rule, J. (1973) *Private Lives, Public Surveillance* (London: Allen-Lane).

Rutherford, A. (1996) *Transforming Criminal Policy: Spheres of Influence
in the United States, the Netherlands and England and Wales during the
1980s* (Winchester: Waterside Press).

Ryan, M. (1983) *The Politics of Penal Reform* (London: Longman).

Rynkiewich, M., and J. Spradley (eds.) (1976) *Ethics and Anthropology:
Dilemmas in Fieldwork* (New York: Wiley).

Sack, F., D. Nogala, and M. Lindenberg (1997) 'Social Control Technologies: Aspekte und Konsequenzen des Technikeinsatzes bei Instanzen strafrechtlicher Sozialkontrolle im nationalen und internationalen Kontext'
Aufbau- und Kontakstudium Kriminologie 295.

Sacks, H. (1978) 'Notes on police assessment of moral character' in van
Maanen and Manning (1978), 190.

Sanders, A., and R. Young (2000) *Criminal Justice*, 2nd edn. (London:
Butterworths).

Santesson, H. (ed.) (1969) *Crime Prevention in the Thirtieth Century* (New
York: Walker Publishing).

Saulsbury, W., J. Mott, and T. Newburn (eds.) (1996) *Themes in Contemporary Policing* (London: Policy Studies Institute/Police Foundation).

Savage, S. P. (1990) 'A war on crime? Law and order policies in the 1980s'
in Savage and Robbins (1990), 89.

——(1998) 'The politics of criminal justice policy' in McKenzie (1998),
172.

——R. Atkinson, and L. Robbins (eds.) (1994) *Public Policy in Britain*
(London: Macmillan).

Savage, S. P., and M. Nash (1994) 'Yet another agenda for law and order'
International Criminal Justice Review 4: 37.

——and L. Robbins (eds.) (1990) *Public Policy under Thatcher* (London:
Macmillan).

Sayer, A. (1992) *Method in Social Science: A Realistic Approach* (London: Hutchinson).

Schlesinger, P., and H. Tumber (1993) 'Fighting the war against crime: television, police and audiences' *British Journal of Criminology* 33(1): 19.

Semple, J. (1993) *Bentham's Prison: A Study of the Panoptic Penitentiary* (Oxford: Clarendon Press).

Seyd, P. (1990) 'Radical Sheffield: from socialism to entrepreneurialism' *Political Studies* 38: 335.

Shapland, J., and J. Vagg (1980) *Policing by the Public* (London: Routledge).

Sharpe, K. (2000) 'Sad, bad and (sometimes) dangerous to know: street corner research with prostitutes, punters and the police' in King and Wincup (2000), 363.

Sharpe, S. (1989) *Electronically Recorded Evidence: A Guide to the Use of Tape and Video Recordings in Criminal and Civil Proceedings* (London: Fourmat).

Shearing, C. (1992) 'The relation between public and private policing' in Tonry and Morris (1992), xv.

—— and P. Stenning (1981) 'Modern private security: its growth and implications' in M. Tonry and N. Morris (eds.) *Crime and Justice: An Annual Review of Research* (Chicago: Chicago University Press), 193.

—— —— (1984) 'From the panopticon to Disneyworld: the development of discipline' in A. Doob and E. Greenspan (eds.) *Perspectives in Criminal Law* (Toronto: Aurora), 336.

—— —— (1987) *Private Policing* (Newbury Park, Calif.: Sage).

Sheptycki, J. (1994) 'It looks different from the outside' *Policing* 10: 125.

—— (1995) 'Transnational policing and the makings of a modern state' *British Journal of Criminology* 35(4): 613.

Sherman, L. W., D. C. Gottfredson, D. L. MacKenzie, J. E. Eck, P. Reuter, and S. D. Bushway (eds.) (1997) *Preventing Crime: What Works, What Doesn't, What's Promising* (Washington: National Institute of Justice).

Short, E. and C. de Than (1998) *Civil Liberties: Legal Principles of Individual Freedom* (London: Sweet & Maxwell Ltd.).

—— and J. Ditton (1995) 'Does CCTV affect crime?' *CCTV Today* 2(2): 10.

—— —— (1996) *Does Closed Circuit Television Prevent Crime? An Evaluation of the Use of CCTV Surveillance Cameras in Airdrie Town Centre* (Edinburgh: The Scottish Office Central Research Unit).

Sibley, D. (1995) *Geographies of Exclusion: Society and Difference in the West* (London: Routledge).

Simpson, L. (1995) *Technology, Time and the Conversations of Modernity* (London: Routledge).

Sivarajasingham, V., and J. P. Shepherd (1999) 'Effect of closed circuit television on urban violence' *Journal of Accident and Emergency Medicine* 16: 225.

Sked, A., and C. Cook (1993) *Post-war Britain: A Political History* 4th edn. (Harmondsworth: Penguin Books).

Skinns, D. (1998) 'Crime reduction, diffusion and displacement: evaluating the effectiveness of CCTV' in Norris *et al.* (1998*b*), 175.

Skogan, W. (1990) *Disorder and Decline* (New York: Free Press).

Skolnick, J. (1966) *Justice without Trial* (New York: Wiley).

—— and D. H. Bayley (1986) *The New Blue Line* (New York: Free Press).

Smandych, R. (ed.) (1999) *Governable Places: Readings on Governmentality and Crime Control* (Dartmouth: Ashgate).

Smart, B. (1985) *Michel Foucault* (London: Tavistock).

Smith, D. (1995) *The Sleep of Reason: The James Bulger Case* (London: Arrow Books).

Sorkin, M. (ed.) (1992) *Variations on a Theme Park: The New American City and the End of Public Space* (New York: Wang and Hill).

Sparks, R. (1992) *Television and the Drama of Crime* (Buckingham: Open University Press).

Speed, M., J. Burrows, and J. Bamfield (1995) *Retail Crime Costs 1993/94 Survey: The Impact of Crime and the Retail Response* (London: British Retail Consortium).

Spitzer, S. (1987) 'Security and control in capitalist societies: the fetishism of security and the secret thereof' in Lowman *et al.* (1987).

Squires, P. (1994) 'Private lives, secluded spaces: privacy as political possibility' *Environment and Planning D: Society and Space* 12: 387.

—— and L. Measor (1996) *Closed Circuit TV Surveillance and Crime Prevention in Brighton: Half Yearly Report* (Brighton: University of Brighton Health and Social Policy Research Centre).

—— —— (1997) *Closed Circuit TV Surveillance and Crime Prevention in Brighton: Follow-up Analysis* (Brighton: University of Brighton Health and Social Policy Research Centre).

Stacey, M. (1969) *Methods of Social Research* (Oxford: Pergamon).

Stenson, K., and D. Cowell (eds.) (1991) *The Politics of Crime Control* (London: Sage).

—— and A. Edwards (2001) 'Rethinking crime control in advanced liberal government: the "third way" and return to the local' in Stenson and Sullivan (2001).

Stenson, K., and R. Sullivan (eds.) (2001) *Crime, Risk and Justice* (Cullompton, Devon: Willan Publishing).

Sternsdorff, H. W. (1983) 'Aktion "Paddy". Die Möglichkeiten der Video-fahndung' in Meyer-Larsen (1983), 95.

Sutton, M. (1996) 'Implementing crime prevention schemes in a multi-agency setting: aspects of process in the Safer Cities Programme', Home Office Research Studies (London: HMSO).

Taylor, I. (1999) *Crime in Context: A Critical Criminology of Market Societies* (Cambridge: Polity Press).

Taylor, N. (2002) 'State surveillance and the right to privacy' *Surveillance and Society* 1(1): 66.

Thomas, T. (1994) 'Covert video surveillance' *New Law Journal* (15 July) 966.

Thrift, N. (1996) 'New urban eras and old technological fears: reconfiguring the goodwill of electronic things' *Urban Studies* 33(8): 1463–93.

Tilley, N. (1992) 'Safer cities and communities safety strategies', CPU Paper 38 (London: Home Office).

—— (1993a) 'Crime prevention and the Safer Cities story' *Howard Journal* 32(1): 40.

—— (1993b) 'Understanding car parks, crime and CCTV: evaluation lessons from Safer Cities' Crime Prevention Unit Paper No. 42, (London: Home Office).

—— (1997) 'Whys and wherefores in evaluating the effectiveness of CCTV' *International Journal of Risk, Security and Crime Prevention* 2(3): 175.

—— (1998) 'Evaluating the effectiveness of CCTV schemes' in Norris *et al.* (1998b), 139.

Tonry, M., and D. Farrington (eds.) (1995) *Building a Safer Society: Strategic Approaches to Crime Prevention*, Crime and Justice Series, vol. 19 (London: The University of Chicago Press).

—— and N. Morris (eds.) (1992) *Modern Policing* (Chicago: University of Chicago Press).

Tunstall, R. (1994) 'Video surveillance in town centres: the implications for urban design', Unpublished MA thesis (Oxford: Oxford Brookes University).

Turner, V. W. (1957) *Schism and Continuity in an African Society: A Study of Ndembu Village Life* (Manchester: University of Manchester Press).

UK CCTV Surveillance Regulation Campaign, 'Who's watching the watchers? Public CCTV in the UK—Beyond 1984', Feature article http://www.spy.org.uk.

Vitalis, A. (1998) 'Big Brother is watching you: they see you but you don't see them' *Le Monde Diplomatique* (Sept.), 15.

—— D. Garland, and A. Wakefield (eds.) (2000) *Ethical and Social Perspectives on Situational Crime Prevention* (Oxford: Hart).

Wade, G. (2001) 'Funding CCTV: the story so far' *CCTV Today* (May).

Walker, A. (1998) 'CCTV works!' *Security Installer* (Mar.), 11.

Walker, C. (1983) 'Review of *The Policing Revolution: Police Technology, Democracy and Liberty in Britain*' *Public Law* 694.

Walklate, S. (1998) *Understanding Criminology* (Buckingham: Open University Press).

Waller, I. (1989) *Current Trends in European Crime Prevention: Implications for Canada* (Ottawa: Canadian Department of Justice).

Walsh, C. (1962) *From Utopia to Nightmare* (New York: Harper and Row).

Walton, P., and J. Young (eds.) (1998) *The New Criminology Revisited* (London: Macmillan).

Warner, M., and M. Stone (1970) *The Data-Bank Society* (London: George Allen and Unwin).

Wax, R. (1971) *Doing Fieldwork: Warnings and Advice* (Chicago: University of Chicago Press).

Weatheritt, M. (1985) *Innovations in Policing* (London: Croom Hill).

——(ed.) (1989) *Police Research: Some Future Prospects* (Aldershot: Avebury).

Webb, B., and G. Laycock (1991) 'Reducing crime on the London Underground: an evaluation of three pilot projects', Crime Prevention Unit Series Paper No. 30 (London: Home Office Police Department).

Webster, C. (2000) 'Relegitimating the democratic polity: the closed circuit television revolution in the UK' in I. Horrocks, J. Moff, and P. Topps (eds.) *Democratic Governance and New Technology: Technologically Mediated Innovations in Political Practices in Western Europe* (London: Routledge).

Welsh, B. C., and D. P. Farrington (2002) 'Crime prevention effects of closed circuit television: a systematic review', Home Office Research Study 252 (London: Development and Statistics Directorate, Home Office).

Wiecek, C., and A. Rudinow Saetnan (2002*a*) 'Working paper No. 4: Restrictive? Permissive? The contradictory framing of video surveillance in Norway and Denmark', Urban eye project: On the threshold to urban Panopticon? Analysing the employment of CCTV in European cities and assessing its social and political impacts (Berlin: Centre for technology and society, Technical University Berlin).

————(2002*b*) 'Working paper No. 5: Geographies of visibility. Zooming in on video surveillance systems in Oslo and Copenhagen', Urban eye project: On the threshold to urban Panopticon? Analysing the employment of CCTV in European cities and assessing its social and political impacts (Berlin: Centre for technology and society, Technical University Berlin).

Williams, K. S., and C. Johnstone (2000) 'The politics of the selective gaze: closed circuit television and the policing of public space' *Crime, Law and Social Change* 34(2): 183.

Wilson, J. Q. (1968) *Varieties of Police Behavior* (Cambridge, Mass.: Harvard University Press).

Winner, L. (1977) *Autonomous Technology: Technics-out-of-Control as a Theme in Political Thought* (Cambridge, Mass.: MIT Press).

Wright, S. (1998) 'An appraisal of the technologies of political control', European Parliament Scientific and Technological Options Assessments working document (consultation version) (Luxembourg: European Parliament).

Young, J. (1994) 'Incessant chatter: recent paradigms in criminology' in Maguire *et al.* (1994), 69.

——(1999) *The Exclusive Society: Social Exclusion, Crime and Difference in Late Modernity* (London: Sage).

Young, M. (1993) *In the Sticks: An Anthropologist in a Shire Force* (Oxford: Oxford University Press).

Younger Committee (1972) *Report of the Committee on Privacy*, Cmnd 5012 (London: HMSO).

Index